PERSPECTIVES ON EVALUATING CRIMINAL JUSTICE AND CORRECTIONS

ADVANCES IN PROGRAM EVALUATION

Series Editors: Saville Kushner

Recent Volumes:

Volume 6: Telling Tales: Evaluation and Narrative – Edited by Tineke Abma

Volume 7: Visions of Quality: How Evaluators Define, Understand and Represent Program Quality – Edited by Alexis P. Benson, D. Michelle Hinn and Claire Lloyd

Volume 8: School-Based Evaluation: An International Perspective – Edited by David Nevo

Volume 9: Evaluating The Upgrading of Technical Courses at Two-Year Colleges: NSF'S Advanced Technological Education Program – Edited by Arlen Gullickson, Frances Lawrenz and Nanette Keiser

Volume 10: Dilemmas of Engagement – Edited by Saville Kushner and Nigel Norris

Volume 11: Assessing Teachers for Professional Certification: The First Decade of the National Board for Professional Teaching Standards – Edited by Robert E. Stake, Saville Kushner, Lawrence Ingvarson and John Hattie

Volume 12: Access, a Zone of Comprehension, and Intrusion – Edited by Brinda Jegatheesan

ADVANCES IN PROGRAM EVALUATION VOLUME 13

PERSPECTIVES ON EVALUATING CRIMINAL JUSTICE AND CORRECTIONS

EDITED BY

ERICA BOWEN
Coventry University, UK

SARAH BROWN
Coventry University, UK

United Kingdom – North America – Japan
India – Malaysia – China

Emerald Group Publishing Limited
Howard House, Wagon Lane, Bingley BD16 1WA, UK

First edition 2012

British Library Cataloguing in Publication Data
A catalogue record for this book is available from the British Library

ISBN: 978-1-78052-644-7
ISSN: 1474-7863 (Series)

CONTENTS

LIST OF CONTRIBUTORS

Brad Astbury	Centre for Program Evaluation, Melbourne Graduate School of Education, University of Melbourne, Melbourne, Australia
Matt Barnard	Evaluation, NSPCC, London, UK
Robert F. Boruch	Graduate School of Education and Statistics Department, Wharton School, University of Pennsylvania, Philadelphia, Pennsylvania, USA
Erica Bowen	Department of Psychology and Behavioural Sciences, Coventry University, Coventry, England
Sarah Brown	Department of Psychology and Behavioural Sciences, Coventry University, Coventry, England
Joe S. Cecil	Research Division, Federal Judicial Center, Washington, DC, USA
Elaine Ellis	National Offender Management Service (NOMS), UK
Nigel Hosking	London Probation Trust, seconded to National Offender Management Service (NOMS), UK
Jordan M. Hyatt	Department of Criminology, University of Pennsylvania, Philadelphia, Pennsylvania, USA
Wendy Hyett	Wales Probation Trust, seconded to National Offender Management Service (NOMS), UK
Julia Ioane	Psychology Department, University of Auckland, Auckland, New Zealand

Barry Kushner	Independent Evaluator, Blue Urban Sky, Liverpool, UK
Saville Kushner	Public Evaluation, Faculty of Education, University of Auckland, Auckland, New Zealand
Ian Lambie	Psychology Department, University of Auckland, Auckland, New Zealand
L. E. Marshall	Rockwood Psychological Services, Kingston, ON, Canada
W. L. Marshall	Rockwood Psychological Services, Kingston, ON, Canada
Sue Rex	National Offender Management Service (NOMS) Ministry of Justice, UK
David Smith	Department of Applied Social Science, Lancaster University, Lancaster, England
Herb Turner III	Analytica, Inc., University of Pennsylvania, USA
Timothy Victor	Science and Strategy, Kantar Health, Princeton, NJ, USA; Quantitative Methods, Graduate School of Education, University of Pennsylvania, Philadelphia, PA, USA

ACKNOWLEDGMENTS

We would like to thank a number of people without whom this book would never have come to fruition. Firstly, I (Erica Bowen) would like to thank Prof. Saville Kushner for supporting the early development of this book after my very impulsive and patchy initial idea at the start of 2011. I would also like to thank my co-editor Sarah Brown for volunteering to help me edit the book after seeing the look of panic on my face when Saville confirmed that he thought it was a good idea.

Sarah and I would like to thank all of the contributors for taking the time to provide some really interesting chapters, and we are delighted that this book has attracted contributors from around the world. Finally, we would like to thank everyone at Emerald for their patience and assistance in getting this book published.

PREFACE

Questions regarding the effectiveness of criminal justice efforts to reduce crime have dominated social and political thinking in this area for more than a century (Bowen, 2011). During this time a number of philosophical shifts regarding the aims of correctional systems have occurred, fuelled typically by the prevailing political standpoint (McGuire, 2005). At the start of the twentieth century, policymakers in the United States and United Kingdom placed faith in the rehabilitative ideal and offender 'treatment'-dominated corrections policies (Cullen & Gendreau, 2000). In this context 'treatment' refers to a range of interventions designed to alter the individual, contextual and social factors that sustain offending behaviour (Hollin, 1999). This remained the prevailing perspective for the subsequent seven decades until questions arose regarding the quality of 'state run' corrections facilities in the United States in the early 1970s. At this point, evaluation science was one of many influences on a change of policy (Hollin, 1999). Martinson's (1974) now infamous research synthesis, described by Glaes (1998, p. 713) as 'a watershed moment', provided politicians and policy-makers with greater justification for changing the focus of corrections policy. Although arguably it was observers misreporting of Martinson's claims about the evidence which were most influential, rather than the review itself. According to Martinson (1974):

> It is just possible that some of our treatment programs are working to some extent, but that our research is so bad that it is incapable of telling. Having entered this very serious caveat, I am bound to say that these data ... give us very little reason to hope that we have in fact found a sure way of reducing recidivism through rehabilitation. This is not to say that we found no instances of success or partial success; it is only to say that these instances have been isolated, producing no clear pattern to indicate the efficacy of any particular method of treatment. (p. 49)

Despite the caveat noted, the results of this review were widely seen as indicating that 'nothing works' in offender rehabilitation. As a result of the range of factors and subsequent debates regarding criminal justice interventions, an emphasis on deterrence and incapacitation within penal policy returned, though a small chorus of dissenting voices (e.g. Garrett, 1985;

Palmer, 1975) could be heard directly questioning Martinson's conclusions. For example, in Palmer's (1975) re-appraisal of the literature Martinson reviewed, positive effects of interventions were identified in 48% of cases.

Despite Martinson's own concession in 1979 that some interventions were effective, and the clear evidence that some interventions elicited positive effects for some offenders and in some circumstances, it was not until the 1990s that the potential of rehabilitation was again at the forefront of penal policy, although questions regarding efficacy remained. Indeed, for the last two decades Governmental policies in the United States, Canada and the United Kingdom have been marketed as 'evidence-based', such that evaluation science now has a central role in the development of penal policy (Petrosino, Boruch, Soydan, Duggan, & Sanchez-Meca, 2001). However, Petrosino et al. (2001) note that there exist many challenges to the implementation of evidence-based policy that reflect issues and debates at the heart of evaluation science, namely the philosophical and methodological approaches that ought to be adopted to elicit reliable evidence.

The question of what works to reduce re-offending is one that has been influenced most greatly by what Alkin and Christie (2004) term the 'methods' branch of evaluation science, that is, the branch that deals with generalisability or 'knowledge construction' (p. 13). Consequently, much of the debate within the corrections literature has concerned the extent to which valid conclusions regarding the causal association between intervention and outcomes can be obtained, drawing on the seminal work of Campbell and Stanley (1966) who specified the conditions for true experimental studies. We are delighted, therefore, that these issues are reflected within this volume and are discussed by key theorists in evaluation science. Of particular focus is the issue of experimentation and the extent to which such methods are (a) appropriate to the evaluation of interventions and (b) can be adopted ethically within the corrections context. The notion of experimentation in the evaluation of criminal justice and corrections interventions is not without its critics, with some arguing that a more pressing issue is to understand *how* interventions elicit change, rather than whether interventions have a net effect of reducing re-offending (e.g. Pawson & Tilley, 1997). An issue that may be better understood with new and innovative qualitative approaches to criminal justice evaluation, and existing quantitative approaches that have yet to be widely employed in criminal justice arenas, both of which are discussed in more detail in this volume.

This book is divided into three sections. In the first section, Theoretical Considerations, Bradley Astbury discusses the use of theory in criminal justice evaluations and Liam Marshall and William Marshall discuss the critical features of responsivity and the implications of this for evaluation research. In criminal justice evaluation research, Bradley Astbury argues in Chapter 1 that there has been little explicit focus on the nature and functions of theory, an issue that is redressed in this chapter. The aim of the chapter is to demonstrate why theory matters and to examine the relationship between theory and practice. The discussion begins with a consideration of why evaluation research is atheoretical, followed by clarification of 'theory' in this context and the distinction between theories of evaluation and theories for evaluation. These theories and the role they play in guiding research are discussed in more detail, with the chapter concluding that they provide an important set of concepts, methods and tools to generate knowledge about the efficacy of a wide range of criminal justice interventions.

In the second chapter, L. E. Marshall and W. L. Marshall discuss the issue of treatment delivery, or the 'responsivity' principle of the Risk, Need and Responsitivity (RNR) model. Although this principle has two components, general and specific responsivity, it is the former which is typically understood to mean that treatment providers should select only interventions that have been shown to be effective, that is the focus of the chapter. Full consideration of the issues discussed in the chapter reveals a number of important implications for evaluation and intervention practices: for example, that researchers should more carefully consider how responsivity issues are included in evaluation research; and that treatment providers should more carefully consider these issues in the delivery of treatment and their reporting of intervention programmes.

The second section of the book, Methodological Considerations', contains four chapters that discuss a range of methodological considerations, the first three of which consider the 'debate' surrounding the use of randomised-control trials (RCTs) in criminal justice evaluation research. David Smith begins this section by outlining contemporary arguments about the strengths and limitations of RCTs using developments in Home Office (UK) policy and practice since 2000 and discussing these in line within the context of the history of RCT use in the United Kingdom. Two recent 'debates' regarding RCT use are then discussed and the types of research studies that have influenced criminal justice policy. David Smith argues that RCTs have no greater chance than other evaluation methodological designs in achieving such influence.

Similar conclusions are drawn by W. L. Marshall and L. E. Marshall who discuss the use of RCTs in relation to sex offender treatment programmes.

Although such programmes are perhaps the most well-researched criminal justice interventions, conclusions regarding their effectiveness are marred by issues regarding methodological rigour and the general absence of RCTs, and in theory the 'conclusive' findings that such RCT studies would produce. These issues are discussed in this chapter, with the reasons why the use of the RCT design is problematic and/or difficult in the evaluation of these interventions. The chapter also includes outlines of the RNR model and a description of a positive strength-based sex offender treatment programme.

The ethical issues encountered in RCTs are the focus of the next chapter in this section of the book. Robert F. Boruch, Timothy Victor, Joe S. Cecil, Herb Turner III and Jordan Hyatt discuss the range of ethical questions and challenges that researchers face when conducting RCTs and they outline how these might be resolved. They argue that ethical issues usually occur in two main areas: firstly that participants/groups/areas randomised to the control condition might be disadvantaged and secondly in relation to participants' privacy. Although the range of issues faced is specific to each RCT, the authors conclude that there are three broad approaches to resolving or reducing such challenges: the use of statistical methods; procedural methods, such as the use of review boards; and finally legal, legislative remedies and that each of these invites further research and development.

In the final chapter in this section, Matt Barnard discusses contemporary developments in the use of qualitative methods in evaluation research. He argues that there has been increasing attention in UK evaluation practice on how and why interventions works, as without such understanding, it is difficult to ensure that interventions are effective when they are used in different contexts, or used more widely. Despite this, however, theoretical and methodological developments have been slow to meet the needs of researchers, as traditional qualitative approaches do not provide insight into how interventions work in a way that can be generalised beyond the data collected for each study. Critical Qualitative Theory (CQT), developed by the National Centre for Social research, and which it is argued fills this methodological gap, is outlined in the chapter. Recently published evaluation studies are used to explain CQT and highlight the strengths of this approach.

In the final section of the book, Evaluation Methods and Practice, the authors focus on the practice of evaluation research with five chapters discussing a range of methods using both quantitative and qualitative approaches. Erica Bowen begins this section by discussing within treatment change. In more traditional treatment and comparison/control group designs, treatment change is measured in relation to change demonstrated between the group average scores at pre-treatment and group averages at post-treatment, with statistically significant differences denoting significant change. However, this method tells us nothing about the range and types of changes across all the individuals in the group (a large change in a small number of offenders with minimal, or no change in most of the group, may demonstrate statistically significant group change), or where the offenders are in relation to 'normal' populations at the end of treatment (although offenders may change from the start of treatment to the end, they may still be a long way off 'normal' functioning at the end of treatment). Measures of clinically significant change, outlined in this chapter, allow us to investigate how each individual changed during treatment and where the post-treatment scores indicate they are in relation to normal and offending populations, which provides the opportunity to assess which offenders need further intervention.

A further weakness with traditional quasi-experimental treatment and comparison group evaluations studies is that it is rarely possible to identify suitable comparison groups that do not differ significantly from treatment groups in a way that might affect the conclusions drawn about the effectiveness of treatment. This issue also means that there is considerable debate about what evaluation studies demonstrate and is linked to debates about the use of RCTs, as discussed in the previous section of the book. Propensity scoring is a statistical method that allows researchers to identify the probability (or propensity) of being assigned to the treatment group. These propensity 'scores' can then be used in a number of ways to compare differences between the treatment and comparison groups more reliably. In Chapter 8, Sarah Brown reviews studies that have used propensity scoring to show how the methods are used in evaluation research and to explain the different ways propensity scores can and have been used. Like the use of clinically significant change, propensity scoring has yet to be utilised in more than a few criminal justice evaluations, and arguments are made in both these chapters that these methods should be used more widely to increase the reliability, validity and utility of evaluation research.

In the next chapter, Sue Rex, Elaine Ellis, Nigel Hosking and Wendy Hyett discuss their experiences of using a collaborative approach to develop models in the National (England and Wales) Offender Management Service (NOMS) that can support effective offender engagement. The Offender Engagement Programme (OEP) draws on desistance research and focused initiatives were developed from practice development from early field work, reviews of the literature and extensive engagement with Probation Trusts. A research strategy was developed early in the OEP to provide evidence of the quality and impact of it. The evaluation took a novel mixed method approach using both internal and external evaluations and is described in this chapter.

Community-based probation practice also provides the context for Chapter 10, where Barry Kushner and Saville Kushner discuss the role that qualitative approaches can have in the development of new practices in the sustainable reduction of offending. It is argued in this chapter that quantitative methods of data collection provide only a 'snapshot' of information that does not focus on the quality of the intervention, which it is suggested is the key driver for change and long-term reductions in offending. Examples of narratives offered by offenders participating in group sessions and extracts from discussions with probation staff are used as 'illustrations' throughout the chapter, which outlines how a probation trust concluded that engagement with offenders is the key to having an impact.

The final chapter in this book is written by Ian Lambie and Julia Ioane who draw on their experiences of conducting evaluation research in New Zealand to discuss making research findings stick at the coal face in everyday clinical work. A series of steps are outlined that aim to guide researchers through the evaluation process and increase the likelihood that the findings will be used in practice. As we can see throughout this book, evaluation research is not easy and there are many challenges throughout this process. This chapter provides a motivational conclusion to the book, with the key message being to keep going, no matter what the challenges are.

Our hopes for this volume were to draw together key thinkers and key issues in evaluation science as applied to evaluating criminal justice programmes, and to provide a sense of how far this sub-field of evaluation has come. What we are reminded of, however, upon reviewing the content of this volume is of how much more there is still to achieve. To this end we hope that you find this volume a source of information and inspiration, and wish you the best of luck in your evaluation endeavours.

Erica Bowen
Sarah Brown
Editors

REFERENCES

Alkin, M. C., & Christie, C. A. (2004). An evaluation theory tree. In M. C. Alkin (Ed.), *Evaluation roots: Tracing theorists' views and influences* (pp. 12–66). Thousand Oaks, CA: Sage.

Bowen, E. (2011). *The rehabilitation of partner-violent men*. Chichester: Wiley-Blackwell.

Campbell, D., & Stanley, J. (1966). *Experimental and quasi-experimental designs for research*. Chicago, IL: Rand McNally.

Cullen, F. T., & Gendreau, P. (2000). Assessing correctional rehabilitation: Policy, practice and prospects. *Criminal Justice*, *3*, 109–175.

Garrett, C. (1985). Effects of residential treatment on adjudicated delinquents: A meta-analysis. *Journal of Research on Crime and Delinquency*, *22*, 287–308. doi:0.1177/00224278850 22004002.

Glaes, G. G. (1998). Corectional treatment. In M. Tonry (Ed.), *The handbook of crime and punishment* (pp. 712–738). Oxford: Oxford University Press.

Hollin, C. R. (1999). Treatment programs for offenders: Meta-analysis 'what works' and beyond. *International Journal of Law and Psychiatry*, *22*, 361–372.

Martinson, R. (1974). What works? Questions and answers about prison reform. *The Public Interest*, *35*, 22–54.

Martinson, R. (1979). New findings, new views: A note of caution regarding sentencing reform. *Hofstra Law Review*, *7*, 243–258.

McGuire, J. (2005). Is research working? Revisiting the research and effective practice agenda. In J. Winstone & F. Pakes (Eds.), *Community justice: Issues for probation and criminal justice* (pp. 257–284). Cullompton: Willan.

Palmer, T. (1975). Martinson revisited. *Journal of Research in Crime and Delinquency*, *12*, 133–152.

Pawson, R., & Tilley, N. (1997). *Realistic evaluation*. London: Sage.

Petrosino, A., Boruch, R., Soydan, H., Duggan, L., & Sanchez-Meca, J. (2001). Meeting the challenges of evidence-based policy: The Campbell collaboration. *Annals of the American Academy of Political and Social Science*, *578*, 14–34.

SECTION 1
THEORETICAL CONSIDERATIONS

USING THEORY IN CRIMINAL JUSTICE EVALUATION

Brad Astbury

ABSTRACT

This chapter examines the nature and role of theory in criminal justice evaluation. A distinction between theories of and theories for evaluation is offered to clarify what is meant by 'theory' in the context of contemporary evaluation practice. Theories of evaluation provide a set of prescriptions and principles that can be used to guide the design, conduct and use of evaluation. Theories for evaluation include programme theory and the application of social science theory to understand how and why criminal justice interventions work to generate desired outcomes. The fundamental features of these three types of theory are discussed in detail, with a particular focus on demonstrating their combined value and utility for informing and improving the practice of criminal justice evaluation.

Criminal justice evaluators are confronted with a myriad of choices: What is the purpose of the evaluation? What are the key evaluation questions? What is the most appropriate design for the study? What methods should be employed? What role should I play in this evaluation? Which stakeholders should be involved? What should be done to ensure that the results are used? What about the legal, political and ethical challenges that may arise? The way in which evaluators respond to these kinds of questions seems to

Perspectives on Evaluating Criminal Justice and Corrections
Advances in Program Evaluation, Volume 13, 3–27

ISSN: 1474-7863/doi:10.1108/S1474-7863(2012)0000013005

depend largely on particular features of the evaluation context, the information needs of decision-makers, as well as the tacit knowledge and experience of the evaluator.

There appears, though, to be little discussion regarding roles for 'theory' in criminal justice evaluation practice. There has been some debate among academic criminologists in Australia and the United Kingdom about political and methodological dimensions of evaluation work and some of this does touch on issues related to theory (see Farrington, 2003; Hope, 2004; Israel, 2000; Walters, 2003; Weatherburn, 2005). However, explicit consideration of the nature and functions of theory in criminal justice evaluation is rare. This could be one of the reasons why some criminologists claim that evaluation research is unreliable, 'lacks academic rigour' and has been corrupted by commercialism and political influence (Travers, 2005, p. 39; White, 2001). A renewed emphasis on theory may go some way towards promoting a more positive image of criminal justice evaluation.

A major aim of this chapter is to unpack the relationship between theory and evaluation practice, and in doing so demonstrate how and why theory matters for practice. I begin by outlining briefly some of the reasons why evaluation research appears to have adopted a primarily method-driven, atheoretical orientation. Next I attempt to clarify what is meant by 'theory' in the context of contemporary evaluation practice by distinguishing between theories *of* and theories *for* evaluation. Theories of evaluation fall into the domain of what is commonly referred to as evaluation theory. Theories for evaluation include programme theory and the application of substantive social science theory to understand how and why criminal justice programmes work to generate desired outcomes. The central features of these various kinds of 'practising theory' are discussed in turn, with particular emphasis on demonstrating the role each type of theory can play in guiding the conduct of criminal justice evaluation.

HISTORICAL NEGLECT OF THEORY IN EVALUATION

The traditional neglect of theory in evaluation practice can be viewed, in the main, as a by-product of the historical development of programme evaluation (Chen, 1990). Compared to many other areas of social science, programme evaluation is still a relatively young discipline. Although systematic evaluation, particularly in the field of education and curriculum assessment, had already been advanced to some extent in the 1930s and 1940s by scholars such as Ralph Tyler it was not until after World War II that evaluation experienced a significant boom. Under the Kennedy and Johnson Administrations of the late 1960s and 1970s social scientists from a variety of disciplinary backgrounds were called upon to conduct programme and policy evaluations of large-scale federal reforms. Researchers studiously applied their analytical and technical skills to the 'rational' assessment of hundreds of new interventions designed to alleviate poverty and improve the human condition.

The general mood at this time was, in hindsight, overly optimistic and perhaps even a little naïve. It was widely believed that through solemn application of sound social science methodology, policy-makers would be able to identify and expand effective social programmes, while at the same time terminating and discarding programmes that did not work. However, distinguishing between programmes that failed because they were a bad idea and those that failed because of poor implementation proved to be much more difficult than anticipated. When clear results were available, many evaluators assumed that politicians and stakeholders, who had funded their work, would eagerly apply findings and recommendations. Experience soon revealed that direct, instrumental use of evaluation findings is frequently an exception rather than the norm.

Since that time, much has been learnt. While programme evaluation is still primarily a practice-driven field, it is also fair to say that it is becoming more sophisticated and theoretically mature (Shadish, 1998). Evaluation is starting to 'crystallize and emerge as a distinct profession' with its own unique and rich language, theories and logic of practice (Stufflebeam & Shinkfield, 2007, p. 41). Over the past two decades the number of articles and books about evaluation has grown dramatically, as has the number of professional evaluation societies. Significant developments in evaluation theory, methodology and practice continue to occur as the field addresses new challenges and becomes increasingly global in orientation.

However, advances in the theoretical knowledge base of programme evaluation appear to have had a negligible impact on how evaluation is practised in the field (Christie, 2003; Shadish & Epstein, 1987; Smith, 1993). This is particularly so in many of the disciplinary areas where evaluations are regularly conducted. For example, in medicine the term 'evaluation' is often still synonymous with experimental impact studies. In psychology, education, health promotion and criminology, where a stronger interdisciplinary focus exists, a broader conception of evaluation is generally encouraged. Nonetheless, the extent to which knowledge of evaluation theory is communicated within and across disciplines appears to be limited. Although the reasons are likely to be varied,[1] 'it is hard to argue that this low level of familiarity with theory is desirable, if for no other reason than the fact that evaluators are deprived of knowledge of options they have available to use in their practice' (Shadish & Epstein, 1987, p. 586).

THE MEANING AND USES OF THEORY IN EVALUATION

There is no universally accepted definition of theory in the natural or social sciences. Depending on the particular field of knowledge and context in which it is used, the term can mean different things. There are important consequences of this for the field of evaluation. The American sociologist Robert Merton, who devoted much of his career to advancing the role of theory in social science, describes the problem as follows:

> Like so many words that are bandied about, the word 'theory' threatens to become meaningless. Because its referents are so diverse – including everything from minor working hypothesis, through comprehensive but vague and unordered speculations, to axiomatic systems of thought – use of the word often obscures rather than creates understanding. (1967, p. 39)

In light of these cautions it is important from the outset to be clear about what is meant by the rather abstract notion of 'theory' and to identify its various applications in evaluation. While it has been recognised for some time that evaluators make use of various kinds of theory in their work, Donaldson and Lipsey (2006) were perhaps the first to clarify some of the different meanings of theory in the context of contemporary evaluation practice. They make a useful distinction between three common forms of theory encountered in evaluation:

1. Evaluation theory
2. Programme theory
3. Social science theory

The first form of theory is best understood as a theory *of* evaluation because it offers a set of prescriptions about what constitutes 'good' evaluation practice. Programme theory and social science theory can be viewed as theories *for* evaluation in that they provide a methodology for understanding how and why programmes bring about change. Of course, the boundaries between these three forms of theory are blurry.[2] Nevertheless, the distinction is helpful because it provides some conceptual clarity regarding the nature and role of theory in evaluation practice.

THEORIES OF EVALUATION

Theories of evaluation attempt to provide a coherent set of principles to guide the study and practice of programme evaluation (Alkin, 2004). According to Shadish, Cook, and Leviton (1991), there are five main components of evaluation theory. These can be summarised briefly as follows:

1. *Social programming*: the nature, internal structure and functioning of social programmes particularly with respect to their role in ameliorating social problems.
2. *Knowledge construction*: philosophical assumptions about the nature of knowledge (epistemology), the nature of reality (ontology) and methods used to generate 'credible' knowledge about social programmes.
3. *Valuing*: the nature and role that various kinds of values play in the evaluation of social programmes.
4. *Knowledge use*: the ways social science information is used to modify programmes and policies and what evaluators can do to increase use.
5. *Evaluation practice*: the role of evaluators, the relationship they form with programme stakeholders and the tactics and strategies evaluators use in their professional work; especially given the constraints of time, money and expertise.

There is no single or ideal theory of evaluation. Evaluation theorists differ considerably in their conceptualisation of the five components of evaluation theory identified above. This has led to a vast (and now almost overwhelming) array of programme evaluation theories that are known more widely as 'models', 'approaches', 'types' or 'forms' of evaluation. Newcomers to the field of evaluation in the 1970s could perhaps be content with understanding the basic distinction between formative and summative evaluation approaches (see Scriven, 1967 and below for more detail). Today the novice evaluator faces a much more difficult prospect of sorting through dozens of competing models of evaluation. One recent attempt at classification, for example, identified 26 alternative evaluation models (Stufflebeam & Shinkfield, 2007).

Table 1 provides a select overview of several well-known and some not so well-known evaluation theories and theorists. The list is certainly not exhaustive, but is intended to demonstrate the depth and variety of theoretical influences on contemporary evaluation practice.

The diversity of evaluation theory is partly due to the influence that different philosophical orientations have had on the nature and development of intellectual thinking in evaluation. During the mid to late 1980s, evaluation, like many disciplines, experienced a heated debate between two prevailing perspectives or paradigms. These two paradigms have been labelled in various ways but most typically are referred to as 'positivism' and 'constructivism'. The 'paradigm wars' have been fought vigorously across many key areas in the philosophy of social science, such as: the nature of reality (ontology); the nature of knowledge (epistemology); the role of values in inquiry (axiology); the possibility of causal linkages; and the ability to establish generalisations (Guba & Lincoln, 1981, 1989).

Traditionally, experimental and quasi-experimental theories of evaluation have dominated mainstream evaluation practice, providing a methodological template for how to do evaluation (e.g. Campbell & Stanley, 1966; Cook & Campbell, 1979). Experimentalism has historical roots in a positivist philosophy of social science. Briefly stated, this position maintains that evaluators should approach the study of social programmes in roughly the same way that the physical sciences such as physics and chemistry approach the study of natural phenomena (Martin & McIntyre, 1994).

Experimental evaluation follows a standard logic – construct two equivalent groups and undertake a 'before' measurement, then apply the intervention to only one of the two groups and then take an 'after' measurement. Any difference or change from first to second measurement in the intervention (experimental/treatment) group compared to the non-intervention (control) group is deemed to be attributable to the intervention. When cases are randomly assigned to each of the two groups, this research design is referred to as a randomised control trial (RCT) or 'true experiment'. When non-random methods are used to create experimental and control groups, or where a control group is absent the design is referred to as a 'quasi-experiment'.

Over the past three decades the orthodoxy of the experimental approach has been challenged by the development of anti-naturalist approaches to evaluation, such as: responsive evaluation (Stake, 1983); fourth-generation evaluation (Guba & Lincoln, 1989); and empowerment evaluation (Fetterman, 1996).

Table 1. Select Overview of Evaluation Theories.

Type	Basic Description	Key Theorist(s)
Objectives-based evaluation	The objectives-oriented approach to evaluation was first formulated in the 1940s, but is still popular today. In essence, it involves operationalising programme goals into measurable objectives that then serve as a benchmark for determining success.	Ralph Tyler William Popham
Experimental evaluation	An evaluation that involves random assignment or the use of matching procedures to allocate participants to treatment and control groups. Quantitative estimates of programme effect are achieved by comparing outcomes between groups.	Donald Campbell Tom Cook William Shadish
CIPP model	The essential features are captured in the acronym CIPP – which stands for evaluations that focus on context, inputs, processes and products. Many evaluation taxonomies are based on the four types of evaluation identified in this model.	Daniel Stufflebeam
Goal-free evaluation	This approach is based on the premise that evaluators should be concerned with what a programme is actually doing rather than official statements of what was intended. The goal-free evaluator deliberately avoids programme goals and attempts to uncover all effects, including unintended positive or negative outcomes.	Michael Scriven
Responsive evaluation	Emphasis is given to holistic observation of programmes in order to support local improvement efforts. The responsive evaluator prefers qualitative case study methods that allow questions and issues to emerge during the evaluation, focuses on programme activities rather than goals, incorporates diverse values and responds to audience information needs.	Robert Stake
Meta-evaluation	Meta-evaluation is a systematic process for evaluating an evaluation, typically against standards such as utility, feasibility, propriety and accuracy. Can be used to improve an ongoing evaluation or inform judgements about the strengths, limitations and overall merit of a completed evaluation.	Michael Scriven Daniel Stufflebeam
Utilisation-focused evaluation	Epitomised by the maxim 'intended use by intended users'. An eclectic and collaborative approach to evaluation that involves identifying stakeholders who have a special interest in an evaluation, obtaining their buy-in, and then orienting the study so that it meets their information needs.	Michael Patton
Adversary evaluation	A concept of evaluation that borrows from the judicial process, where a programme is effectively 'put on trial'. The adversarial or judicial evaluation model seeks to provide a comprehensive, impartial and balanced overview of programme strengths and weaknesses through the presentation of evidence from opposing perspectives. Briefly	Thomas Owens Robert Wolf

Table 1. *(Continued)*

Type	Basic Description	Key Theorist(s)
	used during the context of educational evaluation in the 1970s, but failed to gain widespread acceptance.	
Connoisseurship and criticism	This perspective on evaluation is influenced by art criticism and aesthetic theory. It is concerned fundamentally with the process of making value judgements. The role of the evaluator is somewhat analogous to a good wine connoisseur or art critic who draws on their professional expertise, experience and insights to provide an assessment of programme quality and worth.	Elliot Eisner
Fourth-generation evaluation	Based on constructivist philosophy, fourth-generation evaluation grew out of skepticism towards traditional objectives-based and experimental evaluation approaches. The basic process involves identifying stakeholders, eliciting stakeholders' constructions of the programme and related claims, concerns, and issues, and then facilitating consensus among stakeholders via discussion, negotiation and exchange.	Egon Guba Yvonna Lincoln
Empowerment evaluation	A highly participatory model that uses evaluation methods, concepts, techniques and findings to foster improvement and self-determination. The origins of this approach are based in community psychology and action research. Empowerment evaluators perform the role of a 'coach', providing technical assistance and support to build the capacity of participants to improve their programmes through critical reflection and self-evaluation.	David Fetterman
Deliberative democratic evaluation	An approach to evaluation that draws on the democratic principles of inclusion, dialogue and deliberation to reduce bias and arrive at defensible evaluative conclusions. It involves the use of traditional evaluation methods, but emphasises the need to consider all relevant interests, values and perspectives, engage in stakeholder dialogue and promote reflective deliberation.	Ernest House Kenneth Howe
Developmental evaluation	Patton's most recent contribution to evaluation theory involves the application of systems thinking and complexity theory to the field of evaluation. Developmental evaluators are an integral part of the innovation design team. They assist organisations to develop programmes in complex, dynamic environments.	Michael Patton

Source: Adapted from Mathison (2005).

These are based, to varying degrees, on constructivist philosophies of social science. This position holds the view that evaluators should not investigate social programmes in the same way as natural scientists study nature. The basic argument is a follows: people construct their own subjective reality of social programmes through complex processes of human interaction. As a consequence, knowledge about social programmes cannot exist external to human interactions which occur in specific contexts, spaces and times.

It is difficult to summarise the design 'logic' of constructivist evaluation, as there are many different approaches that fit broadly into the constructive camp. At a fundamental level though, there is usually a tendency to employ qualitative approaches such as case studies, in-depth interviewing and prolonged periods of field observation. This is deemed necessary to understand the complexity and richness of human interactions that occur between various programme stakeholders. Constructivist evaluators also tend to adopt a 'negotiator' role, work closely with stakeholders to facilitate consensus among multiple interpretations of the programme (see Guba & Lincoln, 1989).

The Evolution of Evaluation Theory

The emphasis placed on the five components of evaluation theory has changed over time. Early developments in evaluation theory focused primarily on knowledge construction and valuing (see the work of Donald Campbell and Michael Scriven). In the late 1970s and throughout the 1980s conceptual development turned to theories of use and strategies for responding to the needs of policy-makers (e.g. Carol Weiss, Joseph Wholey and Robert Stake). Evaluation theorists such as Peter Rossi and Lee Cronbach then tried to integrate the work of previous scholars into tailored, systematic evaluation approaches (Shadish et al., 1991).

Over the past decade there have been some notable attempts to further consolidate different perspectives on evaluation. For example, Mark, Henry, and Julnes (2000) present a coherent and practical theory of evaluation, grounded in an emergent realist philosophy of science. They offer a useful distinction between four key purposes of programme evaluation. These are: (1) to assess the merit and worth of programmes; (2) to ensure programme compliance with regulatory mandates, (3) to improve programmes and organisations; and (4) to build theoretical knowledge and cumulate evidence for future programmes. They also identify four modes of evaluative inquiry: description, classification, causal analysis and values inquiry. For practitioners, this integrative framework can guide decisions regarding the most appropriate evaluation approach and methods, given specific circumstances and constraints.

As the field of evaluation continues to grow there has also been a noticeable rise in the number evaluation 'textbooks', as well as new journals, encyclopaedias and handbooks targeted specifically at professional evaluators. In 1972 Carol Weiss published one of the very first evaluation textbooks, and in 1976 the first journal, *Evaluation Review*, was launched by Sage Publications. Today there are over a dozen dedicated evaluation journals that publish scholarly articles reporting on evaluation studies, evaluation methods, theory, use, values and philosophy.

Another indication of growth is the worldwide expansion of professional evaluation associations. In 1980 there were only three regional or national evaluation societies. This grew to nine by the late 1990s and just one decade later there were more than 50 professional evaluation societies. Today, there are over 125 societies and a global network, the International Organisation for Cooperation in Evaluation, has been established to build evaluation capacity and foster the exchange of ideas, practices and insights (http://ioce.net/index.shtml).

These trends and developments suggest that evaluation is becoming much more commonplace in modern democracies as well as in developing countries. We are now experiencing what might be called a 'Second Boom' period in evaluation (Donaldson & Lipsey, 2006). The idealism and heated debates associated with philosophical prescriptions of the past have been tempered by a growing acceptance of the complementary roles that different forms of data can play in evaluation research. A planned eclecticism of approach holds sway. Today's evaluation practitioner typically adopts a pragmatic stance; mixing-methods and tailoring the evaluation to meet the needs of intended users.

Roles for Evaluation Theory in Criminal Justice

Having outlined, very briefly, the nature and evolution of evaluation theory one might ask, why is evaluation theory worth knowing? One way of answering this is to consider the relationship between evaluation theory and methodology. No single research design, methodology or method of data collection is appropriate always and everywhere. Strict adherence to one approach is likely to result in data that is of little use. It may also lead to inaccurate conclusions about the merit or worth of the programme or policy that is being evaluated. The decline of the rehabilitative ideal following Martinson's (1974) now infamous review of 231 quasi-experimental evaluations of offender treatment studies is an instructive example of how the methodological 'law of the hammer[3] 'approach to evaluation can dangerously misinform judgements regarding programme effectiveness.

Shadish et al. (1991) explain that knowledge of evaluation theory encourages appreciation of the range of methods and techniques that can be employed by practising evaluators. Most importantly though, it provides guiding principles for their application across the range of scenarios that criminal justice evaluators are confronted with:

> Evaluation theories are like military strategies and tactics; methods are like military weapons and logistics. The good commander needs to know strategy and tactics to deploy weapons properly or to organise logistics in different situations. The good evaluator needs theories for the same reasons in choosing and deploying methods. Without thorough grounding in evaluation theory, the evaluator is left to trial and error or to professional lore in learning about appropriate methods. (p. 34)

In a similar vein, Stufflebeam and Shinkfield (2007) remind us that evaluation theory is worth knowing because poor theories of evaluation can mislead evaluation practice, resulting in serious negative consequences. They use as an example, the development of objectives-based evaluation theory. This approach was developed by Ralph Tyler in the 1930s, and grew out of his work on the effects of large-scale educational innovation. Objective- or goal-based evaluation narrowly defines the purpose of evaluation as the process of determining whether or not a programme has achieved specified outcomes. This 'theory' of evaluation misled evaluators for decades as there was a strong tendency to focus only on intended outcomes, not on the actual outcomes (positive or negative) that a particular programme might be generating.

Another informative case-in-point comes from the area of evaluation commonly referred to as performance measurement or monitoring (Wholey, 2001). Performance data typically comes in the form of quantitative output measures such as: number of offenders enrolled in a programme; percentage of programme completions; crime 'clearance' rates, recidivism rates and so on. Criminal justice administrators regularly develop and use 'indicators' such as these to track implementation and measure programme impact over time. The application of a measurement or indicator-based approach to evaluation can, however, alter the delivery of an intervention in destructive ways. In the evaluation theory literature this phenomena is commonly referred to as 'Campbell's Law' of goal displacement:

> The more any quantitative indicator is used for social decision-making, the more subject it will be to corruption pressures and the more apt it will be to distort and corrupt the social processes it is intended to monitor. (Campbell, 1979, p. 85)

Consider, for example, the commonly used 'number and rate of completion' measure for correctional programmes. In many jurisdictions new initiatives have been introduced far too rapidly, resulting in perverse effects. In one study, Raynor (2004) found that the three-year time frame for implementing offender programmes in probation agencies across England and Wales was not realistic. Pressure from government and Treasury officials to introduce change quickly occurred mainly as a result of unreasonable targets for programme completions. These targets 'drove the pace of the roll-out of offending programs' but were established 'without any systematic prior assessment of the characteristics of offenders under supervision and their suitability for programmes' (p. 316).

Aside from wasting time and resources, the presence of an unenthusiastic offender in a group programme could have a disruptive or harmful affect on other participants. Even the use of higher-order 'outcome' measures such as recidivism can undermine the intent of correctional programmes. Programme staff, for instance, may recruit lower-risk offenders to make a new programme appear more successful or to gain additional funding (a phenomena known as 'creaming'). While it is difficult to prevent these kinds of scenarios from occurring altogether, prior knowledge of relevant evaluation theory can assist evaluation practitioners to minimise the dysfunctional side-effects of quantitative performance measures.

The benefit of understanding evaluation theory can be demonstrated further through a final illustration. Scriven (1967) first distinguished between the formative and summative roles of evaluation. Formative evaluation asks the question 'How are we doing?' It focuses on generating information about programme processes and implementation. This information is then used primarily by internal staff to inform decisions about programme development and improvement. Summative evaluation asks the question 'How have we done?' It focuses on generating evidence about the worth of the programme in terms of outcomes and ultimate impact of the intervention. Summative evaluation is typically conducted after a programme has had time to settle and mature, and often informs decisions concerning programme continuation, termination, expansion, replication and so on.

The formative–summative typology, although a simplification of reality, is now almost universally accepted in the field and has been instrumental in shaping the way people think about evaluation. Evaluators who lack an understanding of the importance of tailoring an evaluation to the stage of programme development may fall into the trap of conducting a summative evaluation too soon. In the socio-political context of criminal justice programming this can be problematic. For example, where an experimental study conducted on a poorly implemented programme leads to findings of 'no effect', this may result in the premature termination of a potentially effective intervention.

To conclude, evaluation theory serves several purposes. Perhaps most critically, it functions as a guide to practice. It does this in many ways: by informing decisions about when and why to use particular models of evaluation and methods of data collection; by steering evaluators away from narrow or faulty conceptions of what evaluation is and how it should be conducted; and by directing the practising evaluator to common issues, problems and challenges that are likely to arise in particular evaluation contexts.

THEORIES FOR EVALUATION

This section introduces two further notions of theory, which can also be incorporated usefully into the practice of criminal justice evaluation. These two types of theory are referred to here as programme theory and social science theory. Both can be considered theories *for* evaluation because they provide the evaluator with a powerful way of understanding how and why social programmes generate outcomes. This is somewhat different from a theory of evaluation, which as we have seen, focuses on the body of principles, prescriptions and ideas about how to conduct evaluations.

Programme Theory

Many discussions of programme theory seem to imply that it is a new approach – something which has only recently been discovered by the evaluation community. In fact, the concept of 'programme theory' has a relatively long lineage, particularly when one considers the short history of the field of evaluation. The roots of theory-driven evaluation can be traced back to the work of Edward Suchman, who in his 1967 book *Evaluative Research*, was perhaps the first evaluator to argue for the importance of investigating a programme's implicit theory of action (at the time he referred to it as a programme's 'chain of objectives'). Importantly, Suchman suggested that one of the primary purposes of evaluation is 'testing' a programme hypothesis:

> The evaluation study tests some hypothesis that activity A will attain objective B because it is able to influence process C which affects the occurrence of this objective. An understanding of all three factors – program, objective and intervening process – is essential to the conduct of evaluative research. (p. 177)

Perhaps because of Suchman's untimely death shortly after the publication of his book, the importance of focusing evaluation on the theory underlying the action of social programmes was not recognised fully until some years later. Subsequently, evaluation theorists such as Carol Weiss (1972, 1997), Joseph Wholey (1979, 1987), and, in particular, Peter Rossi's student Huey-Tsyh Chen (1990, 2005), have all helped to establish the prominence of programme theory.

There are some important differences in the various approaches to programme theory-based evaluation, but the common underlying theme is that programmes *are* theories. That is, all social programmes contain an assumption (or more likely a set of assumptions) about how and why programme resources and activities will bring about change in the reasoning and behaviour of participants. In this sense, programmes are not 'dosages' given to passive recipients; they are active interventions that only 'work' if people choose to make them work and are placed in the right conditions to enable them to do so' (Pawson & Tilley, 1994, p. 294).

Although there is currently no accepted definition, programme theory-based evaluation has been usefully described by Bickman (1987) as 'the construction of a plausible and sensible model of how a program is supposed to work' with whom, how, why and under what circumstances (p. 5). This definition depicts nicely the idea that programme theories are best thought of as 'small theories' associated with specific social programmes, policies and interventions (Lipsey, 1993).

Unfortunately, the term 'programme theory' all too often invokes images of some grand theory that attempts to account for the functioning of human behaviour in a law-like fashion. This image does not capture the kind of theorising that evaluators apply to the study of social programmes. Theory-oriented evaluations are much more modest. This is one of the reasons why programme theories are often likened (after the sociologist Robert Merton) to middle-range theories which position themselves between universal social laws and description (Pawson, 2000).

Programme theory can be expressed in many ways – a graphic display of boxes and arrows, a table, a narrative description and so on. The methodology for constructing programme theory, as well as the level of detail and complexity, also varies significantly. Some examples include: path analysis and causal modelling; observations of the programme in action; interviews with staff to uncover implicit assumptions about how the programme works; concept mapping exercises; formal (argumentational) analyses of programme and policy documents; and detailed examination of research on similar programmes (Connell, Kubish, Schorr, & Weiss, 1995; Donaldson, 2007; Leeuw, 2003; Smith, 1990; Trochim, 1989). Regardless of the way it is developed and expressed, programme theory should be grounded in the empirically realities of the particular programme, its implementation context, staffing arrangements, funding levels and social and political environment.

As well as helping to build knowledge about how and why programmes work (or fail to work), the literature is replete with further examples of the benefits of programme theory for evaluation. For example, one early advocate of programme theory, Joseph Wholey (1983), used a form of programme theory known as 'evaluability assessment' in his work with the US government to determine whether or not a programme was ready to be evaluated. A good evaluability assessment can save considerable resources by forestalling a premature and potentially costly impact evaluation that would almost certainly yield biased estimates of programme effect.

As interest in programme theory increased throughout the 1990s, evaluators also discovered the importance of programme theory for guiding evaluations and engaging stakeholders. For example, contributors to the *New Directions for Evaluation* compilation on programme theory (see Rogers, Hacsi, Petrosino, & Huebner, 2000) discuss the role of programme theory in formulating and prioritising evaluation questions, directing data collection activities; and augmenting experimental evaluations and meta-analysis. Evaluators also report that the *process* of programme theory development can assist goal clarification, enhance stakeholder buy-in and provide information to improve programme design and delivery.

It is common, however, to discover at the beginning of an evaluation that the theory of change underlying the programme has never been articulated or tested systematically. The programme theory or 'theories' remain hidden, typically in the minds of policy architects and practitioners. Failure to surface assumptions about how programmes are 'supposed to work' can be problematic because if a programme is based on a faulty theory, then it will not bring about desired change, no matter how well it is implemented.

Consider, for example, delinquency prevention programmes such as 'Scared Straight'. These programmes involve young people visiting prison to experience prison life firsthand. The purpose of these visits is usually framed within the context of reducing crime and re-offending. A theory-driven evaluation might start by asking: 'What is it about exposure to prison life and prisoners that is supposed to help reduce crime and re-offending?' One of the (faulty) assumptions underlying 'Scared Straight' programmes is that criminal activity can be prevented by giving wayward teenagers a taste of what it would be like to be locked-up in prison.

However, this hypothesis is not supported by evaluation findings which consistently demonstrate that programmes such as 'Scared Straight' appear to do more harm than good. For example, one comprehensive meta-analysis found that young people who complete these types of programmes have higher rates of re-offending than young people who do not go through the programme (Petrosino, Turpin-Petrosino, & Buehler, 2003). It seems that despite considerable popularity and intuitive appeal 'attempts to scare teenagers into better behaviour [are] not a successful enterprise' (McCord, 2003, p. 26).

A theory-driven evaluation would dig further in an attempt to explain negative outcome patterns. Why is it that 'Scared Straight' programmes produce criminogenic effects? A quick survey of the literature suggests that a number of alternative programme theories seem to be at play. Consider the following three examples that may account for the harmful effects of 'Scared Straight' programmes:

Alternative programme theory #1: Rather than 'deterring' crime, 'Scared Straight' programmes may inadvertently promote deviance among impressionable youths who view prisoners as positive (rather than negative) role models (Finckenauer, 1982).

Alternative programme theory #2: Participants may react to attempts at intimidation by rising to the challenge and 'proving' to themselves, their peers and others that they are not scared of prison (Finckenauer, 1982).

Alternative programme theory #3: Delinquent-prone participants who may already feel alienated from society could form a belief that prison is a place of sanctuary where they can establish new friendships and derive a sense of belonging (Greater Egypt Planning & Development Commission, 1979).

Of course, further investigation would likely reveal several additional, competing 'Scared Straight' programme theories. These would need to be teased out in a similar fashion and empirically tested using a variety of methods of data collection. The important point to emphasise is that programme theory-driven evaluations re-shift the focus of evaluation away from the view that programmes are molar treatments. According to the programme theory perspective, all programmes are based on a set of propositions regarding what goes on in the 'black box' to transform inputs into outcomes. Thus, when conducting programme theory evaluation, the theory or theories underlying programmes (even well-established programmes with high levels of support) are an important focus for the evaluator's scrutiny, not just observable programme effects.

Social Science Theory

A major task of the social sciences[4] is to understand the nature, extent and causes of social problems. Of course, this is not the only task but it is arguably one of the most important. Theories of social problems are based on various kinds of observations, facts and events. When empirical data are packaged into a set of sensible, logical, and interrelated propositions, they form the basis for a verifiable and generalisable theory. Social science theories can be usefully defined as an attempt to explain 'recurrent patterns or regularities in social life' (Blaikie, 2009, p. 124).

Social science theory is relevant for evaluators because programmes are planned efforts to solve social problems. Programmes 'work' by attempting to disrupt social regularities, altering the conditions, behaviours or processes that give rise to recurrent problems like crime, poverty, unemployment, poor educational achievement, substance misuse and so on. Although the evidence base for some social phenomenon is sparse, existing knowledge on prior efforts to prevent or solve social problems often exists. Of course, the knowledge base may not be directly applicable to a specific programme or evaluation, but 'operating within a vacuum when useful information exists, can be a very inefficient way to practice evaluation' (Donaldson & Lipsey, 2006, p. 63).

In the context of criminal justice evaluation, there is an enormous variety of research and empirically based theories that programme planners and evaluations can usefully draw upon. For example, the conceptual basis for offending behaviour programmes is typically based on cognitive social learning theory (McGuire, 2006), and in the area of restorative justice and youth conferencing, Braithwaite's (1989) theory of reintegrative shaming has been applied extensively. Tilley's (1993) realistic evaluation of the way in which surveillance tactics, like closed-circuit television (CCTV), might influence (i.e. 'block') opportunities for criminal behaviour in and around car parks is a clear demonstration of how situational crime prevention theory can be instructive for evaluation.

Social science theory also plays a critical role when evaluators are involved in assessing the need for a programme. Needs assessment is a fundamental stage of criminal justice evaluation 'because a program cannot be effective at ameliorating a social problem if there is no problem to begin with or if the program services do not actually relate to the problem' (Rossi, Lipsey, & Freeman, 2004, p. 102). The Australian criminologist Don Weatherburn provides an insightful critique of car-theft policy in Western Australia that highlights the importance of utilising existing research and theory, especially during needs assessment and programme design.

Weatherburn (2004) explains that in the late 1980s, Western Australia was experiencing a significant rise in the number of officially recorded car thefts. In what was to become the first of two misguided policy responses, law enforcement officials decided to deal with the 'problem' by engaging in high-speed pursuits of stolen cars. The consequences of this policy decision were disastrous (16 deaths during an 18-month period). The Labour Government then introduced severe penalties for repeat juvenile offenders to appease public reaction, which spuriously linked the problem of car theft to a lenient juvenile justice system. A subsequent evaluation revealed that the introduction of new punitive legislation had no effect on the rate of car theft in Western Australia. In a bid to win law and order votes politicians and policy-makers had misdiagnosed the nature of the problem. Weatherburn (2004) writes:

> The crowing irony is that the car theft problem in Western Australia was eventually brought under control, not as a result of tougher penalties, but because a subsequent government passed a law requiring engine immobilisers to be fitted to all vehicles being registered [an example of situational crime prevention theory at work]. (p. 29)

Another significant role for social science theory is to assist evaluators in the development of programme theory. As noted earlier, there are a variety of methods available for reconstructing programme theory. Many popular approaches utilise some form of visual 'logic model' to depict programme operations and outcomes. Typically the programme logic is based on information generated by some kind of elicitation technique, where the evaluator collaboratively develops the model with stakeholders (Leeuw, 2003). However, this does not mean that programme theories always need to be based solely on practitioner wisdom, as stakeholder theories could in fact be wrong (as some of the above examples demonstrate). Where possible, programme theory should also incorporate information from previous research and knowledge of mechanisms derived from social and behavioural science (Astbury & Leeuw, 2010).

From an evaluation perspective, social mechanisms are not programme activities or variables. Mechanisms are the underlying causal processes that generate change in participants, given certain conditions. Put another way, mechanisms focus on the way in which participants respond or react to programme services. A first test of the relevance and 'validity' of a programme or intervention theory can be undertaken by confronting the science with existing knowledge about mechanisms.

Although there are not yet repositories on mechanisms, several scholars have provided useful summaries of the research literature on mechanisms. Jon Elster (2007), for example, draws on insights from psychology to economics and political science to identify and discuss some twenty mechanisms that underlie a range of social phenomena. Similarly, Farnsworth (2007) takes legal arrangements like laws and contracts as a starting point and dissects which types of mechanisms play a role when one wants to understand how these arrangements work. He discusses mechanisms such as the 'slippery slope', the 'endowment effect' and 'framing effects'. Theoreticians within the social sciences have also contributed to knowledge about mechanisms, as work by Festinger (1954), Merton (1968) and Olson (1971) has shown.

If an intervention is based on a mechanism that is known to not work well (in a given context), this is a signal that the programme will probably not be very effective. For example, Pawson (2006) demonstrates that many policies and programmes that appear on the surface to be very different actually rely on the same mechanism to change behaviour. School league tables, sex offender legislation, and car safety indices, for instance, can be conceptualised as a type of *public disclosure intervention* that taps into the same underlying mechanism (in this case, 'naming and shaming'). Evidence suggests, however, that naming and shaming does not work particularly well in the first two contexts. Drawing on Merton's celebrated reference group theory, Pawson (2010) shows that sex offender notification systems often lead to 'naming and evading', driving offenders underground and jeopardising public safety. Meanwhile, school league tables can result in 'naming and gaming', with administrators responding to ranking exercises by deploying tactics such as 'teaching to the test' in order to improve performance data. In contrast, vehicle companies seem to respond much more positively to naming and shaming efforts because they want to protect their position and reputation.

Lastly, a careful examination of social science theory and research literature can be beneficial for guiding decisions about design and method options, such as the selection of constructs and variables, measurement techniques and analysis procedures. Prior research can inform and provide context for interpretation of findings, such as standards and expectations regarding effect sizes for particular kinds of criminal justice interventions. Examination of relevant evaluation studies can also help to identify the types of conceptual and methodological strategies that have worked well, or not so well in the past. Of course, careful adaption for the programme under investigation is likely to be required, as concepts and techniques may not always generalise across different contexts. Nevertheless, the value of drawing on extant theory to anticipate likely pitfalls and leverage from accumulated knowledge should not be underestimated as it can save evaluators and funding agencies considerable time and resources (Donaldson & Lipsey, 2006).

CONCLUSION

In the 1960s, during the first boom-period in social programme evaluation, researchers from a variety of disciplinary backgrounds found themselves conducting evaluations. At this time there was virtually no theoretical foundation to guide practice. As we enter the second boom-period of evaluation, social scientists are again increasingly being called upon to undertake complex and often large-scale evaluations. For the many criminologists (and psychologists, sociologists and economists) now entering the field of evaluation, one of the major messages of this chapter is that evaluation researchers no longer need to rely so heavily on a 'learning-by-doing' or 'trial-and-error' approach.

Of course, good criminal justice evaluation is still good social science. Even so, history has taught us that while technical proficiency in the application of research methodology is important, an understanding of how theory can be incorporated into evaluation practice is also necessary. Drawing on the work of Donaldson and Lipsey (2006), this chapter has identified two broad types of theory and examined some of the ways in which these are useful for evaluation practice in criminal justice settings.

First, theories of evaluation inform decisions regarding evaluation purpose, selection of data collection methods; identification of evaluator roles; techniques for engaging stakeholders and strategies for enhancing use.

There is no such thing as an ideal or perfect theory of evaluation, and practitioners should not adhere rigidly to one approach. Knowledge of evaluation theory tells us how, where, when and why to deploy methods, given the circumstances and constraints. Learning evaluation theory is a professional obligation because it can help evaluators to avoid inadvertent, but potentially harmful practices. For example, selecting an evaluation approach that does not match the stage of programme development or adopting a managerial bias by narrowly defining the success of a programme according to predetermined goals and objectives.

Second, theories for evaluation (i.e. programme theory and social science theory) help to build knowledge about social problems by identifying the causal mechanisms by which criminal justice programmes work (or fail to work). When used as an organising framework, programme theory can also play a valuable role in several stages of an evaluation. During planning, programme theory can inform decisions about whether a programme is even ready to be evaluated. During evaluation design, it assists in determining appropriate questions and can focus the evaluation on critical components of the programme, saving time and resources. When evaluators collaborate with staff, seeking their input into programme theory development, this can enhance stakeholder engagement in the evaluation process and facilitate use of findings.

When combined carefully into evaluation practice, these three forms of theory provide a powerful set of concepts, methods and tools for guiding the conduct of criminal justice evaluation and generating new knowledge about how, why, where and for whom criminal justice interventions work to ameliorate social problems.

NOTES

1. Christie (2003) suggests that this can be explained in part by the fact that many people who conduct evaluations have not received any formal training in evaluation and most are not evaluators; rather their primary identity is with some other field:

> today's evaluators may not use any existing evaluation theory to guide their work … many people conducting evaluation rely on informal theory, derived from their experiences and ideas about evaluation … or use theories offered by their own professional disciplines rather than those offered by the evaluation community. (p. 2)

2. When applied as the dominant framework for organising the conduct of an evaluation, programme theory could be viewed as a distinct model or theory of evaluation. Other forms of theory in evaluation that are sometimes distinguished

include implementation theory and domain theory; although these are arguably subsets of social science theory.

3. This is a reference to Kaplan's (1964) 'Law of the Instrument' – 'give a small boy a hammer, and he will find that everything he encounters needs pounding' (p. 28). Kaplan is describing the similar tendency for researchers to employ their favoured methods and techniques irrespective of the nature and circumstances of the research task.

4. The term 'social science' is used here in a very general sense to refer to the collective wisdom of each of the various substantive disciplines (e.g. history, sociology, economics, psychology, criminology, politics, biology, etc.).

REFERENCES

Alkin, M. C. (Ed.). (2004). *Evaluation roots: Tracing theorists' views and influences*. Thousand Oaks, CA: Sage.

Astbury, B., & Leeuw, F. L. (2010). Unpacking black boxes: Mechanisms and theory building in evaluation. *American Journal of Evaluation, 31*(3), 363–381. doi:10.1177/1098214010371972

Bickman, L. (1987). The importance of program theory. In L. Bickman (Ed.), Using program theory in evaluation. *New Directions for Program Evaluation* (No. 33, pp. 5–18). San Francisco, CA: Jossey-Bass.

Blaikie, N. (2009). *Designing social research*. Cambridge, UK: Polity Press.

Braithwaite, J. (1989). *Crime, shame and reintegration*. Cambridge: Cambridge University Press.

Campbell, D. T. (1979). Assessing the impact of planned social change. *Evaluation and Program Planning, 2*, 67–90. doi:10.1016/0149-7189(79)90048-X

Campbell, D. T., & Stanley, J. C. (1966). *Experimental and quasi-experimental designs for research*. Chicago, IL: Rand McNally.

Chen, H.-T. (1990). *Theory-driven evaluations*. Newbury Park, CA: Sage.

Chen, H.-T. (2005). *Practical program evaluation: Assessing and improving planning, implementation, and effectiveness*. Thousand Oaks, CA: Sage.

Christie, C. A. (2003). What guides evaluation practice? A study of how evaluation practice maps onto evaluation theory. In C. A. Christie (Ed.), The practice-theory relationship in evaluation. *New Directions for Evaluation* (No. 97, pp. 7–36). San Francisco, CA: Jossey-Bass.

Connell, J., Kubish, A., Schorr, L., & Weiss, C. (1995). *New approaches to evaluating community initiatives: Concepts, methods, and contexts*. Washington, DC: Aspen Institute.

Cook, T. D., & Campbell, D. T. (1979). *Quasi-experimentation: Design and analysis issues for field settings*. Boston, MA: Houghton Mifflin.

Donaldson, S. I. (2007). *Program theory-driven evaluation science: Strategies and applications*. Mahwah, NJ: Erlbaum.

Donaldson, S. I., & Lipsey, M. (2006). Roles for theory in contemporary evaluation practice: Developing practical knowledge. In I. Shaw, J. Greene & M. Mark (Eds.), *The Sage handbook of evaluation* (pp. 56–75). Thousand Oaks, CA: Sage.

Elster, J. (2007). *Explaining social behaviour: More nuts and bolts for the social sciences*. Cambridge, UK: Cambridge University Press.

Farnsworth, W. (2007). *The legal analyst: A toolkit for thinking about the law*. Chicago, IL: University of Chicago Press.

Farrington, D. P. (2003). Methodological quality standards for evaluation research. *The Annals of the American Academy of Political and Social Science, 587*(1), 49–68. doi:10.1177/0002716202250789

Festinger, L. (1954). A theory of social comparison processes. *Human Relations, 7*, 117–140. doi:10.1177/001872675400700202

Fetterman, D. M. (1996). Empowerment evaluation: An introduction to theory and practice. In D. M. Fetterman, S. J. Kalflarian & A. Wandersman (Eds.), *Empowerment evaluation: Knowledge and tools for self-assessment and accountability* (pp. 3–46). Thousand Oaks, CA: Sage.

Finckenauer, J. O. (1982). *Scared straight and the panacea phenomenon*. Englewood Cliffs, NJ: Prentice-Hall.

Greater Egypt Regional Planning and Development Commission. (1979). *Menard correctional center: Juvenile tours impact study*. Carbondale, IL: Author.

Guba, E. G., & Lincoln, Y. S. (1981). *Effective evaluation*. San Francisco, CA: Jossey-Bass.

Guba, E. G., & Lincoln, Y. S. (1989). *Fourth generation evaluation*. Newbury Park, CA: Sage.

Hope, T. (2004). Pretend it works: Evidence and governance in the evaluation of the reducing burglary initiative. *Criminology and Criminal Justice, 4*(3), 287–308. doi:10.1177/1466802504048467

Israel, M. (2000). The commercialisation of university-based criminological research in Australia. *Australian and New Zealand Journal of Criminology, 33*(1), 1–20. doi:10.1177/000486580003300102

Kaplan, A. (1964). *The conduct of inquiry: Methodology for behavioural science*. San Francisco, CA: Chandler Publishing Company.

Leeuw, F. L. (2003). Reconstructing program theories: Methods available and problems to be solved. *American Journal of Evaluation, 24*(1), 5–20. doi:10.1177/109821400302400102

Lipsey, M. (1993). Theory as method: Small theories of treatments. In L. B. Sechrest & A. G. Scott (Eds.), Understanding causes and generalizing about them. *New Directions for Program Evaluation* (No. 57, pp. 5–38). San Francisco, CA: Jossey-Bass.

Mark, M. M., Henry, G. T., & Julnes, G. (2000). *Evaluation: An integrated framework for understanding, guiding, and improving policies and programs*. San Francisco, CA: Jossey-Bass.

Martin, M., & McIntyre, L. C. (Eds.). (1994). *Readings in the philosophy of social science*. Cambridge, MA: MIT Press.

Martinson, R. (1974). What works? Questions and answers about prison reform. *The Public Interest, 10*, 22–52.

Mathison, S. (Ed.). (2005). *Encyclopedia of evaluation*. Thousand Oaks, CA: Sage.

McCord, J. (2003). Cures that harm: Unanticipated outcomes of crime prevention programs. *The Annals of the American Academy of Political and Social Science, 587*(1), 16–30. doi:10.1177/0002716202250781

McGuire, J. (2006). General offending behaviour programmes: Concept, theory, and practice. In C. R. Hollin & E. J. Palmer (Eds.), *Offending behaviour programmes: Development, application, and controversies* (pp. 69–111). Chichester: Wiley.

Merton, R. K. (1967). *On theoretical sociology: Five essays, old and new*. New York, NY: Free Press.

Merton, R. K. (1968). *Social theory and social structure* (3rd ed.). New York, NY: Free Press.

Olson, M. (1971). *The logic of collective action: Public goods and the theory of groups*. Harvard: Harvard University Press.

Pawson, R. (2000). Middle-range realism. *Archives Européennes de Sociologie*, *41*(2), 283–325.

Pawson, R. (2006). *Evidence-based policy: A realist perspective*. London: Sage Publications.

Pawson, R. (2010). Middle range theory and program theory evaluation: From provenance to practice. In J. Vaessen & F. L. Leeuw (Eds.), *Mind the gap: Perspectives on policy evaluation and the social sciences*. Comparative Policy Evaluation (Vol. 16, pp. 171–203). London: Transaction Publishers.

Pawson, R., & Tilley, N. (1994). What works in evaluation research? *British Journal of Criminology*, *34*(3), 291–306.

Petrosino, A., Turpin-Petrosino, C., & Buehler, J. (2003). "Scared Straight" and other juvenile awareness programs for preventing juvenile delinquency: A systematic review of the randomized experimental evidence. *The Annals of the American Academy of Political and Social Science*, *589*(1), 41–62. doi:10.1177/0002716203254693

Raynor, P. (2004). The probation service pathfinders: Finding the path and losing the way? *Criminal Justice*, *4*(3), 309–325.

Rogers, P. J., Hacsi, T. A, Petrosino, A., & Huebner, T. A. (Eds.). (2000). Program theory in evaluation: Challenges and opportunities. *New Directions for Evaluation* (No. 87). San Francisco, CA: Jossey-Bass.

Rossi, P. H., Lipsey, M. W., & Freeman, H. E. (2004). *Evaluation: A systematic approach* (7th ed.). Thousand Oaks, CA: Sage Publications.

Scriven, M. (1967). The methodology of evaluation. In R. Tyler, R. Gagne & M. Scriven (Eds.), *Perspectives of curriculum evaluation* (pp. 39–83). Chicago, IL: Rand-McNally.

Shadish, W. R. (1998). Evaluation theory is who we are. *American Journal of Evaluation*, *19*(1), 1–19.

Shadish, W. R., Cook, T. D., & Leviton, L. C. (1991). *Foundations of program evaluation: Theories of practice*. Newbury Park, CA: Sage.

Shadish, W. R., & Epstein, R. (1987). Patterns of program evaluation practice among members of the Evaluation Research Society and Evaluation Network. *Evaluation Review*, *11*(5), 555–590. doi:10.1177/0193841X8701100501

Smith, N. L. (1990). Using path analysis to develop and evaluate program theory and impact. In L. Bickman (Ed.), Using program theory in evaluation. *New Directions for Program Evaluation* (No. 33, pp. 53–57). San Francisco, CA: Jossey-Bass.

Smith, N. L. (1993). Improving evaluation theory through the empirical study of evaluation practice. *Evaluation Practice*, *14*(3), 237–242. doi:10.1016/0886-1633(93)90051-P

Stake, R. E. (1983). Program evaluation, particularly responsive evaluation. In G. F. Madaus, M. Scriven & D. L. Stufflebeam (Eds.), *Evaluation models* (pp. 287–310). Boston, MA: Kluwer-Nijhoff.

Stufflebeam, D. L., & Shinkfield, A. J. (2007). *Evaluation theory, models, and applications*. San Francisco, CA: Jossey-Bass.

Suchman, E. (1967). *Evaluative research: Principles and practice in public service and social programs*. New York, NY: Russell Sage Foundation.

Tilley, N. (1993). *Understanding car parks, crime and CCTV: Evaluation lessons from safer cities*. Crime Prevention Unit Paper 42. London: Home Office.

Travers, M. (2005). Evaluation research and criminal justice: Beyond a political critique. *Australian & New Zealand Journal of Criminology*, *38*(1), 39–58.

Trochim, W. M. K. (1989). Outcome pattern matching and program theory. *Evaluation and Program Planning, 12*, 355–366. doi:10.1375/acri.38.1.39

Walters, R. (2003). *Deviant knowledge: Criminology, politics and policy.* Devon, UK: Willan Publishing.

Weatherburn, D. (2004). *Law and order in Australia: Rhetoric and reality.* Annandale, NSW: Federation Press.

Weatherburn, D. (2005). Critical criminology and its discontents: A response to Travers' critique of criminal justice evaluation. *Australian & New Zealand Journal of Criminology, 38*(3), 416–420.

Weiss, C. H. (1972). *Evaluation.* Upper Saddle River, NJ: Prentice-Hall.

Weiss, C. H. (1997). Theory-based evaluation: Past, present, and future. *New Directions for Evaluation* (No. 76). San Francisco, CA: Jossey-Bass.

White, R. (2001). Criminology for sale: Institutional change and intellectual field. *Current Issues in Criminal Justice, 13*(2), 127–142.

Wholey, J. S. (1979). *Evaluation: Promise and performance.* Washington, DC: Urban Institute.

Wholey, J. S. (1983). *Evaluation and effective public management.* Boston, MA: Little, Brown.

Wholey, J. S. (1987). Evaluability assessment: Developing program theory. In L. Bickman (Ed.), Using program theory in evaluation. *New Directions for Program Evaluation* (No. 33, pp. 77–92). San Francisco, CA: Jossey-Bass.

Wholey, J. S. (2001). Managing for results: Roles for evaluators in a new management era. *American Journal of Evaluation, 22*(3), 343–347. doi:10.1177/109821400102200309

THE RISK/NEEDS/RESPONSIVITY MODEL: THE CRUCIAL FEATURES OF GENERAL RESPONSIVITY

L. E. Marshall and W. L. Marshall

ABSTRACT

This chapter describes Andrews and Bonta's (2006) Principles of Effective Offender Treatment and its relevance for the treatment of sexual offenders. The three principles of this model are Risk, Needs and Responsivity. Each of these is described in some detail with the greatest emphasis being placed on general responsivity which is one of the two parts of the Responsivity Principle. Our interpretation of general responsivity differs from the view of others (e.g. Hanson et al., 2009) who define this aspect of Responsivity in terms of Cognitive Behaviour Therapy (CBT). While Andrews and Bonta indicate that within their meta-analyses, CBT programmes were the ones most likely to succeed; such programmes were not at all effective. It seems to us that a far more important aspect of general responsivity is what Andrews and Bonta describe as the Core Correctional Practices (CCP) which have to do with the way in which treatment is delivered. We review the CCPs in some detail and provide other evidence indicating that the style of treatment delivery is the crucial factor in determining effectiveness.

Perspectives on Evaluating Criminal Justice and Corrections
Advances in Program Evaluation, Volume 13, 29–45

ISSN: 1474-7863/doi:10.1108/S1474-7863(2012)0000013006

INTRODUCTION

The development of sexual offender treatment was, for most of the modern era (see Marshall & Laws, 2003), based on three sources: (1) theoretical propositions about the origin and maintenance of the behaviour; (2) clinically derived notions about what targets needed to be addressed; and (3) the outcome of empirical tests of these clinical ideas.

The initial theory driving treatment was formulated by McGuire, Carlisle, and Young (1965). In keeping with the conditioning bases of the emerging behaviour therapy movement, McGuire et al. proposed that unusual sexual interests arise as the result of the accidental pairing of sexual arousal and images (or actual experiences) of a deviant act. Subsequent masturbation to these images, as McGuire et al. claimed, entrench the deviant sexual interest. This theory directed treatment to the modification of sexual interests, at first by just reducing deviant arousal (Bond & Evans, 1967) with the later addition of enhancing appropriate sexual interests (see Marquis, 1970).

Interventions based on these ideas were soon seen as limited with Marshall (1971) pointing out that changing sexual preferences alone did not guarantee the client would have the skills and confidence necessary to act on his newly acquired prosocial interests. However, Marshall did not provide any evidence to support his plausible proposal. Similarly, but non-empirical, claims were made about the importance of broader social skills (Barlow, 1974), cognitive distortions (Abel, Becker, & Cunningham-Rathner, 1984), empathy (Hoppe & Singer, 1976), self-esteem (Marshall & Christie, 1982) and intimacy and loneliness (Marshall, 1989). Subsequent research (Bumby, 1996; Marshall, 1993; Marshall, Anderson, & Champagne, 1997; McFall, 1990; Pithers, 1994) confirmed that sexual offenders were indeed deficient, compared to other men, in terms of all these features.

Despite these demonstrations it was still not clear that all these factors needed to be changed in treatment. It might be, for example, that although a lack of empathy distinguished sexual offenders, it might be unrelated to a propensity to reoffend and, therefore, not an appropriate target for a treatment programme aimed at reducing future offending. What was needed was an empirical model that identified modifiable features that were related to reoffending. This, however, would not be sufficient; what was also needed was an empirically defined approach to treatment delivery as well as demonstrably effective procedures to change the targets of treatment.

For the present chapter, we will set aside concerns with this latter issue, which we have addressed in detail in descriptions of our treatment programme (Marshall, Anderson, Fernandez, 1999; W. L. Marshall, Marshall,

Serran, & Fernandez, 2006; W. L. Marshall, Marshall, Serran, & O'Brien, 2011). Our focus will, instead, be on Andrews and Bonta's (2006) research-defined *Principles of Effective Offender Treatment*, which provides a framework for identifying the targets of interventions with offenders and how treatment should be delivered. More specifically, we will direct our attention primarily to what this model, and other related research, has to say about the importance of treatment delivery. While Andrews and Bonta's model was developed on the basis of meta-analytic studies of treatment outcome studies with a variety of offenders, Hanson, Bourgon, Helmus, and Hodgson (2009) have shown that these same principles apply to interventions with sexual offenders.

INTRODUCTION TO THE RNR MODEL

In their extensive research on the factors that maximise treatment effectiveness with offenders, Andrews (2001), Andrews and Bonta (2006), Andrews, Bonta, and Hoge (1990), Andrews, Bonta, and Wormith (2006), Andrews and Dowden (1999), Andrews, Zinger et al. (1990), Dowden and Andrews (2003, 2004) and Dowden, Antonowicz, and Andrews (2003) have derived three 'Principles of Effective Offender Treatment'. These three principles are described as: risk, needs and responsivity. Andrews' research has shown that the proper application of these principles results in the effective reduction in recidivism among various types of offenders, and, as noted, Hanson et al. (2009) recently demonstrated that the same is true for the treatment of sexual offenders.

Risk

The risk principle indicates that treatment resources should be allocated according to the offenders' risk levels. Where resources are limited, this principle directs treatment providers to focus only on the high-risk offenders because the rate of reoffending among these individuals is sufficient to allow treatment to be demonstrably effective. Also when these offenders do recidivate they are more likely to do extensive harm. When resources are sufficient to deal with most offenders, treatment should be more extensive and intensive with high-risk offenders and less so with lower risk offenders.

Both Andrews and Bonta (2006) and Hanson et al. (2009) found that of the three principles, the risk principle was the least powerful in producing changes. Andrews and Bonta (2006) report an effect size of .10 for the risk principle, whereas Hanson et al. (2009) report that 'analyses based on the risk principle were not statistically significant in any of the analyses' (p. 884). In their examination of family interventions for juvenile offenders, Dowden and Andrews (2003) also report that their analyses revealed no significant effects for the risk principle. As a result, Hanson et al. suggested that the risk principle should be considered only as a guide to the management of resources, whereas the other two principles, they suggested, are directly applicable to designing and implementing treatment.

Needs

The needs principle directs treatment providers to address identifiable risk factors that are modifiable. Some factors that predict risk are unchangeable (e.g. features of the offenders' criminal history), whereas others are potentially modifiable. These latter factors are known as 'stable dynamic' or 'criminogenic' factors such as deviant sexual interests, sexual preoccupation, offense-supportive attitudes, poor emotional and self-regulation, ineffective problem-solving and inadequate intimacy skills. It is these changeable factors that must be addressed in treatment. Andrews and Bonta (2006) report that when the needs principle is properly adhered to with offenders the effect size is reasonably impressive (ES = .19). Hanson et al. (2009) similarly report significant effects for the Needs Principle.

Although Andrews and Bonta (2006) report that when an excessive number of non-criminogenic factors are targeted, treatment benefits are reduced, there are circumstances when it may be important to target one or two non-criminogenic features. Indeed, Dowden and Andrews (2003) note that 'targeting non-criminogenic needs of offenders may also be important for reasons other than reducing recidivism' (pp. 329–330). For example, some problematic features of sexual offenders present obstacles to full engagement and treatment should attend to these. Basic research has shown that both low self-esteem (Baumeister, 1993) and shame (Tangney & Dearing, 2002) prevent people from engaging effectively in any change-oriented or learning programme. These and other characteristics that block effective participation need to be addressed early in treatment by employing motivational strategies such as those described by Miller and Rollnick (2002). In fact, Andrews and Bonta (2006) specifically point to the need to adopt a motivational approach with offenders. It may also be that some features of sexual offenders (e.g. lack of empathy), which have been shown not to be criminogenic themselves, may play a mediating role in some identified criminogenic need (e.g. relationship skills), and as a result they may also need to be addressed in treatment. These comments, however, should not be taken to justify addressing any non-criminogenic targets in treatment, as this might seriously compromise treatment effects. If treatment providers wish to address features of sexual offenders that have not been shown to predict reoffending, then they must provide sound reasons for so doing.

Fortunately, Hanson (2006), Hanson and Harris (2000) and Mann, Hanson, and Thornton (2010) have identified a set of clearly established criminogenic features, as well as some features that seem likely to be shown to be criminogenic. As a result, treatment programmes for sexual offenders can now direct attention to the modification of factors that are known to predict reoffending. At least in terms of the Needs Principle, sexual offender treatment programmes can be defined in ways that should maximise effectiveness.

Responsivity

It is, however, the third principle described by Andrews and Bonta (2006) that is our major concern. This is the responsivity principle. Andrews and Bonta (2006) show that appropriately adhering to the responsivity principle produces the largest effect size (ES = .23) of all the principles and, in fact, accounts for a substantial amount of the overall effects of all three principles combined (ES = .28). This principle has two components: general and specific responsivity. The latter requires treatment providers to adjust their delivery to meet the unique features of each client (e.g. cultural and social status, personality, cognitive functioning, psychiatric disorder) as well the client's day-to-day fluctuations in mood and focus. Essentially, specific responsivity requirements address the same issue that is referred to as 'flexibility' in the general clinical literature on process features (see Marshall, Fernandez et al., 2003, for a review). Although specific responsivity is important, we want to focus most of our concerns here on general responsivity.

General responsivity is typically understood to mean that treatment providers should select only those approaches that have been shown to be effective. Andrews and Bonta (2006) claim to have shown that among the various approaches they examined, cognitive-behavioural therapy (CBT), with perhaps relapse prevention (RP) elements, consistently produced more effective results across a variety of offenders. The meta-analyses of Hanson et al. (2002) and Lösel and Schmucker (2005) of sexual offender programmes have produced the same results. Andrews and Bonta certainly claim that social learning theory (Bandura, 1977), which characterises CBT programmes, should be the basis upon which treatment programmes for offenders are designed and implemented.

The results of these various meta-analyses, however, should not be understood to mean that all CBT programmes produced benefits, nor should they be taken to mean that all other, non-CBT programmes were ineffective. However, apparently Hanson et al. (2009) read these findings as indicating that if a programme was described as CBT, then it necessarily met criteria for the general responsivity principle. Indeed, Hanson et al. (2009) expressed this unequivocally when they noted that 'cognitive-behavioral programmes were assumed to adhere to the responsivity principle' (p. 874). On this basis they classified all CBT programmes they included in their meta-analysis as meeting the responsivity principle. In doing so, Hanson et al. (2009) specifically refer to Andrews and Bonta (2006). However, in the meta-analysis where they initially demonstrated the importance of the Risk/Needs/Responsivity (RNR) principles, Andrews, Zinger et al. (1990) point out it was only those CBT programmes employing appropriate therapeutic techniques such as modelling, role-plays, reinforcement and graduated practice (i.e. social learning or behavioural features) that were considered to have met this principle. Fernandez, Shingler and Marshall (2006) pointed out, surprisingly few CBT programmes actually employ these or other behavioural techniques, so if these behavioural features are essential to meet the requirements of general responsivity, it cannot be assumed that all CBT programmes adhere to this principle.

CBT programmes, as we discovered, display marked heterogeneity, so to assume they all meet the responsivity principle seems not to match the data. The series of surveys of sexual offender treatment programmes conducted by the Safer Society Press (Burton & Smith-Darden, 2001; McGrath, Cumming, & Buchard, 2003; McGrath, Cumming, Buchard, Zeoli, & Ellerby, 2010) reveal a startling array of differences across CBT programmes in terms of whether or not they address all, or some, or remarkably few established criminogenic features. The majority of these programmes, in fact, clearly addressed numerous non-criminogenic features. In our review of CBT programmes that were described as having an RP approach, we (Marshall & Anderson, 2000) found similar remarkable variations; some programmes provided extensive training in RP strategies and generated seemingly endless RP plans, while others had variable amounts of RP content, and some appeared to have no RP features at all, despite describing their programme as CBT-RP.

In addition, several researchers have expressed reservations about the effectiveness of sexual offender treatment (Hanson, 2010; Rice, 2010; Rice & Harris, 2003; Seto et al., 2008; Quinsey, Rice, Harris, & Lalumière, 1993), although we (W. L. Marshall & Marshall, 2011) offer an alternative, more optimistic interpretation of the available data. If it is accepted that treatment for sexual offenders has not yet been shown to be effective, then it is difficult to know how to identify sexual offender programmes that meet the general responsivity principle which, in essence, requires the adoption of an empirically sound approach to the delivery of treatment.

What then are the defining features of the general responsivity principle that would allow reviewers to determine whether or not a particular programme adhered to this crucial feature of effective treatment? One aspect of Andrews' extensive work that others have either ignored or given little attention is what he refers to as the 'Core Correctional Practices'. It is this rather neglected feature of the RNR model that we wish to address in detail, as we consider it to be a crucial factor in generating positive outcomes in the treatment of all types of offenders, including sexual offenders.

CORE CORRECTIONAL PRACTICES

Andrews and Kiessling (1980) outlined five dimensions that they believed to be essential to effective correctional treatment. Among these were typical social learning principles of treatment such as a clear statement of the group rules, the provision of reinforcement for compliance and an avoidance of dominance and abuse. In addition, they pointed to the importance of modelling and reinforcement of prosocial attitudes and behaviour. Most importantly, Andrews and Kiessling (1980) declared that relationship factors 'are arguably the most important' (p. 205) of the five dimensions. In elaborating this crucial fifth dimension, Andrews and Kiessling pointed out that interpersonal influence 'is maximised under conditions characterised by open, warm, and enthusiastic communication' (p. 205) and that equally important is the development of a respectful relationship.

The initial meta-analysis that demonstrated the effects of the RNR principles (Andrews, Zinger et al., 1990), also examined the influence of these dimensions, which were rephrased as *Core Correctional Practices* (CCP). These practices are described by what Andrews and Bonta (2006) call *Relationship* and *Structuring* principles. The *Relationship* principle was defined as treatment delivered by a therapist who displays warmth, respect, interest, enthusiasm and non-blaming communication. *Structuring* includes number of features, but in particular, effective reinforcement of prosocial attitudes and behaviours and appropriate modelling by the therapist of these characteristics. These features of therapist style were found (see Andrews & Bonta, 2006, for a summary) to be significantly correlated with treatment effect sizes. The correlations with overall effect size for each of the CCP features were as follows: (a) the relationship skills of staff, $r = .26$; (b) structuring, $r = .37$; (c) effective reinforcement, $r = .25$; and (d) appropriate modelling, $r = .36$.

In a more detailed report, Dowden and Andrews (2004) described the results of two meta-analyses of a large number of studies ($k = 154$ in the first study; $k = 273$ in the second) where they specifically looked at the influence of the CCP. Again they found that the way in which treatment was delivered exerted a profound influence on treatment outcome. It is important to note that these effects were magnified in those programmes targeting high-risk offenders; in other words, the more problematic the offenders were, the more important were the CCP elements.

Dowden and Andrews (2004) concluded that those programmes that appropriately incorporated the CCP elements (i.e. emphasised the appropriate delivery of treatment) 'were associated with substantially higher mean effect sizes than programmes that did not' (p. 210). To illustrate this, Dowden and Andrews reported that when all CCP features were present the correlations with overall effect sizes were significant across treatment programmes for male offenders ($r = .41$), female offenders ($r = .67$), adult offenders ($r = .46$) and juvenile offenders ($r = .42$), as well as for institutional programmes ($r = .42$), and for community-based programmes ($r = .47$). These are, indeed, compelling data that ought to result in a greater focus on both research and treatment on the mode and style of treatment delivery.

Unfortunately only 16% of the programmes Dowden and Andrews (2004) examined properly adhered to CCP principles, despite the fact that most of the programmes were described as CBT. Again we see that describing a programme as CBT offers little reassurance that it meets any of the criteria for the general responsivity principle. Dowden and Andrews (2004) lamented that the 'emphasis placed on developing and utilizing appropriate staff techniques has been sorely lacking with correctional treatment programs' (p. 209). We suggest same is true for sexual offender programmes.

To further illustrate the importance of failing to properly employ CCP principles, we referred to Dowden and Andrews' (2003) examination of studies of family interventions with young offenders (only some of which employed CBT). Dowden and Andrews (2003) found that when both the relationship and structuring principles were met, the effect size was impressive (ES = .39); when only one of these two was met the effect size was lower (ES = .24); and when neither was met the effect size was meaningless (ES = .04). This latter observation is most significant and seems likely to explain why some CBT programmes are ineffective. Andrews and Bonta's (2006) summary of the results of their various meta-analyses of offender programmes indicate that carefully selecting staff for the presence of the requisite relationship skills is significantly correlated with overall treatment effect sizes ($r = .26$), and the same is true for the effects of training staff in these skills ($r = .26$). Citing the results of Andrews' various studies, as well as their own, Dowden and Andrews (2003) declare, that 'the general responsivity principle is predominantly concerned with the *style of program delivery*' (p. 330, italics added), not, as is generally suggested, with the deployment of CBT.

Our view of the importance of the CCP features of responsivity is bolstered by other evidence indicating that the way treatment is delivered is far more important than the procedures employed to produce the desired changes, and perhaps more important than the theoretical orientation of the programme (see Marshall, in press). For example, in the examination of programmes for various disorders (other than the paraphilias) it has been consistently shown across various theoretical approaches that the delivery of treatment is the crucial factor. Research shows, for example, that the therapeutic alliance accounts for between 25% and 30% of the benefits used by the interventions, while the deployment of specific procedures to modify treatment targets accounts for just 15% (Norcross, 2002). Add these two sources of variance together and there is likely little left for the influence of theoretical orientation given the rather noisy circumstances of the therapeutic context.

With respect to sexual offender treatment programmes, we (Marshall, Serran, Fernandez et al., 2003; Marshall et al., 2002) demonstrated that the way in which therapists deliver treatment (i.e. their therapeutic skills and style) accounts for at least 30% and as much as 60% of the treatment-induced changes. Note that this is a larger amount of the variance accounted for by the style of treatment delivery to sexual offenders than is true for other disorders. Our studies indicated that when therapists display warmth and empathy, and a rewarding and somewhat directive style, treatment benefits with sexual offenders are maximised. These therapist features and delivery style identified in our studies as influential are essentially a match for Andrews and Bonta's (2006) CCP. Studies of the perspective sexual offenders have of treatment, indicate that they identify as crucial the role of the therapist (Drapeau, 2005; Drapeau, Korner, Brunet, & Granger, 2004) while acknowledging that certain procedures are also helpful. The views expressed by these clients indicate that they respond positively to therapists who are empathic, warm, respectful and supportive, and who model and reinforce prosocial attitudes and behaviours, while they are resistant or non-compliant with therapists who are confrontational and lacking in the virtues that define effective therapists. It is also important to note that CCP features, and their counterparts identified in other research, not only produce clear beneficial changes, but also reduce drop-outs and increase completion rates (Eisenthal, Emery, Lazare, & Udin, 1979). In sexual offender treatment, drop-outs have been shown to have higher rates of reoffending than do those who refuse to enter treatment (Abel, Mittelman, Becker, Rathner, & Rouleau, 1988; Browne, Foreman, & Middleton, 1998) and sexual offenders who fail to comply with treatment requirements do not achieve the targets of treatment. Only those who are compliant with treatment and attain the targets have lowered reoffense rates (Marques, Weideranders, Day, Nelson, & van Ommeren, 2005).

Finally, Beech and Fordham (1997) and Beech and Hamilton-Giachritsis (2005) (see chapter by Bowen, this volume, for a discussion of these studies) have shown that the way in which therapists facilitate the creation of the group climate is also critical. They found that when therapists created a group climate that was cohesive and expressive, treatment benefits were maximised. Cohesion refers to the way in which group members support and bond with one another, while expressiveness indicates the degree of active participation and emotional expression among the participants. It is clear that a warm, empathic and rewarding group therapist (i.e., one who embodies the CCP features) is the necessary ingredient to maximise cohesion and expressiveness.

There is now, then, a compelling body of literature both within the general offender field (Marshall & Burton, 2010; Marshall, Burton, & Marshall, in press) and in the sexual offender–specific field (Serran & Marshall, 2010) indicating the powerful influence on treatment changes of these various features of treatment delivery. These are precisely the features Andrews and Bonta (2006) point to as defining the Responsivity Principle, namely, the CCPs. This body of research, in fact, indicates that the way in which treatment is delivered is the most important aspect in ensuring effective outcomes. So long as treatment is delivered in a way consistent with the CCPs that emphasises respect and concern for the clients, and so long as criminogenic factors are the targets, we can be reasonably confident of generating positive outcomes.

IMPLICATIONS

The observations made in this chapter have numerous implications for research and practice. First, when selecting programmes within a meta-analytic study to determine the influence of particular programme features, researchers should require an adjustment to the presently employed guide to the criteria for meeting the general aspect of the responsivity principle. As we have shown, it is not satisfactory to consider all programmes that are described as CBT for meeting this principle. Aside from the above-mentioned considerations, we note that Multisystemic Therapy (MST) appears to be effective with juvenile sexual offenders (Borduin, Schaeffer, & Heiblum, 2009). From our reading of the relevant literature on MST, it appears that the therapists are concerned to employ the very characteristics that Andrews and Bonta (2006) describe as CCP. These MST programmes also clearly target known criminogenic features and high-risk offenders. Thus, they meet all three of the Principles of Effective Offender Treatment. In addition, a well-designed psychodynamic treatment programme (i.e. one that addressed criminogenic features and employed an appropriate delivery style) demonstrably reduced long-term recidivism (Kriegman, 2006). These results are all the more impressive as the treatment programme targeted the highest risk sexual offenders. Kreigman's findings should not be seen as surprising since psychodynamic treatment programmes for a variety of non-offending disorders have been shown to be very effective in number of random controlled trials (see Shedler, 2010, for a review). In these studies, the beneficial effects of psychodynamic therapies were long-lasting, something that has not always been shown to be true of CBT programmes for non-offending Axis 1 disorders (Barbaree, 2006).

Perhaps within meta-analyses, researchers should set aside concerns about the theoretical orientation of programmes when identifying those that meet or do not meet criteria for general responsivity. Rather, researchers should focus on how well each programme meets the requirements of carefully selecting, training and supervising therapists to ensure that they are able to meet the CCP requirements. As we have seen, only those offender programmes that met the important general responsivity criteria (i.e., have staff to enact appropriate therapeutic skills) effectively reduce recidivism. As a result, we suggest that if only those sexual offender programmes that meet the Needs Principle and deliver treatment consistent with the CCP were to be entered into meta-analyses, the results might more clearly support the effectiveness of treatment.

Indirect support for this claim comes from studies examining the effectiveness programmes for men who physically assault their partners. Babcock, Green, and Robie (2004) conducted a meta-analysis including a mixture of CBT programmes and approaches that followed the Duluth Model (Pence & Paymar, 1993). This meta-analysis revealed an overall small but meaningful effect size. Closer examination (Fisher, 2008) revealed that the programmes included in this meta-analysis in fact produced a remarkable range of effect sizes. Some of the programmes produced small but negative effects, some generated marginal positive effects, others produced meaningful positive effects, but most importantly a small number produced impressive results (ES $\geq$ .4). The distinctive features of the programmes generating larger effects, as Fisher (2008) demonstrated, were that the therapists delivered them in a motivational way, the therapists' skills were emphasised and the therapeutic alliance was effectively in place. In the less effective programmes, these elements were either absent or insufficiently enacted. These observations, along with the findings showing the importance of the delivery style in treating sexual offenders, and Dowden and Andrews'(2003, 2004) results concerning therapist training and skills all point to the overriding importance of the qualities of therapists and the style of treatment delivery in the effectiveness of treatment for all types of offenders.

It is important to reiterate that Andrews, Bonta et al.'s (1990) study and Hanson et al.'s (2009) replication with sexual offender programmes found that the most effective of the three principles in producing treatment benefits was Responsivity. On the basis of all the observations we have made, we suggest that researchers examining the effectiveness of sexual offender treatment give greater attention to selecting programmes that adhere to the components of the Responsivity Principle and, in particular, to the features of treatment delivery that ensure the CCPs are effectively enacted. Identifying treatment programmes as meeting the requirements of general responsivity on the basis of particular theoretical approach, such as CBT, seems not only overly restrictive but also inconsistent with the evidence. Indeed, the most compelling conclusion that can be drawn from the meta-analyses conducted to date on treatment of sexual offenders is that CBT programmes do not all produce positive outcomes. We need to look beyond particular theoretical approaches when selecting evaluations for meta-analyses. Instead, researchers should focus on the way treatment is delivered (i.e. all aspects of the Responsivity Principle, particularly the CCPs), plus whether or not the Needs Principle is properly adhered to.

Finally, we strongly recommend that treatment providers, both in terms of how they conduct treatment and in terms of how they report their programme, give greater emphasis to the CCP factors to ensure that the way in which treatment is delivered is maximally effective. This, along with targeting known criminogenic factors, is far more important than describing the theoretical orientation that guides treatment and is, apparently, rather more important than describing specific procedures used to alter particular behaviours, cognitions or emotions. In our view, programmes derived from the various aspects of what has been called *Positive Psychology* (Linley & Joseph, 2004; Peterson, 2006; Seligman & Csikszentmihalyi, 2000; Snyder & Lopez, 2005) and incorporate features of Miller and Rollnick's (2002) *Motivational Interviewing* are likely to maximise treatment benefits. We (see Marshall et al., 2005, 2011) prefer these types of approaches since they focus on building strengths rather than on simply eliminating deficits. By focusing on strength-building in the areas of identified criminogenic needs we can achieve the elimination of problematic functioning, while at the same time giving clients the capacities to have more fulfilling, offense-free lifestyles. The best currently available model in the sexual offender field that epitomises this approach is Ward's (2002) *Good Lives Model*. Our belief is that a well-functioning and satisfied person is unlikely to return to crime in order to meet his needs and the long-term outcome of our programme supports this contention (Marshall et al., 2011).

REFERENCES

Abel, G. G., Becker, J. V., & Cunningham-Rathner, J. (1984). Complications, consent and cognitions in sex between children and adults. *International Journal of Law and Psychiatry*, *7*, 89–103.

Abel, G. G., Mittelman, M., Becker, J. V., Rathner, J., & Rouleau, J. L. (1988). Predicting child molesters' response to treatment. *Annals of the New York Academy of Sciences*, *528*, 223–234.

Andrews, D. A. (2001). Principles of effective correctional programming. In L. L. Motiuk & R. C. Serin (Eds.), *Compendium 2000 on effective correctional programming* (pp. 9–17). Ottawa: Correctional Services of Canada.

Andrews, D. A., & Bonta, J. (2006). *The psychology of criminal conduct* (4th ed.). Cincinnati, OH: Anderson Publishing.

Andrews, D. A., Bonta, J., & Hoge, R. D. (1990). Classification for effective rehabilitation: Rediscovering psychology. *Criminal Justice and Behavior*, *17*, 19–52.

Andrews, D. A., Bonta, J., & Wormith, S. J. (2006). The recent past and near future of risk and/or need assessment. *Crime & Delinquency*, *52*, 7–27.

Andrews, D. A., & Dowden, C. (1999). A meta-analytic investigation into effective correctional intervention for female offenders. *Forum on Corrections Research*, *11*, 18–21.

Andrews, D. A., & Kiessling, J. J. (1980). Program structure and effective correctional practices: A summary of the CaVIC research. In R. R. Ross & P. Gendreau (Eds.), *Effective correctional treatment* (pp. 439–463). Toronto: Butterworth.

Andrews, D. A., Zinger, I., Hoge, R. D., Bonta, J., Gendreau, P., & Cullen, F. T. (1990). Does correctional treatment work? A psychologically informed meta-analysis. *Criminology, 28*, 369–404.

Babcock, J. C., Green, C. E., & Robie, C. (2004). Does batterers' treatment work? A meta-analytic review of domestic violence treatment. *Clinical Psychology Review, 23*, 1023–1053.

Bandura, A. (1977). *Social learning theory*. Englewood Cliffs, NJ: Prentice-Hall.

Barbaree, H. E. (2006, September). Treatment of sexual offenders: Where do we go from here? Paper presented at the 25th annual research and treatment conference of the Association for the Treatment of Sexual Abusers, Chicago, IL.

Barlow, D. H. (1974). The treatment of sexual deviation: Toward a comprehensive behavioral approach. In K. S. Calhoun, H. E. Adams & K. M. Mitchell (Eds.), *Innovative treatment methods in psychopathology* (pp. 121–147). New York, NY: Wiley.

Baumeister, R. F. (Ed.). (1993). *Self-esteem: The puzzle of low self-regard.* New York, NY: Plenum Press.

Beech, A. R., & Fordham, A. S. (1997). Therapeutic climate of sexual offender treatment programs. *Sexual Abuse: A Journal of Research and Treatment, 9*, 219–237.

Beech, A. R., & Hamilton-Giachritsis, C. E. (2005). Relationship between therapeutic climate and treatment outcome in a group-based sexual offender program. *Sexual Abuse: A Journal of Research and Treatment, 17*, 127–140.

Bond, I. K., & Evans, D. R. (1967). Avoidance therapy: Its use in two cases of underwear fetishism. *Canadian Medical Association Journal, 96*, 1160–1162.

Borduin, C., Schaeffer, C. M., & Heiblum, N. (2009). A randomised clinical trial of Multisystemic Therapy with juvenile sexual offenders: Effect in youth social ecology and criminal activity. *Journal of Consulting and Clinical Psychology, 77*, 26–37.

Browne, K. D., Foreman, L., & Middleton, D. (1998). Predicting treatment dropout in sex offenders. *Child Abuse Review, 7*, 402–419.

Bumby, K. M. (1996). Assessing the cognitive distortions of child molesters and rapists: Development and validation of the MOLEST and RAPE scales. *Sexual Abuse: A Journal of Research and Therapy, 8*, 37–54.

Burton, D. L., & Smith-Darden, J. (2001). *North American survey of sexual abuser treatment and models: Summary data 2000*. Brandon, VT: Safer Society Press.

Dowden, C., & Andrews, D. A. (2003). Does family intervention work for delinquents? Results of a meta-analysis. *Canadian Journal of Criminology and Criminal Justice, 45*, 327–342.

Dowden, C., & Andrews, D. A. (2004). The importance of staff practice in delivering effective correctional treatment: A meta-analysis. *International Journal of Offender Therapy and Comparative Criminology, 48*, 203–214.

Dowden, C., Antonowicz, D., & Andrews, D. A. (2003). The effectiveness of relapse prevention with offenders: A meta-analysis. *International Journal of Offender Therapy and Comparative Criminology, 47*, 516–528.

Drapeau, M. (2005). Research on the processes involved in treating sexual offenders. *Sexual Abuse: A Journal of Research and Treatment, 17*, 117–125.

Drapeau, M., Korner, C. A., Brunet, L., & Granger, L. (2004). Treatment at La Macaza clinic: A qualitative study of the sexual offenders' perspective. *Canadian Journal of Criminology and Criminal Justice, 46*, 27–44.

Eisenthal, S., Emery, R., Lazare, A., & Udin, H. (1979). 'Adherence' and the negotiated approach to patienthood. *Archives of General Psychiatry*, *36*, 393–398.

Fernandez, Y. M., Shingler, J., & Marshall, W. L. (2006). Putting 'behavior' back into cognitive 'behavioral' treatment for sexual offenders. In W. L. Marshall, Y. M. Fernandez, L. E. Marshall & G. A. Serran (Eds.), *Sexual offender treatment: Controversial issues* (pp. 211–224). Chichester: Wiley.

Fisher, A. (2008, March). Revisioning male violence: Men of courage. Paper presented at the first provincial conference on male sexual victimization, Toronto, Canada.

Hanson, R. K. (2006). Stability and change: Dynamic risk factors for sexual offenders. In W. L. Marshall, Y. M. Fernandez, L. E. Marshall & G. A. Serran (Eds.), *Sexual offender treatment: Controversial issues* (pp. 17–31). Chichester: Wiley.

Hanson, R. K. (2010, September). Meta-analysis of treatment outcome in sexual offenders. Paper presented at the 11th conference of the International Association for the Treatment of Sexual Offenders, Oslo.

Hanson, R. K., Bourgon, G., Helmus, L., & Hodgson, S. (2009). The principles of effective correctional treatment also apply to sexual offenders: A meta-analysis. *Criminal Justice and Behavior*, *36*, 865–981.

Hanson, R. K., Gordon, A., Harris, A. J. R., Marques, J. K., Murphy, W., Quinsey, V. L., & Seto, M. C. (2002). First report of the collaborative outcome data project on the effectiveness of psychological treatment for sex offenders. *Sexual Abuse: A Journal of Research and Treatment*, *14*, 167–192.

Hanson, R. K., & Harris, A. J. R. (2000). Where should we intervene? Dynamic predictors of sex offender recidivism. *Criminal Justice and Behavior*, *27*, 6–35.

Hoppe, C. M., & Singer, R. D. (1976). Overcontrolled hostility, empathy, and egocentric balance in violent and non-violent psychiatric offenders. *Psychological Reports*, *39*, 1303–1308.

Kriegman, D. (2006). The reduction of sexual offense recidivism following commitment and psychodynamic treatment. *Journal of Sexual Offender Civil Commitment: Science and the Law*, *1*, 90–98.

Linley, P. A., & Joseph, S. (Eds.). (2004). *Positive psychology in practice*. Hoboken, NJ: Wiley.

Lösel, F., & Schmucker, M. (2005). The effectiveness of treatment for sexual offenders: A comprehensive meta-analysis. *Journal of Experimental Criminology*, *1*, 117–146.

Mann, R. E., Hanson, R. K., & Thornton, D. (2010). Assessing risk for sexual recidivism: Some proposals on the nature of psychologically meaningful risk factors. *Sexual Abuse: A Journal of Research and Treatment*, *22*, 191–217.

Marques, J. K., Weideranders, M., Day, D. M., Nelson, C., & van Ommeren, A. (2005). Effects of a relapse prevention program on sexual recidivism: Final results from California's Sex Offender Treatment and Evaluation Project (SOTEP). *Sexual Abuse: A Journal of Research and Treatment*, *17*, 79–107.

Marquis, J. N. (1970). Orgasmic reconditioning: Changing sexual object choice through controlling masturbation fantasies. *Journal of Behavior Therapy and Experimental Psychiatry*, *1*, 263–271.

Marshall, W. L. (1971). A combined treatment method for certain sexual deviations. *Behaviour Research and Therapy*, *9*, 292–294.

Marshall, W. L. (1989). Invited essay: Intimacy, loneliness and sexual offenders. *Behaviour Research and Therapy*, *27*, 491–503.

Marshall, W. L. (1993). The role of attachment, intimacy, and loneliness in the etiology and maintenance of sexual offending. *Sexual and Marital Therapy*, *8*, 109–121.

Marshall, W. L. (in press). Elements of effective sexual offender treatment. In L. E. Marshall and D. Boer (Eds.), *Theory, assessment and treatment of sexual offenders*. Chichester: Wiley.

Marshall, W. L., & Anderson, D. (2000). Do relapse prevention components enhance treatment effectiveness? In D. R. Laws, S. M. Hudson & T. Ward (Eds.), *Remaking relapse prevention with sex offenders: A sourcebook* (pp. 39–55). Newbury Park, CA: Sage Publications.

Marshall, W. L., Anderson, D., & Champagne, F. (1997). Self-esteem and its relationship to sexual offending. *Psychology, Crime & Law*, *3*, 161–186.

Marshall, W. L., Anderson, D., & Fernandez, Y. M. (1999). *Cognitive behavioural treatment of sexual offenders*. Chichester: Wiley.

Marshall, W. L., & Burton, D. L. (2010). The importance of therapeutic processes in offender treatment. *Aggression and Violent Behavior: A Review Journal*, *15*, 141–149.

Marshall, W. L., Burton, D. L., & Marshall, L. E. (in press). Features of treatment delivery and group processes that maximize the effects of offender programs. In J. L. Woods & T. A. Gannon (Eds.), *Group influence: Criminal activity and crime reduction*. London: Willan-Routledge.

Marshall, W. L., & Christie, M. M. (1982). The enhancement of social self-esteem. *Canadian Counsellor*, *16*, 82–89.

Marshall, W. L., Fernandez, Y. M., Serran, G. A., Mulloy, R., Thornton, D., Mann, R. E., & Anderson, D. (2003). Process variables in the treatment of sexual offenders: Review of the relevant literature. *Aggressive and Violent Behavior: A Review Journal*, *8*, 205–234.

Marshall, W. L., & Laws, D. R. (2003). A brief history of behavioral and cognitive behavioral approaches to sexual offender treatment: Part 2. The modern era. *Sexual Abuse: A Journal of Research and Treatment*, *15*, 93–120.

Marshall, W. L., & Marshall, L. E. (2011). Can treatment be effective with sexual offenders or does it do harm? A response to Hanson (2010) and Rice (2010). *Sexual Offender Treatment*, *2*. Retrieved from http://iatso.org/ejournal/

Marshall, W. L., Marshall, L. E., Serran, G. A., & Fernandez, Y. M. (2006). *Treating sexual offenders: An integrated approach*. New York, NY: Routledge.

Marshall, W. L., Marshall, L. E., Serran, G. A., & O'Brien, M. D. (2011). *Rehabilitating sexual offenders: A strength-based approach*. Washington, DC: American Psychological Association.

Marshall, W. L., Serran, G. A., Fernandez, Y. M., Mulloy, R., Mann, R. E., & Thornton, D. (2003). Therapist characteristics in the treatment of sexual offenders: Tentative data on their relationship with indices of behavior change. *Journal of Sexual Aggression*, *9*, 25–30.

Marshall, W. L., Serran, G. A., Moulden, H., Mulloy, R., Fernandez, Y. M., Mann, R. E., & Thornton, D. (2002). Therapist features in sexual offender treatment: Their reliable identification and influence on behavior change. *Clinical Psychology and Psychotherapy*, *9*, 395–405.

Marshall, W. L., Ward, T., Mann, R. E., Moulden, H., Fernandez, Y. M., Serran, G. A., & Marshall, L. E. (2005). Working positively with sexual offenders: Maximizing the effectiveness of treatment. *Journal of Interpersonal Violence*, *20*, 1096–1114.

McFall, R. M. (1990). The enhancement of social skills: An information processing analysis. In W. L. Marshall, D. R. Laws & H. E. Barbaree (Eds.), *Handbook of sexual assault: Issues, theories, and treatment of the offender* (pp. 311–330). New York, NY: Plenum Press.

McGrath, R. J., Cumming, G. F., & Buchard, B. L. (2003). *Current practices and trends in sexual abuser management: Safer Society 2002 nationwide survey*. Brandon, VT: Safer Society Press.

McGrath, R. J., Cumming, G. R., Buchard, B. L., Zeoli, S., & Ellerby, L. (2010). *Current practices and emerging trends in sexual abuser management*. Brandon, VT: Safer Society Press.

McGuire, R. J., Carlisle, J. M., & Young, B. G. (1965). Sexual deviation as conditioned behaviour: A hypothesis. *Behaviour Research and Therapy, 3*, 185–190.

Miller, W. R., & Rollnick, S. (2002). *Motivational interviewing: Preparing people for change* (2nd ed.). New York, NY: Guilford Publishing.

Norcross, J. C. (2002). Empirically supported therapy relationships. In J. C. Norcross (Ed.), *Psychotherapy relationships that work: Therapist contributions and responsiveness to patient needs* (pp. 1–10). New York, NY: Oxford University Press.

Pence, E., & Paymar, M. (1993). *Education groups for men who batter: The Duluth model*. New York, NY: Springer.

Peterson, C. (2006). *A primer in positive psychology*. New York, NY: Oxford University Press.

Pithers, W. D. (1994). Process evaluation of a group therapy component designed to enhance sex offenders' empathy for sexual abuse survivors. *Behaviour Research and Therapy, 32*, 565–570.

Quinsey, V. L., Harris, G. T., Rice, M. E., & Lalumière, M. L. (1993). Assessing treatment efficacy in outcome studies of sex offenders. *Journal of Interpersonal Violence, 8*, 512–523.

Rice, M. E. (2010, September). Treatment for adult sex offenders: May we reject the null hypothesis? Paper presented at the 11th conference of the International Association for the treatment of Sexual Offenders, Oslo.

Rice, M. E., & Harris, G. T. (2003). The size and sign of treatment effects in sex offender therapy. *Annals of the New York Academy of Sciences, 989*, 428–440.

Seligman, M. E. P., & Csikszentmihalyi, M. (2000). Positive psychology: An introduction. *American Psychologist, 55*, 5–14.

Serran, G. A., & Marshall, W. L. (2010). Therapeutic processes in the treatment of sexual offenders: A review article. *British Journal of Forensic Practice, 12*, 4–16.

Seto, M. C., Marques, J. K., Harris, G. T., Chaffin, K. M., Lalumière, M. L., Miner, M. H., … Quinsey, V. L. (2008). Good science and progress in sex offender treatment are intertwined: A response to Marshall & Marshall (2009). *Sexual Abuse: A Journal of Research and Treatment, 2*, 247–255.

Shedler, J. (2010). The efficacy of psychodynamic psychotherapy. *American Psychologist, 65*, 98–109.

Snyder, C. R., & Lopez, S. J. (Eds.). (2005). *Handbook of positive psychology*. New York, NY: Oxford University Press.

Tangney, J. P., & Dearing, R. L. (2002). *Shame and guilt*. New York, NY: Guilford Press.

Ward, T. (2002). Good lives and the rehabilitation of offenders: Promises and problems. *Aggression and Violent Behavior, 7*, 513–528.

SECTION 2
METHODOLOGICAL CONSIDERATIONS

ARGUMENTS ABOUT METHODS IN CRIMINAL JUSTICE EVALUATION

David Smith

ABSTRACT

The chapter considers the change of position of the Home Office on the value of randomised controlled trials (RCTs) in England and Wales which took place around 2003 after the end of the Crime Reduction Programme (CRP). Before the CRP Home Office researchers had shown little interest in RCTs; after it, they came close to arguing that no other kinds of evaluation research were worth doing. This represented a reversal of a position that had dominated Home Office thinking on the issue for almost 30 years – that RCTs were in general impractical and unlikely to produce clear-cut results. This view was based in part on the experience of RCTs in the 1970s, which led influential researchers to conclude that the method could not be transferred from medicine to criminal justice. But, disappointed with the lack of definite results from the CRP, the Home Office turned back to RCTs as a potential source of certainty about what works. The chapter considers two recent scholarly exchanges on the question, in relation to an evaluation of a community crime reduction programme, for which an experimental design was attempted but not achieved, and to Lawrence Sherman's recent advocacy of RCTs and his use of research on restorative justice as an example of

Perspectives on Evaluating Criminal Justice and Corrections
Advances in Program Evaluation, Volume 13, 49–69

ISSN: 1474-7863/doi:10.1108/S1474-7863(2012)0000013007

the successful use of the method. The chapter argues that the restorative justice research, while of very high quality, does not provide as clear an example of the use of an RCT as Sherman claims, and concludes with some reflections on the inherent difficulties of criminal justice evaluation, and on the lack of a predictable, rational relationship between research quality and policy influence.

INTRODUCTION

Without seeking to re-open the 'paradigm wars' (Pawson & Tilley, 1998a; see also Astbury, this volume) among competing schools of evaluation, I try in this chapter to give an account of some recent arguments about the merits or otherwise of randomised controlled trials (RCTs) in criminal justice evaluation. The starting point for this is the change in attitude of Home Office researchers between 2000 and 2004, when they shifted from apparently accepting that RCTs would rarely be feasible to (in some accounts at least) apparently claiming that no other kinds of research were worth doing. After discussing this *volte-face*, the chapter briefly reviews the history of criminological RCTs in Britain, before considering two recent exchanges between enthusiasts for RCTs and advocates of more 'realist', non-experimental methods. The example of research on restorative justice schemes, claimed as experimental but (inevitably) rougher in some respects than this designation implies, is used to suggest that the practicality of pure RCTs in the field of criminal justice is limited, a point further illustrated from my own experience. Finally, I offer some brief reflections on what kinds of research have influenced or arguably ought to have influenced policy and conclude that there is no reason to think that RCTs have a better chance than other methods of achieving such influence (see also W. L. Marshall & Marshall, this volume).

THE CRIME REDUCTION PROGRAMME AND AFTER

The Crime Reduction Programme (CRP) which ran in England and Wales from 1999 to 2001 emerged in a period of official optimism that it was possible to identify (at least tentatively) what was likely to work in crime prevention efforts, and that evaluative research could turn these tentative conclusions into more definite ones. Goldblatt and Lewis (1998), under the direction of Chris Nuttall, then head of Research, Development and Statistics at the Home Office, edited a wide-ranging review of evidence on 'ways of dealing with offending behaviour' that came to conclusions that were a long way from the 'nothing works' line that had dominated official and academic thinking on the topic from the mid-1970s to the early 1990s. Approaches that were judged particularly promising (Maguire, 2004) were multi-agency partnerships, situational crime prevention (especially in relation to burglary), problem-oriented and intelligence-led policing, and cognitive behavioural programmes for offenders in prison and the community (the last of these had been the focus of a considerable volume of Canadian research whose positive results had begun to influence practice in Britain from the early 1990s).

The time therefore seemed propitious for the launch of the largest and best-funded crime reduction programme ever attempted in Britain – and the Home Office also displayed an apparent commitment to the independent evaluation of all the elements of the programme, and funded around 1,500 projects. Ten per cent of the original budget of £250 million was to be allocated to evaluation, an unprecedented sum that brought criminologists flocking to the launch of the CRP in late 1998. The Home Office helpfully produced guidance for evaluators on how to assess programmes for offenders (Colledge, Collier, & Brand, 1999), how to produce an analysis of costs and benefits (Dhiri & Brand, 1999) and how to measure 'inputs' (Legg & Powell, 2000). The first of these provided 'very basic guidance' (Raynor, 2004, p. 314) on how to carry out a reconviction study; the latter two sought to lay down a common approach to the analysis of project costs and benefits – an ambitious enterprise, as Raynor (2004) notes, given the diversity of projects funded under the CRP. Colledge et al. (1999, p. 16) mentioned the RCT as an evaluation method, only to dismiss it as being 'usually ... not possible for practical reasons'. There was certainly no suggestion anywhere in the guidance that RCTs were the best – or only valid – method of evaluating projects' success or failure.

After the CRP had ended, the position of Home Office researchers was very different. The introduction to the review edited by Harper and Chitty (2005) presented it as building on the 1998 review by Goldblatt and Lewis (Friendship, Street, Cann, & Harper, 2005), but rather than building on the earlier foundations, the new review in effect tore them up. It was much more sceptical about whether we really know anything about what works in 'correctional services' interventions with adult offenders' (p. 1), pointing to the difficulty of transferring results obtained in one

(Canadian) context to another, and lamenting the supposedly poor quality of most British evaluative research on the topic. It drew on the work of Sherman et al. (1998) to produce a 'Scientific Methods Scale adapted for reconviction studies' (Friendship et al., 2005, p. 7) in which 'random assignment of offenders to the intervention and control conditions' was awarded Level 5 and studies with a well-matched comparison group (but no random allocation) were placed at Level 4. Anything below Level 4 was regarded as close to worthless – and certainly unlikely to be funded. Friendship et al. (p. 8) went on to warn that methodological rigour was not enough: sample sizes needed to be sufficient for robust conclusions to be drawn. The requirements on sample size were demanding: for an expected reduction of 10 percentage points in the rate of reconviction, the minimum number needed in both treatment and control groups was 325; for an expected reduction of 2.5 percentage points, it was 5,024. The authors remarked that (not surprisingly, one might add), few UK studies have met these requirements, and that Level 5 has rarely been achieved in reconviction studies.

An intelligible and perhaps sensible reaction to the sample size requirements might be that they are so large as to make RCTs and probably Level 4 studies impossible. In the review's conclusion, however, Chitty (2005, p. 80) again emphasised the superiority of RCTs over other methods and called for their use 'in the correctional services, so that our knowledge of what works is truly improved and the existing equivocal evidence is replaced with greater certainty'. Supposedly, only RCTs can deliver the certain knowledge that will allow the staff of these services (prison and probation) to be sure that what they are doing is effective. This position is reiterated in the 'minimum standards for reconviction studies' produced by the Home Office in February 2004 and then incorporated into the Youth Justice Board Research Strategy for 2008–2011.[1] This actually makes relatively modest claims for the superiority of RCTs over all other methods, but reproduces the table of minimum sample sizes without comment (as in Harper & Chitty, 2005) on its implications for the feasibility of RCTs. But the Home Office (and now the Ministry of Justice) position is clear: RCTs are unquestionably the best methodology for reconviction studies, and as Raynor (2008) remarked, this is asserted in a firmly managerial language – instead of being offered guidance, prospective evaluators are now presented with minimum standards. It is safe to predict that more of them will be deterred from attempting studies of reconviction, given the near-inevitability of falling short of these exacting requirements.

Back to the 1970s?

In its preference for RCTs following what it perceived as the disappointing results of much of the CRP research, the Home Office was perhaps inadvertently harking back to the late 1960s and early 1970s, when, without being as exclusive as the 2004 'minimum standards', it had funded RCTs along with other kinds of evaluation. There were, as Nuttall (2003) reminded us, four projects that were concerned with the effect of 'treatment' on reconvictions that used an RCT design in that period. These were a study of Kingswood Approved School by Clarke and Cornish (1972, 1975); a study of social work in prison by Margaret Shaw (1974); the IMPACT study of the effects of intensive probation (Folkard, Smith, & Smith, 1976; Folkard et al., 1974); and what was presented as a replication of Shaw's study by Fowles (1978). If Harper and Chitty (2005) and the authors of the Youth Justice Board standards are right, these studies, being RCTs, ought to have produced clear, definitive, unarguable answers that would go on to inform future practice in prisons, probation offices and residential schools for delinquent juveniles. It is fair to say that they did not produce such answers.

Enthusiasts for RCTs might argue that this was because of inadequate sample sizes. The Kingswood study, which Nuttall (2003) judges to have been the most influential of the four, albeit in a negative way, had data on 86 boys in the experimental 'house' (run on therapeutic community lines) and 87 in the comparison house, which had a traditional authoritarian regime. Shaw's study used data on 75 men in each of the experimental and comparison groups: the experimental group received 'extended contact' in the last six months of their sentence from probation officers seconded to the prisons, while the control group had only the normal amount of contact, largely initiated by the prisoners. Fowles's study had a total sample of 290; although it was treated as a replication of Shaw's work, it took place in a different kind of prison and with a different kind of prisoner (short-term rather than long-term), so it is not surprising that it produced a different result. The largest sample was in the IMPACT study, with a total initial intake of 1,379 men (around 300 of whom were withdrawn from the experiment by their probation officers before random allocation to the intensive or routine supervision groups). This did not mean that it produced clear-cut results.

Out of a set of results that Nuttall (2003, p. 274) describes as 'a mixed bag', the most clear-cut positive result came from the study with the smallest sample size – Shaw's study of social work in Ashwell and Gartree prisons.

The two-year reconviction rate for the experimental group was 57%, and for the control group it was 76% – a statistically significant difference. Even at the time, before 'nothing works' became fully established as the professional and academic orthodoxy, this success seems to have been regarded as an annoying anomaly: I. J. Croft, then Head of the Home Office Research Unit, wrote in his Foreword:

> At various times, claims have been made for treatments and the types of offender likely to benefit from them. In the long run few of these claims for the relative effectiveness of treatment have stood the test of rigorous examination in terms of scientific method ... and it is this context that Miss Shaw's report deserves to be considered. And if I venture to strike a cautionary note when I suggest that, until they have been repeated, the experiments in social casework described in this report should not necessarily be regarded as the answer to the penologists' prayer, it is in no sense to depreciate the work of the author in this endeavour. (Shaw, 1974, p. iii)

This reads, if not like a depreciation, at least like a damnation with faint praise. The equilibrium of penological pessimism was re-established by the results of Fowles's study, which were not so troublingly positive – although, as Nuttall (2003, p. 276) points out, they were not as reassuringly negative as they were presented as being.

The same could be said of the IMPACT results (Folkard et al., 1974). The authors' main conclusion was that in respect of one-year reconviction rates there was no significant difference between the experimental and control groups, but there were subtler effects when the variables of degree of criminality and level of personal problems were factored in. Roughly, offenders with low or medium levels of personal problems did worse in the experimental conditions, and much worse if they scored high on criminality; offenders with high levels of problems and low criminality did better in the experimental group, and those with medium or high levels of criminality did no worse. Nuttall (2003, p. 276) suggests 'that at a different time ... the results of the Impact experiment would not have been interpreted as basically supporting "nothing works" but would have been used at least to support further work in the area'. He writes (p. 283) that he is still mystified by the way the criminological establishment in the United Kingdom embraced the 'nothing works' message when the available research did not compel it to do so, and suggests a number of explanations, some of them local and specific to the Home Office. More generally, the response to this research could be seen as a sign of the emerging disillusionment with treatment approaches, which Garland (2001) and others have identified as one element of a much broader movement away from penal modernism and faith in rehabilitative expertise towards a more populist and punitive set of policy assumptions (Pratt, Brown, Brown, Hallsworth, & Morrison, 2005). An intermediate-level explanation would include the recognition that while the results of these experiments were not as negative as they were portrayed as being they – like earlier results of non-experimental research on rehabilitative programmes – were not as positive as the most enthusiastic advocates of treatment would have liked them to be.

Among the local explanations listed by Nuttall is Ron Clarke's disillusionment with RCTs as a result of the Kingswood experience and his consequent interest in other forms of research and other approaches to crime reduction, notably situational preventive measures with the aim of opportunity reduction (there was no difference in two-year reconviction rates between the experimental and control houses – both were high). Clarke (2004) showed how he carried both his rejection of RCTs and his preference for changing situations over changing people into what he and others claimed to be the new discipline of 'crime science' – so that while they are committed to scientific method in most respects, crime scientists – with varying degrees of fervour – reject RCTs. With his colleague Derek Cornish, Clarke concluded that RCTs were not the most appropriate method for penological research (even in an institutional setting in which one might have thought it should be relatively easy to control the environment – a point dealt with at greater length below) (Clarke & Cornish, 1972). They mention problems of ethics, the difficulty of deciding what success criteria should be, practical problems of random allocation, the limited generalisability of the results, and the problem of taking account of changes in treatment during the research period – all of which, they argued, apply to the use of RCTs in a setting like Kingswood in a way they do not apply to their use in medical trials. The Kingswood research had to be terminated early because social workers became reluctant to refer boys to an institution in which they knew an experiment was being conducted that might lead to their clients' being denied potentially helpful treatment. There was also a built-in selection effect, since boys assessed as unlikely to respond to treatment were allocated to a third house that did not form part of the experiment.

The Revival of RCTs

There were thus various problems with the implementation of the RCT design at Kingswood, the memory of which stayed with the Home Office and kept it from privileging RCTs over other methods for almost 30 years.

It is therefore not at all surprising that the guidance to evaluators before the CRP began showed little interest in the method. More surprising was the enthusiasm for it which appeared after the CRP had ended. The Home Office was disappointed in the results of the evaluations associated with it, and placed the blame in part on researchers who 'did the wrong kind of research' (Raynor, 2004, p. 319). The Maryland Scale of Scientific Methods (Sherman et al., 1998) was available as an attractive guide to what kinds of research would be better, in the sense of more rigorous, with higher internal validity, and supposedly with a greater chance of producing results that would satisfy the managerial requirements of certainty and predictability (MacIntyre, 1985). The Campbell Collaboration, established in 2000 on the model of the Cochrane Collaboration in medicine to conduct and make available systematic reviews of research, was also available as an apparently authoritative source that endorsed the idea that RCTs were the 'gold standard' of research in criminal justice, as in medical trials.[2] Hence Clarke and Cornish's warnings about the differences between medical and criminological research were forgotten, and interest in the use of RCTs revived, not only in the Home Office but in the relevant academic journals.

Not that interest in RCTs had entirely disappeared: among their persistent supporters, as well as Lawrence Sherman, was David Farrington, who became the first chair of the Campbell Collaboration Crime and Justice Group. From a wide range of possible examples of the 'paradigm wars' (Pawson & Tilley, 1998a, p. 73) between experimentalists and other kinds of evaluation researcher two exchanges will be used here for illustrative purposes – the first between Farrington on the one side and Pawson and Tilley on the other over the feasibility of an experimental (or quasi-experimental) design for the evaluation of Communities that Care (CTC), a community-level crime reduction programme imported, at Farrington's suggestion (1997, p. 158), from the United States to the United Kingdom in the late 1990s, the second between Lawrence Sherman and critics of his advocacy of RCTs in his 2008 inaugural lecture at Cambridge.

Arguments About RCTs

Farrington (1997) offered a brief outline of a quasi-experimental approach to the evaluation of CTC, which he hoped would be 'feasible and realistic' even though the 'precise features of the intervention program are not fully specified' (p. 160). He assumed that a 'randomized experiment' would not be possible; instead, 'In my opinion, the minimum acceptable design would have one experimental community and one comparable control community drawn from the same area' (p. 161). In fact he suggested three experimental and three control communities, 'community' being roughly defined as 'a large, well-defined housing estate containing several thousand people and at least one secondary school' (p. 161). The experimental and control communities should be geographically close but not adjacent, to reduce the risk of resentment in the control community (p. 165), and communication between the communities 'should be minimized as far as possible' (p. 167) – for the same reason but also to maintain the differences between experimental and control areas. (He did not say how communication was to be kept to a minimum.) Farrington explicitly criticised Pawson and Tilley's (1994) dismissal of experimental methods in criminal justice evaluation, and saw a precedent for his proposal in the design of Foster and Hope's (1993) evaluation of the Priority Estates Project (though whether Hope would be happy to find his earlier work being used in this way is uncertain (Hope, 2005)).

In responding to Farrington, Pawson and Tilley (1998a) did not – as they might have been expected to do from their earlier work – reject experimental principles per se. They accepted (p. 74) that experimental methods could sometimes be useful, when, for example the programme being evaluated was based on a single theory, the researcher could control the 'treatment', and the outcomes were well defined and likely to be quickly detectable. But they argued that CTC, 'with its scatter of underlying program ideas, its diversity of personnel and agencies, its flexible, iterative and evolving construction, is indubitably *not* one of them' (p. 74, emphasis in original). They argued that, because of the inherent complexity of CTC, no two initiatives 'will ever be sufficiently alike to act as "treatment" and "control"' (p. 83). In his reply, Farrington (1998) argued that CTC was (unlike the Safer Cities project of the 1980s) a well-defined, empirically based programme that would be the same everywhere because the staff who implemented it would follow the manual of instructions; that the failure to evaluate it in the United States was because an RCT, which was regarded as 'the most convincing and rigorous design' (p. 205) and therefore the only acceptable approach, would have been prohibitively expensive[3] (and not, as Pawson and Tilley had suggested, because its elements were poorly specified); and that it was 'a discrete, distinctive technology package that can be evaluated' by quasi-experimental means. Pawson and Tilley (1998b) in a brief reply reiterated their criticism of Farrington's 'cook-book quasi-experimentalism' (p. 211) and their preference for a scientific realist methodology, concluding: 'The UK evaluation of CTC will be under way by the time this exchange is published. Let us see what happens!'

Who was right? According to the evaluators (Crow, France, Hacking, & Hart, 2004, pp. 63–64),[4] Pawson and Tilley were. Crow and his colleagues wrote that as a result of their evaluation they were able to make a contribution to this debate. Unable to say much about the outcomes of the three CTC demonstration projects they evaluated, they were able to say a good deal about the process, including this:

> They [Pawson and Tilley] argued that it was unlikely that there would be only one model of CTC. Our evaluation supports such a position. In our process of evaluation it has been clear that CTC has been adapted to local circumstances and that we have been examining not one but three very different projects. These have evolved as a result of complex negotiations between their historical circumstances and their present-day context. All the projects ... have involved different sets of people, used different methods of evaluating risk audits and undertaken resource audits in different ways. (Crow et al., 2004, p. 64)

A provisional conclusion might be that whatever else it may be suitable for, the experimental method – even in its quasi-experimental form – is not suitable for the evaluation of complex, multi-faceted, multi-agency community-level crime reduction programmes. It is just not possible to control the multitude of environmental variables such programmes entail in the way that the experimental method requires, if it is to retain its claim to high internal validity. Furthermore, as Hope (2005) points out, in community programmes participation is essentially voluntary, unlike participation in the settings which have most often been subjected to (quasi-) experimental evaluation (courts and prisons, for example), where 'there is a greater level of resource available for engineering the compliance of subjects available to agencies with the authority and legitimacy to bring about change' (Hope, 2005, p. 278).

The second exchange was between Sherman (2009) and three critics, two of them already cited here, who replied to his strong and optimistic advocacy of the potential of experimental criminology (Hope, 2009; Hough, 2010; Tilley, 2009). In a wide-ranging discussion Sherman argued that the dearth of reliable evidence in criminology – illustrated by the gulf between the impressive number of reviews of medical research on the Cochrane Collaboration website and the much less impressive number in the Crime and Justice section of the Campbell Collaboration site – showed how important the task of experimental criminology was. He envisaged the development of an institution analogous to the National Institute of Health and Clinical Excellence (NICE) that would provide top-down guidance to criminal justice practitioners, based on systematic Campbell-style reviews of experimental evidence. He advocated 'randomized experiments where possible' and 'quasi-experiments where better designs are not possible' (p. 22). All the good evidence on any selected problem would be synthesised and presented to committees of experts who would develop 'succinct operational guidance' and communicate it to relevant audiences. Sherman's 'prime example' of how experimental criminology can 'produce evidence supporting incremental contributions to freedom from crime and excessive punishment' is the work by Joanna Shapland and her colleagues on restorative justice. Sherman (2009, p. 11) notes that the report of Shapland and her colleagues was based 'on the first randomized controlled trials in British criminal justice in three decades'. Cumulatively, the pattern of findings reported by Shapland et al. (2008)[5] from combining a number of small-scale studies (which on their own produced few statistically significant results) showed that offenders who experienced some form of restorative justice were convicted of significantly fewer offences in a two-year follow-up period than offenders in control groups who were dealt with in other ways.

This optimistic and in many ways appealing vision met with predictable kinds of criticism. Of the three main critics, Hope (2009) is the most thoroughgoing in his rejection of the experimental model. Using the examples of research on 'hotspot' policing by Sherman himself, and on Neighbourhood Watch, he argues (p. 129) that 'selection and treatment processes are likely to be correlated in many situations, since both treatment and subject share the same world' – exactly the kind of interaction effect that RCTs are meant to guard against. And he repeats the point quoted above from his 2005 paper, that RCTs cannot eradicate the uncertainty inherent in the social world, and that this is especially a problem in hard-to-control, open, community contexts, as opposed to institutional settings. In contrast, Tilley (2009) is relatively hospitable to RCTs, but also gives a clear summary of the main 'realist' arguments against their application to social programmes:

> ... most social programmes change over time. Differing sub-groups interact with programme components in different ways. Stakeholders, including subjects, adapt over time, meaning not only that the intervention but also responses to it change over time ... . Moreover, most social programmes involve multiple interventions and it is unclear on the basis of any simple experiment what worked, where there is an apparent effect and hence what needs to be replicated reasonably to expect similar outcomes. (p. 138)

This is a statement of the realist case against experimental evaluation of social programmes without – perhaps helpfully for some readers – the customary realist language of contexts and mechanisms. The final point is perhaps the most frequent and longest-lasting criticism of RCTs, and one not confined to declared scientific realists (e.g. Smith, 1987) – that even if they provide clear results in terms of outcomes, they are less good at specifying what the processes were that led to these outcomes – that is, if something worked, what was it? Shaw (1974, pp. 94–95) noted this as a deficiency in what was clearly a successfully conducted experiment and suggested that it was an inherent limitation of experimental studies. The extent to which Shapland et al. (2008) were able to overcome this problem is considered below.

Hough's (2010) response to Sherman argues that he over-sold the experimental method and over-promised on what it could deliver. Hough acknowledges that experiments have a place in establishing what works in reducing reoffending, but argues that it would be a mistake to privilege them over other methods, that they will not deliver the conclusive evidence their advocates aspire to and that they have been associated with an over-emphasis on managerially approved programmes and an under-emphasis on 'models that see "people changing" as a complex social skill' (Hough, 2010, p. 12). His example, also used by others, of the difficulty of generalising from a promising initial study (i.e. the problem of external validity) is of a series of studies carried out by the Home Office on cognitive behavioural programmes for prisoners (Cann, Falshaw, Nugent, & Friendship, 2003; Falshaw, Friendship, Travers, & Nugent, 2003; Friendship, Blud, Erikson, & Travers, 2002). These showed, respectively, that these programmes apparently worked in reducing reconvictions, that they apparently did not, and that they seemed sometimes to work with some people. The crucial difference seemed to be that the enthusiasm and commitment of staff, and the management support available to them, were lower when the programmes were 'rolled out' than when they were first delivered on a smaller scale (as I have argued elsewhere: Smith, 2006). Hough goes on to argue that there is a great deal that experimental methods miss out in the form of middle-range theories of what makes a difference that have been developed from descriptive rather than experimental research. As one example, Hough cites the work of Alison Liebling (2004) on prison regimes, which has identified important differences among them that are associated with different perceptions by prisoners of the justice and decency of their treatment: some regimes are better, in specifiable ways, than others. This work, Hough states, has been influential on prison managers, and it is plausible that regime quality could have an effect on the risk of reoffending after release, but on Campbell Collaboration principles it would have to be excluded as evidence for practice on the grounds that it does not reach the required standard of methodological rigour. The exclusiveness of the Campbell approach (and by implication of Sherman's proposal of a NICE-style institute for criminal justice) can thus be seen as a form of what, in a different context and with a different basis for his complaint, the late Don Andrews called 'knowledge destruction' (Andrews, 2010, p. 17).

EXPERIMENTAL (OR ALMOST EXPERIMENTAL) RESEARCH ON RESTORATIVE JUSTICE

The prime example Sherman (2009) gives is that of Shapland et al. (2008) on the effect of restorative justice on reconviction – a late flower of the CRP, which funded the research from mid-2001. Earlier reports by Shapland her colleagues looked at implementation, participants' expectations and take-up rates, and victims' and offenders' views on process and outcomes. Taken together, these four reports provide a wealth of material on both process and outcomes, and go some way – but not all the way – towards answering the question most RCTs fail to answer: what was it about the intervention that made the difference? In this and other respects, including its description of the research process, its analytical rigour, and the care with which inferences are drawn, this research is probably about as good as research on criminal justice programmes in this country is likely to get. But it is not quite, as Sherman claimed it to be, a clear example of the superiority of the RCT method. As Shapland et al. say, only one of the three schemes they evaluated, although the largest by some way, used random allocation to restorative justice conferencing; for the other two schemes the researchers had to identify a comparison group, matched as far as possible on relevant variables (but not on criminal history). On the Maryland scale, Shapland et al. (2008, pp. 4–5) therefore claim Level 5 (the highest) only for the evaluation of the schemes run in London, Northumbria and the Thames Valley by the Justice Research Consortium (JRC), with which Sherman was actively involved. For the other two evaluations, which used matched comparison groups, they rank themselves at Level 4.[6] These were of smaller schemes in London and Sheffield.

The researchers concluded that overall offenders who participated in restorative justice were convicted for fewer offences in the subsequent two years than those in the control and comparison groups, to a statistically significant degree. While, with one exception, individual schemes worked with numbers that were too small for a statistically significant result to be expected, the total number across the schemes was sufficient for statistical significance to emerge. The exception was the JRC scheme in Northumbria that offered restorative justice to offenders prosecuted for property offences. Here there was such a large effect on likelihood and seriousness of reconviction that there was a statistically significant difference between the group who attended a conference ($N = 31$) and the control group. Shapland et al. (2008) do not attempt to explain this result, but they do (p. 42) offer a plausible general theory of how restorative justice conferences work:

> The authors think that, in order to agree sincerely to participate in restorative justice at all, offenders have to be at least on the cusp of trying to desist. They have to be prepared to admit responsibility for the offence, hear that they have inflicted harm, think about the problems related to their offending and agree to meet both the victim and their supporters, who are often members of their family. This, for JRC, was so for both the restorative justice and control groups. The conference itself, however, could provide an extra boost.

So far, so good; but a possible problem arises: if the conference provided a boost for offenders randomly allocated to it, might allocation to the control group act as a drag or a barrier to desistance for equally well-motivated offenders who were denied the opportunity of a conference? And there are further questions about the meaning of Shapland et al.'s findings. Their theoretical interpretation of what the causal mechanism may have been applies only to conferences. This was the form that restorative justice took in the JRC schemes, but not, for the most part, in the CONNECT or REMEDI interventions. CONNECT dealt with 50 cases in the evaluation period, 37 by indirect mediation (in which victim and offender do not meet), 11 by direct mediation, and 2 by conferences. REMEDI dealt with 132 cases, 97 by indirect mediation and 35 by direct mediation. Thus restorative justice meant different things across the schemes, and even when it ostensibly meant the same thing, as in the JRC schemes, the conferences were run in three distinct locations – and of course by different staff.

This is not to disparage the work of Shapland et al.; it would be unreasonable to expect it to answer every question that might be asked about restorative justice. But it is to suggest how difficult it is to conduct high-quality evaluations with a focus on both process and outcomes that provides genuine illumination of the mechanisms involved in the process of change – in this case, what is it about restorative justice that sometimes 'worked'? And what kinds of restorative justice practice are most likely to lead to positive results? There are indications in Shapland et al.'s report that the JRC scheme in Northumbria, which used conferencing, was particularly effective in reducing the reconviction rate. But the majority of cases in the smaller schemes were dealt with by indirect mediation, in which the parties do not meet, and which therefore cannot do for offenders what Shapland et al., as quoted above, think is important if restorative justice is to reduce the reconviction risk. Rather than evaluating one kind of intervention, Shapland et al. (2008) evaluated three (like the evaluators of CTC). The results of their research are therefore not as clear cut as Sherman (2009) suggested: while important and persuasive (and encouraging for advocates of criminal justice reform), they leave several questions unanswered.

THE DIFFICULTY OF EVALUATIVE RESEARCH

As suggested above, one explanation for this is that evaluative research on the crime reduction effect of criminal justice interventions is very difficult to do well. This is certainly my own experience, and I tried to set out the evidence that it is difficult – and why it is difficult – in an account of evaluations of two projects for persistent juvenile offending in Scotland (Lobley & Smith, 2007). These evaluations benefited from strong support from the funder (the Scottish Office, which became the Scottish Executive); we also had the full co-operation of the project staff and their managers; in both cases we had full access to Scottish Criminal Records; and in one case there was a broad inter-agency commitment to the evaluation, which included the supply of data from the police on a scale and of a quality unlikely to be repeated. Despite all this, the process of finding suitable comparison groups was protracted and complicated, and I would not claim that those we finally obtained were as closely matched as they ought to have been, at least by Maryland scale standards; certainly the match was much rougher than the funders had originally hoped it would be. If pressed, I would rate the research at Level 3 on the Maryland scale, with some hope that it might be judged close to Level 4, but the main value of the research, in my view, is the illumination it provides into the conditions for the survival of specialist projects: that they need strong and consistent inter-agency support, and that constant work is needed to maintain this. On the basis of this experience, I would argue that evaluative research in this field will usually involve (in addition to close attention to processes) quasi-experimental rather than fully experimental methods, and therefore be less tidy and more provisional in its findings than advocates of RCTs would like.

This conclusion also seems to apply to the work of Shapland et al. – and if anything with more force, because the scale and duration – and the methodological quality – of their work are likely to remain exceptional. The research took seven years from initial funding to the fourth report, which was the first to deal with reconvictions; 10 authors contributed to the report; according to Joanna Shapland's web page at the University of Sheffield (accessed on 14 July 2011), the total grant for the research was approximately £1,300.000. It is safe to say that there will not be many evaluative research projects of this scale and quality in Britain in the near future – and that there will be even fewer if random allocation is included as a requirement in specifications for research.

CONCLUSION: WHAT KINDS OF RESEARCH MAKE A DIFFERENCE?

Sherman (2009) made large claims not only for the virtues and technical feasibility of RCTs but for their potential to improve criminal justice policy decisions, and the effectiveness of practice, in a way that would increase the liberty of citizens. It might be unfair to ask the reader to reflect on whether the RCT or even quasi-experimentation has been the method employed in research that actually has been influential in these ways, because – at least in Britain (and Europe as a whole) – there have been so few of them. As argued above, there are good reasons for this, which amount to far more than the 'folklore' that Weisburd (2010) sees as having irrationally restricted the use of RCTs; and it seems reasonable to believe that most useful criminal justice-related research in the future, as in the past, will not use RCTs as its primary method. Leaving aside the vexed and much disputed question of how far policy can be evidence-based, especially in a field as politically sensitive as criminal justice policy, and how to make it more so,[7] it also seems reasonable to suggest that there are examples of good, policy-relevant research that (1) have influenced policy and practice and (2) have not done so, but should have done.

In the first category one might think of the American evidence on early intervention (summarised in Karoly et al., 1998) that allowed Sure Start to be claimed as an evidence-based programme; of the work on cognitive behavioural programmes for offenders by the 'RNR gang', the '"what works" bunch' or the 'Canadians' (Andrews, 2010, p. 7) that influenced probation and prison practice from the early 1990s, mainly through findings not from RCTs but from quasi-experimental designs (Hollin, 2008); the work of Liebling (2004) on prison regimes cited above; or – an example of research whose influence waned as the political climate changed – the work of Thorpe, Smith, Green, and Paley (1980) on the risks of over-intervention with juveniles who had committed relatively minor offences. In the second category, as I have suggested elsewhere in reflecting on this last example (Smith, 2010), there is recent work that provides much stronger evidence than was available in the late 1970s that contact with formal systems is likely to lead to more, not less, offending by young people (McAra & McVie, 2007; Soothill, Ackerley, & Francis, 2008), but there is very little sign that the apparent policy implications of this research have been taken seriously where they need to be. Goldson (2010) provides a wider-ranging analysis of the apparently determined neglect of evidence in recent youth justice policy in England and Wales, and it might be added that the enthusiasm with which my own work in Scotland (Lobley & Smith, 2007) was initially greeted did not lead to any lasting policy shift in the direction implied by the research.

The research sketched above, whether influential or not, is of various kinds – from ethnographic observation through file studies to large-scale survey work – but none of it is experimental, though in the case of McAra and McVie (2007) the findings arose from what might be thought of as a naturally occurring quasi-experiment. With all due respect to the advocates and practitioners of RCTs, there is every reason to expect that the research that has an effect in future will continue to span a range of methods, and that RCTs will remain relatively rare, not only because of practical considerations (including but not confined to cost), but because complex interventions cannot be controlled in the way that RCTs require them to be. In the real world of criminal justice practice, there are not many interventions that are or can be as controlled and well defined as in a classic clinical trial in medicine. Given this, even work that aspires as far as possible to the condition of the RCT is liable to be compromised by recourse to quasi-experimental methods (as in Shapland et al., 2008). And rather than lamenting this as a falling away from the ideal of the RCT, we should welcome such compromises, as increasing the amount and enriching the quality of the data, and as recognising the real complexity of criminal justice programmes and the unpredictability of social life itself.

NOTES

1. Available at http://www.justice.gov.uk/downloads/publications/research-and-analysis/yjb/ResearchStrategy200811.pdf. Accessed on 6 July 2011.

2. See http://www.campbellcollaboration.org/background/index.php. Accessed on 7 July 2011.

3. This, of course, would mean that CTC was beyond evaluation, if the only acceptable method was impractical on grounds of cost.

4. Available at http://www.jrf.org.uk/sites/files/jrf/1859351840.pdf. Accessed on 7 July 2011.

5. Available at http://webarchive.nationalarchives.gov.uk/+/http://www.justice.gov.uk/docs/restorative-justice-report_06-08.pdf. Accessed on 12 July 2011.

6. As did Tuffin, Morris, and Poole (2006) in their evaluation of reassurance policing – where, in comparisons across neighbourhoods, the variables were much harder to control than they were for Shapland and her team.

7. For an informed discussion of how far the UK governments of 1997 and 2001, ostensibly committed to using evidence to shape policy, actually did so, see Davies (2004a, 2004b). Available at, respectively, http://www.nationalschool.gov.uk/policyhub/downloads/JerryLeeLecture1202041.pdf and http://www.nationalschool.gov.uk/policyhub/docs/policy_evaluation_uk.pdf. Accessed on 15 July 2011.

REFERENCES

Andrews, D. A. (2010). The impact of nonprogrammatic factors on criminal-justice interventions. *Legal and Criminal Psychology*, *16*, 1–23. doi:10.1348/135532510 × 521485

Astbury, B. (this volume). Using theory in criminal justice evaluation. In E. Bowen & S. Brown (Eds.), *Perspectives on evaluating criminal justice and corrections*. Advances in Program Evaluation (Vol. 13). Bingley, UK: Emerald Group Publishing.

Cann, J., Falshaw, L., Nugent, F., & Friendship, C. (2003). *Understanding what works: Accredited cognitive skills programmes for adult men and young offenders*. Home Office Research Findings No. 226. London: Home Office.

Chitty, C. (2005). The impact of corrections on re-offending: Conclusions and the way forward. In G. Harper & C. Chitty (Eds.), *The impact of corrections on re-offending: A review of 'what works'*. Home Office Research Study No. 291. London: Home Office.

Clarke, R. V. (2004). Technology, criminology and crime science. *European Journal on Criminal Policy and Research*, *10*(1), 55–63. doi:10.1023/B:CRIM.0000037557.42894.f7

Clarke, R. V. G., & Cornish, D. B. (1972). *The controlled trial in institutional settings: Paradigm or pitfall for penal evaluators?* Home Office Research Study No. 15. London: HMSO.

Clarke, R. V. G., & Cornish, D. B. (1975). *Residential treatment and its effects on delinquency*. Home Office Research Study No. 32. London: Home Office.

Colledge, M., Collier, P., & Brand, S. (1999). *Programmes for offenders: Guidance for evaluators*. CRP Guidance Note 2. London: Home Office.

Crow, I., France, A., Hacking, S., & Hart, M. (2004). *Does Communities That Care Work?* York: Joseph Rowntree Foundation.

Davies, P. (2004a, February 19). *Is evidence-based government possible?*, The Jerry Lee lecture. Presented at the Campbell Collaboration Symposium, Washington, DC. Retrieved from http://www.nationalschool.gov.uk/policyhub/downloads/JerryLeeLecture1202041.pdf

Davies, P. (2004b). *Policy evaluation in the United Kingdom.* Paper presented at the KDI International Policy Forum, Seoul. Retrieved from http://www.nationalschool.gov.uk/policyhub/docs/policy_evaluation_uk.pdf

Dhiri, S., & Brand, S. (1999). *Analysis of costs and benefits: Guidance for evaluators.* CRP Guidance Note 1. London: Home Office.

Falshaw, L., Friendship, C., Travers, R., & Nugent, F. (2003). *Searching for 'what works': An evaluation of cognitive skills programmes.* Home Office Research Findings No. 206. London: Home Office.

Farrington, D. P. (1997). Evaluating a community crime prevention program. *Evaluation, 3*(2), 157–173. doi:10.1177/135638909700300203

Farrington, D. P. (1998). Evaluating "Communities That Care": Realistic scientific considerations. *Evaluation, 4*(2), 204–210. doi:10.1177/13563899822208536

Folkard, M. S., Fowles, A. J., McWilliams, B. C., McWilliams, W., Smith, D. D., & Walmsley, G. R. (1974). *IMPACT: Intensive matched probation and after-care treatment, Volume I: The design of the experiment and an interim evaluation.* Home Office Research Study No. 24. London: HMSO.

Folkard, M. S., Smith, D. E., & Smith, D. E. (1976). *IMPACT Volume II: The results of the experiment.* Home Office Research Study No. 36. London: HMSO.

Foster, J., & Hope, T. (1993). *Housing, community and crime: The impact of the priority estates project.* Home Office Research Study No. 131. London: HMSO.

Fowles, A. J. (1978). *Prison welfare: An account of an experiment at Liverpool.* Home Office Research Study No. 45. London: HMSO.

Friendship, C., Blud, L., Erikson, M., & Travers, R. (2002). *An evaluation of cognitive behavioural treatment for prisoners.* Home Office Research Findings No. 161. London: Home Office.

Friendship, C., Street, R., Cann, J., & Harper, G. (2005). Introduction: Assessing the evidence. In G. Harper & C. Chitty (Eds.), *The impact of corrections on re-offending: A review of 'what works'.* Home Office Research Study No. 291. London: Home Office.

Garland, D. (2001). *The culture of control: Crime and social order in late modernity.* Oxford: Clarendon Press.

Goldblatt, P., & Lewis, C. (1998). *Reducing offending: An assessment of research evidence on ways of dealing with offending behaviour.* Home Office Research Study No. 187. London: Home Office.

Goldson, B. (2010). The sleep of (criminological) reason: Policy rupture and New Labour's youth justice legacy. *Criminology and Criminal Justice, 10*(2), 155–178. doi:10.1177/1748895809360964

Harper, G., & Chitty, C. (Eds.). (2005). *The impact of corrections on re-offending: A review of 'what works'.* Home Office Research Study No. 291. London: Home Office.

Hollin, C. R. (2008). Evaluating offender behaviour programmes: Does only randomization glister? *Criminology and Criminal Justice, 8*(1), 89–106. doi:10.1177/1748895807085871

Hope, T. (2005). Pretend it doesn't work: The "anti-social" bias in the Maryland Scientific Methods Scale. *European Journal on Criminal Policy and Research, 11*(3/4), 275–296. doi:10.1007/s10610-005-9000-1

Hope, T. (2009). The illusion of control: A response to Professor Sherman. *Criminology and Criminal Justice*, *9*(2), 125–134. doi:10.1177/1748895809102548

Hough, M. (2010). Gold standard or fool's gold? The pursuit of certainty in experimental criminology. *Criminology and Criminal Justice*, *10*(1), 11–22. doi:10.1177/1748895809352597

Karoly, L. A., Greenwood, P. W., Everingham, S. S., Houbé, J., Kilburn, R., Rydell, C. P., … & Chiesa, J. (1998). *Investing in our children: What we know and don't know about the costs and benefits of early childhood interventions*. Santa Monica, CA: RAND Corporation.

Legg, D., & Powell, J. (2000). *Measuring inputs – guidance for evaluators*. CRP Guidance Note 3. London: Home Office.

Liebling, A. (2004). *Prisons and their moral performance*. Oxford: Oxford University Press.

Lobley, D., & Smith, D. (2007). *Persistent young offenders: An evaluation of two projects*. Aldershot: Ashgate.

MacIntyre, A. (1985). *After virtue: A study in moral theory* (2nd ed.). London: Duckworth.

Maguire, M. (2004). The crime reduction programme in England and Wales: Reflections on the vision and the reality. *Criminal Justice*, *4*(3), 213–237.

Marshall, W. L., & Marshall L. E. (this volume). Treatment of sexual offenders: Effective elements and appropriate outcome evaluations. In E. Bowen & S. Brown (Eds.), *Perspectives on evaluating criminal justice and corrections*. Advances in Program Evaluation (Vol. 13). Bingley, UK: Emerald Group Publishing.

McAra, L., & McVie, S. (2007). Youth justice? The impact of system contact on patterns of desistance from offending. *European Journal of Criminology*, *4*(3), 315–345. doi:10.1177/1477370807077186

Nuttall, C. (2003). The Home Office and random allocation experiments. *Evaluation Review*, *27*(3), 267–289.

Pawson, R., & Tilley, N. (1994). What works in evaluation research? *British Journal of Criminology*, *34*(3), 291–306.

Pawson, R., & Tilley, N. (1998a). Caring communities, paradigm polemics, design debates. *Evaluation*, *4*(1), 73–90. doi:10.1177/13563899822208400

Pawson, R., & Tilley, N. (1998b). Cook-book methods and disastrous recipes: A rejoinder to Farrington. *Evaluation*, *4*(2), 211–213. doi:10.1177/13563899822208545

Pratt, J., Brown, D., Brown, M., Hallsworth, S., & Morrison, W. (Eds.). *The new punitiveness: Trends, theories, perspectives*. Cullompton: Willan.

Raynor, P. (2004). The probation service "pathfinders": Finding the path and losing the way? *Criminal Justice*, *4*(3), 309–325.

Raynor, P. (2008). Community penalties and Home Office research: On the way back to "nothing works"?. *Criminology and Criminal Justice*, *8*(1), 73–87.

Shapland, J., Atkinson, A., Atkinson, H., Dignan, J., Edwards, L., Hibbert, J, … & Sorsby, A. (2008). *Does restorative justice affect reconviction? The fourth report from the evaluation of three schemes*. Ministry of Justice Research Series 10/08. London: Ministry of Justice.

Shaw, M. (1974). *Social work in prison*. Home Office Research Study No. 22. London: HMSO.

Sherman, L. W. (2009). Evidence and liberty: The promise of experimental criminology. *Criminology and Criminal Justice*, *9*(1), 5–28. doi:10.1177/1748895808099178

Sherman, L. W., Gottfredson, D. C., MacKenzie, D., Eck, J., Reuter, P., & Bushway, S. (1998). *Preventing crime: What works, what doesn't, what's promising*. Washington, DC: National Institute of Justice.

Smith, D. (1987). The limits of positivism in social work research. *British Journal of Social Work*, *17*(4), 401–416.

Smith, D. (2006). Youth crime and justice: Research, evaluation and "evidence". In B. Goldson & J. Muncie (Eds.), *Youth crime and justice: Critical issues*. London: Sage.

Smith, D. (2010). *Out of Care* 30 years on. *Criminology and Criminal Justice*, *10*(2), 119–135.

Soothill, K., Ackerley, E., & Francis, B. (2008). Criminal convictions among children and young adults: Changes over time. *Criminology and Criminal Justice*, *8*(3), 297–315. doi:10.1177/1748895808092431

Thorpe, D. H., Smith, D., Green, C. J., & Paley, J. H. (1980). *Out of care: The community support of juvenile offenders*. London: Allen and Unwin.

Tilley, N. (2009). Sherman vs. Sherman: Realism vs rhetoric. *Criminology and Criminal Justice*, *9*(2), 135–144. doi:10.1177/1748895809102549

Tuffin, R., Morris, J., & Poole, A. (2006). *An evaluation of the reassurance policing programme*. Home Office Research Study No. 296. London: Home Office.

Weisburd, D. (2010). Justifying the use of non-experimental methods and disqualifying the use of randomized controlled trials: Challenging folklore in evaluation research in crime and justice. *Journal of Experimental Criminology*, *6*, 209–227. doi:10.1007/s11292-010-9096-2

TREATMENT OF SEXUAL OFFENDERS: EFFECTIVE ELEMENTS AND APPROPRIATE OUTCOME EVALUATIONS

W. L. Marshall and L. E. Marshall

ABSTRACT

In this chapter, we first describe the all governing principles of treatment for sexual offenders that maximise effectiveness. These are derived from Andrews and Bonta's (2006) summary of a variety of meta-analyses of outcome studies. From this source and others, we then claim that there are three elements essential to effective treatment: (1) targeting criminogenic features; (2) employing empirically sound procedures to modify these targets; and (3) delivering treatment in an effective psychotherapeutic way. Next we describe our treatment approach that emphasises these crucial elements within a strength-based programme that is motivational and provides Ward's (2002) Good Lives Model *as the framework. We then challenge the broadly accepted idea that the* Random Controlled Trial *(RCT) is the only basis upon which inferences about treatment effectiveness can be derived. We point to methodological, practical and ethical problems associated with implementing an RCT study and offer at least two alternatives: the so-called 'incidental design' which compares the outcome of the treated group with a matched (but not randomly assigned)*

Perspectives on Evaluating Criminal Justice and Corrections
Advances in Program Evaluation, Volume 13, 71–94

ISSN: 1474-7863/doi:10.1108/S1474-7863(2012)0000013008

group from the same or similar setting to the treated group; and a strategy where the recidivism rate of treated group is compared with what would be expected on the basis of risk assessments of each of the treated subjects.

INTRODUCTION

The treatment of sexual offenders is beset by controversy. For example, there is a debate about the need to include relapse prevention elements in treatment (Carich, Dobkowski, & Delehanty, 2009; Yates & Ward, 2009) or at least how extensive these elements should be if they are included (W. L. Marshall, Marshall, Serran, & O'Brien, 2011). There is disagreement about the value of detailed treatment manuals (see Mann, 2009; Marshall, 2009, for differing points of view). While many clinicians and researchers (e.g. Abel, Becker, & Cunningham-Rathner, 1984; Bumby, 1996; Carich & Calder, 2003; Salter, 1988) point to the need to modify what are called 'cognitive distortions', some claim that such an approach is unnecessary since the majority of distortions are not related to the propensity to reoffend (W. L. Marshall, Marshall, & Kingston, 2011; W. L. Marshall, Marshall, & Ware, 2009). Perhaps more importantly, some have claimed that the treatment of sexual offenders has not yet been shown to be effective (Quinsey, Harris, Rice, & Lalumière, 1993; Rice & Harris, 2003; Seto et al., 2008), while others (W. L. Marshall, Marshall, Serran, et al., 2011) suggest there is sufficiently convincing evidence of its efficacy.

In this chapter we will outline the effective principles of treatment, then we will describe what we believe to be an effective approach to treating sexual offenders, and finally we will consider how treatment programmes for sexual offenders can be satisfactorily evaluated.

THE PRINCIPLES OF EFFECTIVE TREATMENT

Andrews and Bonta (2006) have integrated the vast body of research appraising treatment effectiveness with offenders of various types. In particular they report the results of several meta-analyses conducted by the Carleton Criminology group (Andrews & Dowden, 1999; Andrews, Zinger et al., 1990; Dowden & Andrews, 1999a, 1999b, 2003, 2004; Dowden, Antonowicz, & Andrews, 2003) plus the meta-analyses of other researchers

(Lipsey, 1995, 1999; Lipsey & Wilson, 1993; Lösel, 1995; Redondo, Garrido, & Sanchez-Meca, 1999; Whitehead & Lab, 1989). From this vast array of data Andrews and Bonta (2006) have extracted three principles of effective offender treatment that they demonstrate account for the majority of the variance in outcome across studies. These three principles are described as: the risk principle, the needs principle and the responsivity principle. Collectively they are known as the RNR principles of effective treatment and they have been shown to apply to adult offenders of various types, including male and female offenders as well as juvenile offenders, and to be equally applicable to institutional and community-based programmes. Hanson, Bourgon, Helmus, and Hodgson (2009) have shown that these principles also apply to sexual offender treatment.

The Risk Principle indicates that treatment should be differentially applied to offenders who are assessed as having different levels of risk for future reoffending. When resources are limited the risk principle demands that treatment be directed at the highest risk offenders; when resources are more generously available treatment should be more extensive and intensive with the highest risk group and less so for offenders at lower risk. This principle accounts for only a small proportion of the variance in outcome, so Hanson et al. (2009) suggest it should be seen as an administrative principle for allocating offenders to treatment, whereas the remaining two principles are crucial to treatment design and implementation.

The Needs Principle demands that treatment addresses those features of offenders that research has shown to be predictive of recidivism. The more of these criminogenic features that are targeted in treatment, the more effective treatment is. While Dowden and Andrews (2003) and Hanson et al. (2009) indicate that there are some non-criminogenic factors that need to be addressed in order to motivate or engage offenders, it is clear that spending too much time in treatment of non-criminongenic issues reduces effectiveness proportional to the number of such issues that are addressed (Gendreau, French, & Gionet, 2004). This principle is, then, quite straightforward and clearly accounts for a meaningful number of the benefits derived from treatment.

The Responsivity Principle, on the other hand, is rather more complex and has, in our view, been repeatedly misinterpreted. L. E. Marshall and Marshall (this volume) have addressed the complexity of the responsivity principle and the meaning of its subcomponents. This principle is said to have two major components: general responsivity and specific responsivity. Both are primarily concerned with the way in which treatment is delivered and research indicates quite consistently that in combination these two components account for the greatest amount of beneficial change generated by treatment (Andrews & Bonta, 2006; Dowden & Andrews, 2004; Hanson et al., 2009). Specific responsivity essentially describes the quintessentially psychotherapeutic principle of flexibility (Kottler, Sexton, & Whiston, 1994; Walborn, 1996). Adjusting the delivery of treatment in response to generic features such as culture, gender and age (i.e. juvenile or adult), as well as for intellectual differences, seems obvious and several authors have described programmes for such special populations (see Marshall, Fernandez, Hudson, & Wards, 1998). Adjustments also need to be made for each client's day-to-day fluctuations in mood and motivation. It is the general component of responsivity, however, that is the more complex and often misinterpreted feature.

Having reviewed the results of the various meta-analyses of treatment outcome with offenders, Andrews and Bonta (2006) conclude that 'the most powerful influence strategies available are cognitive-behavioural strategies' (p. 283). This, however, does not mean that because programmes are described as cognitive-behavioural therapy (CBT) they will necessarily be effective. Indeed, the series of meta-analyses of sexual offender treatment outcome (Alexander, 1999; Gallagher, Wilson, Hirschfield, Coggeshall, & MacKenzie, 1999; Hall, 1995; Hanson et al., 2002, 2009; Lösel & Schmucker, 2005), while confirming Andrews and Bonta's observation that the most effective programmes were CBT, also revealed that a significant number of CBT programmes were ineffective. What is important to note, is that sexual offender programmes described as CBT are not all the same, as is clearly revealed by the results of three surveys reported by the Safer Society over the past 10 years (Burton & Smith-Darden, 2001; McGrath, Cumming, & Buchard, 2003; McGrath, Cumming, Buchard, Zeoli, & Ellerby, 2010). Most of the surveyed programmes address some, but not all, known criminogenic factors, as well as a variable number of non-criminogenic factors. As Fernandez, Shingler, and Marshall (2006) pointed out, many so-called CBT programmes employ very little in the way of behavioural procedures and practices, and even fewer address the components of emotional self-regulation (W. L. Marshall, Marshall, Serran, & Fernandez, 2006) that underpin behavioural self-regulation; the latter is a known criminogenic factor. In fact, in Andrews, Zinger et al.'s (1990) seminal meta-analysis, the only CBT programmes that were effective were those that appropriately employed techniques such as modelling, role-plays, reinforcement and graduated practice.

We cannot, therefore, assume that if a programme is described as CBT that it will, as a consequence, be effective. More importantly, we cannot assume that all CBT programmes meet the requirements of general responsivity but that is what Hanson et al. (2009) assumed in their attempt to evaluate the effects of programmes adhering to this principle. In fairness to Hanson et al., Andrews has not always been as clear on this issue as he might have been. What a detailed examination of Andrews' series of studies reveals is that responsivity is more to do with the way treatment is delivered rather than the theoretical approach that guides the programme.

In the general clinical literature, programmes addressing various Axis 1 and Axis 2 disorders (others than the paraphilias) have been examined in order to detect the critically effective elements. In summarising these extensive findings, Norcross (2002) concluded that some 20–30% of the variance in beneficial changes resulted from the formation of an effective therapeutic alliance. An effective alliance is maximally secured when the therapists have a variety of positive qualities (e.g. confidence, skill, fairness, empathy, respectfulness, genuineness, warmth) and deliver treatment in an effective way (e.g. being supporting, listening, rewarding appropriate behaviours, displaying flexibility, being appropriately directive). Norcross also showed that the employment of effective procedures or techniques directed at the client's problems accounted for a further 15% of the observed benefits. Combining the effects of these two aspects of treatment (alliance and procedures) results in the explanation of 35–45% of the variance in measures of change, thereby leaving little or no variance to be explained by theoretical orientation.

In the treatment of sexual offenders, we (Marshall, Serran, Fernandez et al., 2003; Marshall, Serran, Moulden et al., 2002) found therapist features similar to those found with other Axis 1 disorders explained between 30% and 60% of the changes evident on measures of criminogenic factors. Clearly this is greater than the effects of these features evident in the treatment of non-offenders. When we combine this with the observations of Beech Beech and Fordham (1997) and Beech and Hamilton-Giachritsis (2005) of the powerful influence (although not reported in terms of variance accounted for) of the group climate on treatment benefits to sexual offenders, there is little or nothing left to be explained either by the use of specific procedures/techniques or by theoretical orientation. It seems likely that the reason why CBT programmes appear to do better than other approaches with offenders is simply that, properly applied, CBT entails many of the elements (e.g. modelling and rewarding) that are essential to effective treatment. However, it is also clear that CBT programmes do not always incorporate the various other critical features of effective treatment delivery.

Returning to Andrews and Bonta's (2006) work, we find that they identified what they call 'core correctional practices' as the crucial elements of the general responsivity principle. Core correctional practices (CCP) include what Andrews and Bonta describe as 'relationship' and 'structuring' principles. They define the relationship principle in terms identical to what Norcross (2002) found created an effective therapeutic alliance and what Marshall and his colleagues found maximised treatment effectiveness with sexual offenders, that is, empathy, warmth, respect, support and flexibility. The structuring principle encompasses some of the other elements found in Norcross' (2002) review and in Marshall's studies (rewardingness, directiveness), as well as effective modelling by the therapist particularly of prosocial attitudes and behaviours.

From our reading of the general clinical literature, as well as the literature on the treatment of both non-sex offenders and sexual offenders, we (L. E. Marshall & Marshall, this volume) have concluded that so long as treatment directs attention to all the known criminogenic features and delivers treatment according to Andrews' CCPs, the likelihood of successful outcome is maximised. However, given the evident, and understandable, reluctance of sexual offenders to either enter treatment or openly discuss problematic issues, a motivational component also seems necessary and, not surprisingly, Andrews and Bonta (2006) point to this need. When sexual offenders are offered a place in treatment many refuse (Jones, Pelissier, & Klein-Saffran, 2006; Mann & Webster, 2002; Seager, Jellicoe, & Dhaliwal, 2004) and of those who enter treatment, too many withdraw or are removed typically because they are deemed non-cooperative or resistant (Lee, Proeve, Lancaster, & Jackson, 1996; McPherson, Chein, Van Maren, & Swenson, 1994; Shaw, Herkov, & Greer, 1995). These are serious problems because refusers have high recidivism rates (Seager et al., 2004) and treatment drop-outs have even higher reoffence rates than do sexual offenders who do not enter treatment (Abel, Mittelman, Becker, Rathner, & Rouleau, 1988; Browne, Foreman, & Middleton, 1998; Lee et al., 1996; McGrath, Cumming, Livingston, & Hoke, 2003). Accordingly the first step in an effective programme should be motivational and aimed at full engagement.

We will now describe our programme which not only is motivational but also emphasises the offenders' strengths and aims at enhancing strengths in a variety of areas of functioning. The programme is framed in terms of the various aspects of positive psychology (see Linley & Joseph, 2004; Peterson, 2006; Snyder & Lopez, 2005) including, in particular, Ward's *Good Lives Model* (Ward & Mann, 2004; Ward & Marshall, 2004). We choose to use our programme as a model because it seems to represent the direction in which many treatment approaches with sexual offenders are going and it is certainly the direction taken by recent programmes for other disorders (see Smith (2006) for a review).

A POSITIVE STRENGTH-BASED PROGRAMME

We have made continual changes to our programme from the early 1970s (Marshall, 1971; Marshall & Williams, 1975) through the 1980s (Marshall & Barbaree, 1988; Marshall, Earls, Segal, & Darke, 1983) and the 1990s (Marshall, Anderson, & Fernandez, 1999) to the present century (W. L. Marshall, Marshall, Serran, et al., 2011; Marshall, Ward et al., 2005). These changes reflect a continual move away from a deficit-oriented focus associated with an insistence on full offence disclosure and the development of relapse prevention strategies, towards a more strength-based view of the clients that emphasises the instillation of self-respect, and optimism and hope for the future. The framework on which these changes are based derive from Ward's (2002), Ward and Gannon (2006), Ward and Mann (2004) and Ward and Stewart (2003) persuasive articulation of the *Good Lives Model*, as well as the recent developments in positive psychology (Linley & Joseph, 2004; Peterson, 2006; Snyder & Lopez, 2005), although most of the changes in our programme predate these developments. We have described our programme in our most recent book (W. L. Marshall, Marshall, Serran, et al., 2011) and the interested reader is referred to that for details. Here we will provide a brief overview.

The programme is conceptualised as a three-phase approach. In the first phase, the approach is motivational as it is throughout treatment. In Phase 1 our aim is simply to engage the client by (a) outlining our outcome data (see later section); (b) pointing out that our intention is to give clients the skills and self-confidence to be able to live a more satisfying life; and (c) addressing some issues (e.g. shame, self-esteem and coping skills) that are seen by clients as non-threatening and personally beneficial. Both shame and low self-esteem present obstacles to full engagement and commitment to any learning or change process (Baumeister, 1993; Tangney & Dearing, 2002) but when they are effectively addressed, clients of various types not only fully engage in treatment, but also significantly benefit in terms of reduced relapses (Cliska, 1990; Heatherton & Polivy, 1991; Miller, 1983; Needles & Abramson, 1990).

In this initial motivational phase of treatment, we do not require the clients to disclose what they did during their offence(s). Indeed, we do not require this at any point in treatment. Most programmes we have examined in various countries require sexual offenders to not only give, as a first step in treatment, a detailed offence description but this description must match the victim's account. We (W. L. Marshall et al., 2009; W. L. Marshall, Marshall, & Kingston, 2011) have challenged the wisdom and empirical bases of this requirement but suffice to say that no one has ever provided us with a satisfactory rationale for doing this. In our experience, requiring a full disclosure of the offence typically generates resistance in the client and suspicion of the therapist's motives. This resistance often elicits a confrontational response from the therapist, which all too often leads the client to withdraw or to falsely agree to the victim's account in order to continue in treatment.

Once clients are sufficiently engaged when we turn our attention in Phase 2 to addressing the known criminogenic features. These criminogenic features can be usefully clustered into four categories: (a) a limited set of dysfunctional attitudes and cognitions; (b) self-regulation issues; (c) relationship problems; and (d) sexual issues. The attitudes and cognitions we address are not those that are usually subsumed under the rather nebulous title of 'cognitive distortions'. Few of these so-called distortions are actually criminogenic (see W. L. Marshall et al., 2009; W. L. Marshall, Marshall, & Kingston, 2011), so there is little or no justification for targeting them. The attitudes and cognitions that we aim to change are primarily those that interfere with attaining the goals of the truly criminogenic features (e.g. attitudes towards women or adults in general, attitudes about relationships, beliefs about sex, self-beliefs). However, it is important to note that we do not address these in the abstract. Many programmes have a separate module addressing cognitive distortions which we see as artificial. Beneficial or problematic attitudes and cognitions can only satisfactorily be elicited and addressed in the context in which they are naturally embedded. Appropriate attitudes towards women, for example, are unlikely to be expressed when discussing women in the abstract; when an offender discusses his past history of unsatisfactory relationships with women, however, it is quite common for him to indicate that he construes all women as having what he sees as the negative traits of his past partners. Similarly distorted views of sexuality arise when sex is a topic of discussion. Accordingly we address dysfunctional attitudes and cognitions when they arise as we discuss other criminogenic issues or future plans.

One of the central features of our programme is aimed at enhancing the clients' relationship skills. Clients are assisted in recognising the value of forming effective adult relationships including an intimate sexual relationship and we also stress the importance of family and friendships. It is pointed out that maximal satisfaction in a sexual/romantic relationship is attained only when both partners participate equally in all important decisions (e.g. buying a house or car, disciplining children, where to vacation), and when each partner treats the other with respect. Satisfaction of various basic human needs (i.e. intimacy, sexual, nurturing and attachment) cannot be met in inequitable relationships such as those involved in sexual abuse. Most clients recognise quite readily that although they felt some degree of satisfaction as a result of offending, this was only partial and typically fleeting. Recognising this, and their past dysfunctional approaches to adult relationships, serves as a strong motivator to acquire the skills, attitudes and self-confidence necessary to achieve the goal of meeting their needs prosocially. We assist them in recognising the various strengths relevant to addressing these issues, and the encouragement and confidence-boosting remarks from the other group members enhance their belief that they can achieve, with some effort, the goal of satisfying their needs in appropriate ways.

As we noted earlier, behavioural self-regulation problems can be seen as primarily problems of emotional dysregulation. Accordingly helping clients identify their own emotions and those of others, differentiating emotional states, and coping appropriately with emotional distress is a significant first step in the development of overall self-regulation. However, since a substantial number of sexual offenders meet criteria for sexual preoccupation (L. E. Marshall & Marshall, 2001, 2006; L. E. Marshall, Marshall, Moulden, & Serran, 2008), which is often referred to as 'sexual addiction' (Carnes, 1989), there is an evident need to expand self-regulatory functioning beyond the usual realm of behavioural regulation. Indeed, this is essential since sexual preoccupation has been identified as the dynamic factor most strongly predictive of reoffending (Hanson & Morton-Bourgon, 2005). While there are sound psychological programmes for sexual preoccupation (Delmonico, Griffin, & Carnes, 2002; Goodman, 1998), it appears useful to complement, in some cases, these approaches with the administration of one of the selective serotonin re-uptake inhibitors (Kafka, 1994; Kafka & Prentky, 1992), at least as a first step to get clients in the frame of mind where they are amenable to psychological treatment.

With respect to deviant sexual interests it is important to note that only a limited number of sexual offenders display deviant arousal at phallometric assessments (Marshall & Fernandez, 2003) and a similarly limited number meet criteria for a paraphilia based on their history and presentation (Marshall, 2007, 2008). However, for those who display or report deviant interests, there are readily available behavioural procedures that, presented in the appropriate way, are effective in reorganising sexual interests so that they become acceptable (Marshall et al., 2009).

In the final part of our programme (i.e. Phase 3), we help each client integrate what they have learned into an abbreviated version of the *Good Lives Model*. Based on this they identify plans aimed at developing their personal 'good life' after discharge. We particularly emphasise the importance of developing personally enjoyable leisure activities both because we want their non-work time to be meaningfully occupied and because such activities are functionally related to better mental and physical health (Mutrie & Faulkner, 2004; Taylor & Faulkner, 2007). Clients also typically generate plans for education or for upgrading their work skills. They are also asked to identify people (friends, family, professionals) who will provide them with support upon release. However, we emphasise the importance of them taking responsibility for achieving the goals they have set, since there is evidence indicating that over-reliance on a confidante can diminish the active pursuit of personal goals (Fitzsimmons & Finkel, 2011).

Finally, we limit them to generating one, or at most two, simple avoidance strategies (e.g. for a child molester 'never be alone with a child'). This is done partly because avoidance plans are rarely maintained even in healthy well-functioning people (Gollwitzer & Bargh, 1996), and also because our overall approach throughout treatment is to encourage clients to adopt a positive approach to their futures. Adopting a positive stance towards the future increases optimism and hope in all people (Seligman, 1991; Snyder, 2000), which enhances the likelihood of a beneficial outcome (Snyder et al., 2000). Increasing optimism not only leads to better outcomes, but also improves mental and physical health (Gillham, 2000; Peterson, 2000; Peterson & Bossio, 1991).

ISSUES IN THE EVALUATION OF TREATMENT OUTCOME

As we indicated earlier, the question of whether treatment for sexual offenders is effective has been an enduring issue that has not been resolved to the satisfaction of everyone. The two most respected meta-analyses of outcome (Hanson et al., 2002; Lösel & Schmucker, 2005) concluded that treatment of sexual offenders appeared to be effective, although these conclusions were couched in reservations about the quality of the studies. Both sets of authors declared that the most convincing evidence would come from studies employing the *Random Controlled Trial* (RCT), a declaration echoed by others (Quinsey et al., 1993; Rice & Harris, 2003;

Seto et al., 2008) in even stronger form; the latter group claim that no 'satisfactory' (read RCT) studies have yet provided any grounds for optimism. We (Marshall, 1993, 2006; Marshall, Jones, Ward, Johnston, & Barbaree, 1991; W. L. Marshall & Marshall, 2011; Marshall & Pithers, 1994) have consistently taken a more positive view which we admit was, in our earlier statements, rather overly optimistic based on the evidence available at that time. Now, however, we are satisfied that the evidence is sufficiently convincing.

The argument for employing the RCT design is clearly articulated by the various authors cited above. They point out that several respected researchers have declared the superiority of RCT designs over alternatives with the Cochrane Collaboration (www.cochrane.org) and the Campbell Collaboration (www.campbellcollaboration.org) consolidating this point of view. While we do not have any reservations about the scientific status of the members of these collaborations, their conclusions, we should point out, are not empirically based but rather represent the consensus of experienced researchers. As the noted sociobiologist, and Pulitzer Prize winning author, Edward Wilson once said, scientific knowledge is not the product of consensus. He might have added that disagreement is the lifeblood of research and theory and, in this case, of research design. We take the option of respectfully disagreeing with the collaborative consensus about the value of RCT designs. We do note that at least the Cochrane group pointed to some serious practical limitations to the implementation of the 'ideal' design, a point we have repeated several times (Marshall, 1993, 2006; W. L. Marshall & Marshall, 2007; Marshall & Pithers, 1994).

In their response to our (W. L. Marshall & Marshall, 2007) detailed criticisms of the RCT design, Seto et al. (2008) claimed that the first step in evaluating treatment is to determine if it works in principle, which they describe as an 'efficacy study' (i.e. the RCT design). Seto et al. go on to say that after efficacy is established, subsequent studies are conducted to evaluate effectiveness. Again this declaration simply reflects the agreement of certain researchers. From the perspective of clinicians, it is the effectiveness of treatment (i.e. the reduction of problematic behaviours) conducted under the typical constraints and complexities of clinical delivery, that matters. Conducting efficacy studies under the artificial conditions demanded by the RCT design can provide misleading information. Indeed, we believe that these artificial (read clinically inappropriate) conditions minimise the possibility of finding positive results since they take out of the equation most, if not all, the factors we have outlined above as essential to effective treatment.

While we agree that the RCT design is elegant, we believe it has several inherent problems: methodological, ethical and practical. Our reading of the various authoritative documents on the RCT design indicates that several requirements must be met. First, as the title indicates, available volunteers must be randomly allocated to either treatment or no treatment. When approaching sexual offenders for treatment, as we noted above, a number of them refuse and the number of these refusers varies considerably across programmes. When offenders are told they are in a study where they might be allocated to no treatment, our guess is the refusal rate would increase, particularly in circumstances where completion of treatment is a necessary condition for receiving parole. It may be that sexual offenders who refuse to participate in an *RCT* study are at higher risk to reoffend than are those who agree to participate but are allocated to the no-treatment condition. Thus an RCT design may inadvertently eliminate those offenders most in need of treatment. However, Seto (2011) has offered an alternative RCT design that we find more palatable and that may obviate the above concerns. He suggested that since current treatments appear to be moving away from the tenets of the earlier relapse prevention model, the newer approach could be compared, in an RCT design, to a relapse prevention programme.

The setting where we work (Correctional Service of Canada (CSC) prisons) constitutes one of the world's most extensive set of programmes for sexual offenders and one of the most productive sources of research on these felons. In these prisons, sexual offenders are told upon entry to the system that unless they effectively engage in treatment they will not be granted parole. The important effect of this is that were we to request the offenders to enter a study where they had a 50–50 chance of being allocated to no treatment, most would quite sensibly refuse, making it unlikely that we could conduct an RCT study. Were sufficient numbers to agree to enter the study, those in the no-treatment group would languish in prison longer, which would in itself introduce confound, and they would no doubt be emotionally distressed by this consequence introducing yet another confound. Not only would the possibility of being allocated to a no-treatment group be likely to increase refusal rates and confound the RCT design, but also a proposal to conduct such a study would likely be turned down by institutional authorities due to fears of a negative public backlash. The tenor of public dialogue regarding sexual offenders is extremely negative, punitive and risk aversive. The tabloid media, in particular, portray all sexual offenders as high risk, often reporting reoffence rates that bear no relation to the reality of evidence-based data. Thus, Seto's (2011) suggested approach not only may placate the authorities, but also would likely reduce the rate of refusals and eliminate potential confounds.

Another design requirement of an RCT study is aimed at ensuring internal validity. This refers to the need to ensure that the treatment programme is implemented with integrity and uniformity applied to all participants. Unless this is done it cannot be said that the programme as described has been truly evaluated. In the view of several leading researchers/clinicians in the general clinical field (Goldfried & Wolfe, 1996; Howard, Moras, Brill, Martinovich, & Lutz, 1996; Persons, 1991; Persons & Silberschaltz, 1998; Seligman, 1995, 1996), the results of RCT studies have little or no relevance for practical clinical work as they do not address 'therapy as it is actually delivered in the field' (Seligman & Levant, 1998, p. 211). As Hollin (2006) points out, the RCT design sacrifices external validity (i.e. relevance to clinic work) for internal validity (i.e. rigorous adherence to a prescriptive manual). While manuals can vary in their structure and the detail of their prescriptive nature (see discussions by Hollin (2009), Mann (2009) and Marshall (2009)), the advocates of the RCT design (i.e. the collaborative groups referred to earlier) demand rigorous adherence to the manual. Slavishly adhering to the details of a manual restricts the flexibility and the application of the specific responsivity principle, both of which, as we have pointed out above, are essential to effective treatment. From this point of view, we might anticipate that RCT studies, properly implemented, would minimise, if not eliminate, any potential benefits of treatment.

On a related issue, the adherence to a detailed manual is likely to result in all participants receiving the same degree of treatment. To maintain internal integrity, the RCT design requires the clear specifications of the targets and procedures and demands that the number of treatment sessions and the duration of treatment be uniform across participants. This contradicts the responsivity principle and generally agreed upon best practice considerations (Seligman, 1995). It has been found that incomplete or inappropriate treatment (as would result from a 'one size fits all' approach) significantly reduces treatment effectiveness (Boruch & Gomez, 1977; Hunter & Schmidt, 1990; Lipsey, 1990; Lipsey & Wilson, 1993). This same point has been made for sexual offender programmes (Laws & Ward, 2006). In any case, the inability to exercise the flexibility necessary to avoid these potential pitfalls of the RCT design contradicts the essence of a cognitive-behavioural approach to treatment (Wilson, 1996). As we have seen earlier, the role of therapists' skills and interpersonal characteristics significantly influence the effects of treatment and these features cannot easily be operationalised within the structure of a manual.

We (Marshall, 1993; Marshall & Pithers, 1994) have noted a number of ethical issues with RCT studies but the primary problems relate to (a) the issue of consent and (b) the need, at some point, to provide the most effective treatment to the control group. Both these problems emerge when the proposal for the study is submitted for scrutiny to an ethics committee, as should all studies involving human subjects. In our experience of conducting RCT and other evaluation studies of the treatment of various Axis 1 disorders (Hayes & Marshall, 1984; Kleiner, Marshall, & Spevack, 1987; Marshall, Parker, & Hayes, 1982; Taylor & Marshall, 1977), ethics committees require freely given informed consent by the target group and the provision of treatment for the control group at the earliest possible date. Consent in these studies can appropriately be given by the participants and, of course, this must happen in studies of sexual offender treatment. However, ethics committees should be properly concerned about minimising any possible harm to others (e.g. in the present case potential victims) resulting from failing to provide the most effective treatment to the control group. In order for an RCT design to allow for the possibility that treatment might work, the assumption has to be made that a significantly greater number of the control group must be expected to reoffend by abusing a woman or child. Therefore, an ethically appropriate study should ask women and the guardians of children or at the very least a representative sample of them for approval to conduct the research. It seems to us that since women and children's guardians are likely to be acutely aware of the potential for harm that would befall victims at the hands of sexual offenders, they would be unlikely to condone an RCT study.

In their response to our (W. L. Marshall & Marshall, 2007) expressed concern about the ethics of an RCT study of sexual offender treatment, Seto et al. (2008) note that this 'does not recognise the possibility that unproven treatments (which is how they regarded sexual offender treatment) might have harmful effects, unintentionally increasing recidivism' (p. 250, section in parentheses added). This reprises earlier statements by Quinsey et al. (1993) and was restated by Rice (2010). To strengthen this claim, Rice reported studies of established medical procedures that, when examined in an RCT study, proved to be harmful. We (W. L. Marshall & Marshall, 2011) responded to Rice's claim by pointing out that we could find no published study of sexual offender treatment that has shown an increase in reoffences over that expected by well-established base rates. Indeed, the RCT report that Seto et al. (2008) and Rice (2010) hold to be exemplary, namely the California SOTEP study, reported no evidence of higher recidivism among the treated offenders compared to either the no-treatment volunteers or those who refused to participate in the project (Marques, Weideranders, Day, Nelson, & van Ommeren, 2005).

The other demand of ethics committees, namely the need to provide the control group with effective therapy at the earliest date, is more difficult to address with sexual offenders than with most other Axis 1 disorders. For example, the bulk of relapses among treated clients with anxiety disorders occur within the first six months after discharge, and these clients can typically be readily contacted and offered treatment. With sexual offenders, researchers would have to wait at least 4–5 years after discharge for the bulk of reoffences to occur and by then contacting the untreated group would be difficult, if not unethical and disruptive to their lives.

TREATMENT OUTCOME STUDIES

The first report that carefully selected sexual offender treatment studies for a meta-analysis of effectiveness was the result of the Collaborative Outcome Data Project reported by Hanson et al. (2002). Each of the 43 studies entering this analysis had to have at least a matched group of untreated subjects as the comparison with the treatment group. This meta-analysis, therefore, included RCT designs and also studies employing an alternative design. Those studies meeting these requirements that were not random controlled designs were described as 'incidental assignment' studies. All studies also had to employ official recidivism data as the index of long-term outcome. Hanson et al. found that 12.3% of the treated subjects and 16.8% of the untreated subjects sexually recidivated over an average time at risk of 5 years. When Hanson et al. compared CBT programmes with others; it was only the CBT group of studies that showed effectiveness: 9.9% recidivism versus 17.4% for the other programmes. Having access to a larger number of studies ($k = 80$), Lösel and Schmucker (2005) found almost identical results. In Hanson et al.'s (2009) more recent meta-analysis, the results were again remarkably similar: 10.9% sexual recidivism in the treated group versus 19.8% among the untreated subjects. In all three studies, treatment also markedly reduced non-sexual offending; for example, in Hanson et al.'s (2009) report, 48.3% of the untreated sexual offenders committed non-sexual crimes after release compared with 31.8% of the treated offenders.

The CSC provides treatment for sexual offenders in several prisons across the country with treatment dosage being adjusted according to risk level. A number of these programmes have reported long-term evaluations. In the very highest risk programme, Looman, Abracen, and Nicholaichuk (2000), employing an incidental design, found that over a 10-year follow-up period, 23.6% of the treated subjects and 51.7% of the untreated subjects sexually reoffended. Employing a similar incidental design, Nicholaichuk, Gordon, Gu, and Wong (2000) evaluated a programme for high-risk sexual offenders. Among the treated subjects 14.5% reoffended, whereas 33.2% of the untreated group committed further sexual crimes. Barbaree, Langton, and Peacock, 2003 and Langton, Barbaree, Seto, Harkins, and Peacock (2006) reported a reoffence rate of 11.1% in the moderate/high-risk treated group ($N = 468$) over 6 years. Like our programme, Barbaree's programme has a low refusal rate and there are therefore no available untreated offenders. However, like us, Barbaree's group of researchers compared the treated group's outcome with the expected rate of recidivism derived from established risk assessment instruments (i.e. STATIC-99 and RRASOR). The expected rate of sexual recidivism for untreated offenders reported in Barbaree's studies was 18%.

The latest outcome evaluation of our prison-based programme is reported in our recent book (W. L. Marshall, Marshall, & Kingston, 2011). To date, we have followed 535 sexual offenders who have been at risk in the community for 8.4 years. As against an expected rate of 23.8% (again using the STATIC-99 and RRASOR), only 5.6% of these treated offenders recidivated on a sexual crime. In terms of other reoffending, 8.4% of the treated group committed a violent (sexual or non-sexual) offence during the follow-up period against an expected rate (using the VRAG) of 34.8%. Additional analysis revealed that among possible predictors of sexual reoffending, scores on Hare's PCL-R (Hare, 1991) were not significantly related to recidivism. Categorising offenders as psychopaths, using a cut-off of either 25 or 30, failed to predict reoffending (AUC = .53; $p = .77$; ACU = .55, $p = .64$ respectively), nor did entering PCL-R scores as a continuous variable (AUC = .62, $p = .16$). However, entering therapist ratings of the achievement of treatment goals (see W. L. Marshall, Marshall, & Kingston, 2011, for details of this measure) did prove to be a reliable predictor (AUC = .64; $p < .05$).

There are, of course, other effective programmes reported in the literature as the reader will realise given Hanson et al.'s two reports (2002, 2009) and Lösel and Schmucker's (2005) study. Indeed, our view of the literature persuades us that treatment for sexual offenders can be effective. Note that we say 'can be effective'. Clearly a number of reports reveal that particular programmes are ineffective. We believe that if only those programmes that meet criteria for the needs and responsivity principles were entered into meta-analyses, the results would be favourable. We leave it to future researchers to examine this hypothesis.

REFERENCES

Abel, G. G., Becker, J. V., & Cunningham-Rathner, J. (1984). Complications, consent and cognitions in sex between children and adults. *International Journal of Law and Psychiatry*, *7*, 89–103.

Abel, G. G., Mittelman, M., Becker, J. V., Rathner, J., & Rouleau, J. L. (1988). Predicting child molesters' response to treatment. *Annals of the New York Academy of Sciences*, *528*, 223–234.

Alexander, M. A. (1999). Sexual offender treatment efficacy revisited. *Sexual Abuse: A Journal of Research and Treatment*, *11*, 101–116.

Andrews, D. A., & Bonta, J. (2006). *The psychology of criminal conduct* (4th ed.). Newark, NJ: LexisNexis/Anderson.

Andrews, D. A., & Dowden, C. (1999). A meta-analytic investigation into effective correctional intervention for female offenders. *Forum on Corrections Research*, *11*, 18–21.

Andrews, D. A., Zinger, I., Hoge, R. D., Bonta, J., Gendreau, P., & Cullen, F. T. (1990). Does correctional treatment work? A clinically relevant and psychologically informed meta-analysis. *Criminology*, *28*, 369–404.

Barbaree, H. E., Langton, C. M., & Peacock, E. J. (2003, October). The evaluation of sex offender treatment efficacy using samples stratified by levels of actuarial risk. Paper presented at the 22nd annual research and treatment conference of the Association for the Treatment of Sexual Abusers, St. Louis, MO.

Baumeister, R. F. (Ed.). (1993). *Self-esteem: The puzzle of low self-regard*. New York, NY: Plenum Press.

Beech, A. R., & Fordham, A. S. (1997). Therapeutic climate of sexual offender treatment programs. *Sexual Abuse: A Journal of Research and Treatment*, *9*, 219–237.

Beech, A. R., & Hamilton-Giachritsis, C. E. (2005). Relationship between therapeutic climate and treatment outcome in group-based sexual offender treatment programs. *Sexual Abuse: A Journal of Research and Treatment*, *17*, 127–140.

Boruch, R. F., & Gomez, J. (1977). Sensitivity, bias, and theory in impact evaluations. *Professional Psychology*, *8*, 411–434.

Browne, K. D., Foreman, L., & Middleton, D. (1998). Predicting treatment dropout in sex offenders. *Child Abuse Review*, *7*, 402–419.

Bumby, K. M. (1996). Assessing the cognitive distortions of child molesters and rapists: Development and validation of the MOLEST and RAPE scales. *Sexual Abuse: A Journal of Research and Treatment*, *8*, 37–54.

Burton, D. L., & Smith-Darden, J. (2001). *North American survey of sexual abuser treatment and models: Summary data 2000*. Brandon, VT: Safer Society Press.

Carich, M. S., & Calder, M. C. (2003). *Contemporary treatment of adult male sex offenders*. Lime Regis: Russell House.

Carich, M. S., Dobkowski, G., & Delehanty, N. (2009). No, the spirit of RP is important: A response to Yates & Ward (2009) on abandoning RP. *ATSA Forum*, *21*, 1–8.

Carnes, P. J. (1989). *Contrary to love: Helping the sexual addict*. Minneapolis, MN: CompCare.

Cliska, D. (1990). *Beyond dieting – psychoeducational interventions for chronically obese women: A non-dieting approach*. New York, NY: Brunner/Mazel.

Delmonico, D. L., Griffin, E., & Carnes, P. J. (2002). Treating online compulsive sexual behavior: When cybersex is the drug of choice. In A. Cooper (Ed.), *Sex and the internet: A guidebook for clinicians* (pp. 147–167). New York, NY: Brunner-Routledge.

Dowden, C., & Andrews, D. A. (1999a). What works for female offenders: A meta-analytic review. *Crime & Delinquency*, *45*, 438–452.

Dowden, C., & Andrews, D. A. (1999b). What works in young offender treatment: A meta-analysis. *Forum on Corrections Research*, *11*, 21–24.

Dowden, C., & Andrews, D. A. (2003). Does family intervention work for delinquents? Results of a meta-analysis. *Canadian Journal of Criminology and Criminal Justice*, *45*, 327–342.

Dowden, C., & Andrews, D. A. (2004). The importance of staff practice in delivering effective correctional treatment: A meta-analytic review of core correctional practice. *International Journal of Offender Therapy and Comparative Criminology*, *48*, 203–214.

Dowden, C., Antonowicz, D., & Andrews, D. A. (2003). The effectiveness of relapse prevention with offenders: A meta-analysis. *International Journal of Offender Therapy and Comparative Criminology*, *47*, 516–528.

Fernandez, Y. M., Shingler, J., & Marshall, W. L. (2006). Putting 'behavior' back into the cognitive-behavioral treatment of sexual offenders. In W. L. Marshall, Y. M. Fernandez, L. E. Marshall & G. A. Serran (Eds.), *Sexual offender treatment: Controversial issues* (pp. 211–224). Chichester: Wiley.

Fitzsimmons, G. M., & Finkel, E. J. (2011). Outsourcing self-regulation. *Psychological Science*. Retrieved from http://pss.sagepub.com/content/early/2011/02/07/0956797610397955

Gallagher, C. A., Wilson, D. B., Hirschfield, P., Coggeshall, M. B., & MacKenzie, D. L. (1999). A quantitative review of the effects of sexual offender treatment on sexual reoffending. *Corrections Management Quarterly*, *3*, 19–29.

Gendreau, P., French, S. A., & Gionet, A. (2004). What works (what doesn't work): The principles of effective correctional treatment. *Journal of Community Corrections*, *13*, 4–6.

Gillham, J. E. (Ed.). (2000). *The science of optimism and hope: Research essays in honor of Martin E. P. Seligman*. Radnor, PA: Templeton Foundation Press.

Goldfried, M. R., & Wolfe, B. (1996). Psychotherapy practice and research: Repairing a strained alliance. *American Psychologist*, *51*, 1007–1016.

Gollwitzer, P. W., & Bargh, J. A. (Eds.). (1996). *The psychology of action: Linking cognition and motivation to behavior*. New York, NY: Guilford Press.

Goodman, A. (1998). *Sexual addiction: An integrated approach*. Madison, CT: International Universities Press.

Hall, G. C. N. (1995). Sexual offender recidivism revisited: A meta-analysis of recent treatment studies. *Journal of Consulting and Clinical Psychology*, *63*, 802–809.

Hanson, R. K., Bourgon, G., Helmus, L., & Hodgson, S. (2009). The principles of effective correctional treatment also apply to sexual offenders: A meta-analysis. *Criminal Justice and Behavior*, *36*, 865–891.

Hanson, R. K., Gordon, A., Harris, A. J. R., Marques, J. K., Murphy, W. D., Quinsey, V. L., & Seto, M. C. (2002). First report of the Collaborative Outcome Data Project on the effectiveness of psychological treatment of sex offenders. *Sexual Abuse: A Journal of Research and Treatment*, *14*, 169–194.

Hanson, R. K., & Morton-Bourgon, K. E. (2005). The characteristics of persistent sexual offenders: A meta-analysis of recidivism studies. *Journal of Consulting and Clinical Psychology*, *73*, 1154–1163.

Hare, R. D. (1991). *Manual for the revised psychopathy checklist*. Toronto: Multi-Health Systems.

Hayes, B. J., & Marshall, W. L. (1984). Generalization of treatment effects in training public speakers. *Behaviour Research and Therapy*, *22*, 519–533.

Heatherton, T. F., & Polivy, J. (1991). Development and validation of a scale for measuring self-esteem. *Journal of Personality and Social Psychology*, *60*, 895–910.

Hollin, C. R. (2006). Offending behaviour programmes and contention: Evidence-based practice, manuals, and programme evaluation. In C. R. Hollin & E. J. Palmer (Eds.), *Offending behaviour programmes: Development, application, and controversies* (pp. 33–67). Chichester: Wiley.

Hollin, C. R. (2009). Treatment manuals: The good, the bad and the useful. *Journal of Sexual Aggression*, *15*, 133–137.

Howard, K. I., Moras, K., Brill, P. L., Martinovich, Z., & Lutz, W. (1996). Evaluation of psychotherapy: Efficacy, effectiveness, and patient progress. *American Psychologist*, *51*, 1059–1064.

Hunter, J. E., & Schmidt, F. L. (1990). *Methods of meta-analysis: Correcting error and bias in research findings*. Newbury Park, CA: Sage.

Jones, N., Pelissier, B., & Klein-Saffran, J. (2006). Predicting sex offender treatment entry among individuals convicted of sexual offence crimes. *Sexual Abuse: A Journal of Research and Treatment*, *18*, 83–98.

Kafka, M. P. (1994). Sertraline pharmacotherapy for paraphilias and paraphilia-related disorders: An open trial. *Annals of Clinical Psychiatry*, *6*, 189–195.

Kafka, M. P., & Prentky, R. (1992). Fluoxetine treatment of non-paraphilic sexual addictions and paraphilias in men. *The Journal of Clinical Psychiatry*, *53*, 351–358.

Kleiner, L., Marshall, W. L., & Spevack, M. (1987). Training in problem-solving and exposure treatment for agoraphobics with panic attacks. *Journal of Anxiety Disorders*, *1*, 219–238.

Kottler, J. A., Sexton, T. L., & Whiston, S. C. (1994). *The heart of healing: Relationship in therapy*. San Francisco, CA: Jossey-Bass.

Langton, C. M., Barbaree, H. E., Seto, M. C., Harkins, L., & Peacock, E. J. (2006). Sexual offenders' response to treatment and its association with recidivism as a function of psychopathy. *Sexual Abuse: A Journal of Research and Treatment*, *18*, 99–120.

Laws, D. R., & Ward, T. (2006). When one size doesn't fit all. In W. L. Marshall, Y. M. Fernandez, L. E. Marshall & G. A. Serran (Eds.), *Sexual offender treatment: Controversial issues* (pp. 241–254). Chichester: Wiley.

Lee, J. K. P., Proeve, M. J., Lancaster, M., & Jackson, H. J. (1996). An evaluation and 1-year follow-up study of a community-based treatment program for sex offenders. *Australian Psychologist*, *31*, 147–152.

Linley, P. A., & Joseph, S. (Eds.). (2004). *Positive psychology in practice*. Hoboken, NJ: Wiley.

Lipsey, M. W. (1990). *Design sensitivity: Statistical power for experimental research*. Newbury Park, CA: Sage.

Lipsey, M. W. (1995). What do we learn from 400 research studies on the effectiveness of treatment with juvenile delinquency? In J. McGuire (Ed.), *What works: Reducing reoffending, guidelines from research to practice* (pp. 63–78). West Sussex: Wiley.

Lipsey, M. W. (1999). Can rehabilitative programs reduce the recidivism of juvenile offenders? An inquiry into the effectiveness of practical programs. *Virginia Journal of Social Policy and the Law*, *6*, 611–641.

Lipsey, M. W., & Wilson, D. B. (1993). The efficacy of psychological, educational, and behavioral treatment: Confirmation from meta-analysis. *American Psychologist*, *48*, 1181–1209.

Looman, J., Abracen, J., & Nicholaichuk, T. P. (2000). Recidivism among treated sexual offenders and matched controls: Data from the Regional Treatment Centre (Ontario). *Journal of Interpersonal Violence*, *15*, 279–290.

Lösel, F. (1995). The efficacy of correctional treatment: A review and synthesis of meta-evaluations. In J. McGuire (Ed.), *What works: Reducing reoffending, guidelines from research to practice* (pp. 79–111). Chichester: Wiley.

Lösel, F., & Schmucker, M. (2005). The effectiveness of treatment for sexual offenders: A comprehensive meta-analysis. *Journal of Experimental Criminology*, *1*, 117–146.

Mann, R. E. (2009). Sex offender treatment: The case for manualization. *Journal of Sexual Aggression*, *15*, 121–131.

Mann, R. E., & Webster, S. D. (2002, October). Understanding resistance and denial. Paper presented at the 21st annual research and treatment conference of the Association for the Treatment of Sexual Abusers, Montreal, Canada.

Marques, J. K., Weideranders, M., Day, D. M., Nelson, C., & van Ommeren, A. (2005). Effects of a relapse prevention program on sexual recidivism: Final results from California's Sex Offender Treatment and Evaluation Project (SOTEP). *Sexual Abuse: A Journal of Research and Treatment*, *17*, 79–107.

Marshall, L. E., & Marshall, W. L. (this volume). The Risk/Needs/Responsivity Model: The crucial features of general responsivity. In E. Bowen & S. J. Brown (Eds.), *Perspectives on evaluating criminal justice and corrections* (pp. 29–45). Bingley, UK: Emerald Publishing.

Marshall, L. E., & Marshall, W. L. (2001). Excessive sexual desire disorder among sexual offenders: The development of a research project. *Sexual Addiction & Compulsivity: The Journal of Treatment and Prevention*, *8*, 301–307.

Marshall, L. E., & Marshall, W. L. (2006). Sexual addiction in incarcerated sexual offenders. *Sexual Addiction & Compulsivity: The Journal of Treatment and Prevention*, *13*, 377–390.

Marshall, L. E., Marshall, W. L., Moulden, H. M., & Serran, G. A. (2008). The prevalence of sexual addiction in incarcerated sexual offenders and matched community nonoffenders. *Sexual Addiction & Compulsivity: The Journal of Treatment and Prevention*, *15*, 271–283.

Marshall, W. L. (1971). A combined treatment method for certain sexual deviations. *Behaviour Research and Therapy*, *9*, 293–294.

Marshall, W. L. (1993). The treatment of sex offenders: What does the outcome data tell us? A reply to Quinsey et al. *Journal of Interpersonal Violence*, *8*, 524–530.

Marshall, W. L. (2006). Appraising treatment outcome with sexual offenders. In W. L. Marshall, Y. M. Fernandez, L. E. Marshall & G. A. Serran (Eds.), *Sexual offender treatment: Controversial issues* (pp. 255–273). Chichester: Wiley.

Marshall, W. L. (2007). Diagnostic issues, multiple paraphilias, and comorbid disorders in sexual offenders: Their incidence and treatment. *Aggression and Violent Behavior*, *12*, 16–35.

Marshall, W. L. (2008). Czy pedofilia jest uleczalna? Wyniki badań pólnocnoamerykańskich (Are pedophiles treatable? Evidence from North American studies). *Seksuologia Polska*, *6*, 1–6.

Marshall, W. L. (2009). Manualization: A blessing or a curse? *Journal of Sexual Aggression, 15*, 109–120.

Marshall, W. L., & Barbaree, H. E. (1988). The long-term evaluation of a behavioural treatment program for child molesters. *Behaviour Research and Therapy, 26*, 499–511.

Marshall, W. L., & Fernandez, Y. M. (2003). *Phallometric testing with sexual offenders: Theory, research, and practice*. Brandon, VT: Safer Society Press.

Marshall, W. L., & Marshall, L. E. (2007). The utility of the Random Controlled Trial for evaluating sexual offender treatment: The gold standard or an inappropriate strategy? *Sexual Abuse: A Journal of Research and Treatment, 19*, 175–191.

Marshall, W. L., & Marshall, L. E. (2011). Can treatment be effective with sexual offenders or does it do harm? A response to Hanson (2010) and Rice (2010). *Sexual Offender Treatment, 2*. Retrieved from http://iatso.org.ejournal/

Marshall, W. L., & Pithers, W. D. (1994). A reconsideration of treatment outcome with sex offenders. *Criminal Justice and Behavior, 21*, 10–27.

Marshall, W. L., & Williams, S. (1975). A behavioural approach to the modification of rape. *Quarterly Bulletin of the British Association for Behavioural Psychotherapy, 4*, 78.

Marshall, W. L., Anderson, D., & Fernandez, Y. M. (1999). *Cognitive behavioural treatment of sexual offenders*. Chichester: Wiley.

Marshall, W. L., Earls, C. M., Segal, Z. V., & Darke, J. (1983). A behavioral program for the assessment and treatment of sexual aggressors. In K. Craig & R. McMahon (Eds.), *Advances in clinical behavior therapy* (pp. 148–174). New York, NY: Brunner/Mazel.

Marshall, W. L., Fernandez, Y. M., Hudson, S. M., & Ward, T. (Eds.). (1998). *Sourcebook of treatment programs for sexual offenders*. New York, NY: Plenum Press.

Marshall, W. L., Jones, R., Ward, T., Johnston, P., & Barbaree, H. E. (1991). Treatment outcome with sex offenders. *Clinical Psychology Review, 11*, 465–485.

Marshall, W. L., Marshall, L. E., & Kingston, D. A. (2011). Are the cognitive distortions of child molesters in need of treatment? *Journal of Sexual Aggression, 17*(2), 118–129.

Marshall, W. L., O'Brien, M. D., & Marshall, L. E. (2009). Modifying sexual preferences. In A. R. Beech, L. A. Craig & K. D. Browne (Eds.), *Assessment and treatment of sex offenders: A handbook* (pp. 311–327). Chichester: Wiley.

Marshall, W. L., Parker, L., & Hayes, B. J. (1982). Treating public speaking problems: A study using flooding and the elements of skills training. *Behavior Modification, 6*, 147–170.

Marshall, W. L., Marshall, L. E., & Ware, J. (2009). Cognitive distortions in sexual offenders: Should they all be treatment targets? *Sexual Abuse in Australia and New Zealand: An Interdisciplinary Journal, 2*, 70–78.

Marshall, W. L., Marshall, L. E., Serran, G. A., & Fernandez, Y. M. (2006). *Treating sexual offenders: An integrated approach*. New York, NY: Routledge.

Marshall, W. L., Marshall, L. E., Serran, G. A., & O'Brien, M. D. (2011). *The rehabilitation of sexual offenders: A strength based approach*. Washington, DC: American Psychological Association.

Marshall, W. L., Serran, G. A., Fernandez, Y. M., Mulloy, R., Mann, R. E., & Thornton, D. (2003). Therapist characteristics in the treatment of sexual offenders: Tentative data on their relationship with indices of behaviour change. *Journal of Sexual Aggression, 9*, 25–30.

Marshall, W. L., Serran, G. A., Moulden, H., Mulloy, R., Fernandez, Y. M., Mann, R. E., & Thornton, D. (2002). Therapist features in sexual offender treatment: Their reliable identification and influence on behaviour change. *Clinical Psychology & Psychotherapy*, *9*, 395–405.

Marshall, W. L., Ward, T., Mann, R. E., Moulden, H., Fernandez, Y. M., Serran, G. A., & Marshall, L. E. (2005). Working positively with sexual offenders: Maximizing the effectiveness of treatment. *Journal of Interpersonal Violence*, *20*, 1096–1114.

McGrath, R. J., Cumming, G. F., & Buchard, B. L. (2003). *Current practices and trends in sexual abuser management: Safer Society 2002 nationwide survey*. Brandon, VT: Safer Society Press.

McGrath, R. J., Cumming, G. F., Buchard, B. L., Zeoli, S., & Ellerby, L. (2010). *Current practices and emerging trends in sexual abuser management*. Brandon, VT: Safer Society Press.

McGrath, R. J., Cumming, G. F., Livingston, J. A., & Hoke, S. E. (2003). Outcome of a treatment program for adult sex offenders: From prison to community. *Journal of Interpersonal Violence*, *18*, 3–17.

McPherson, M., Chein, D., Van Maren, N., & Swenson, D. (1994). *Sex offender treatment programs*. Saint Paul, MN: Program Evaluation Division, Office of the Legislative Auditor.

Miller, W. R. (1983). Motivational interviewing with problem drinkers. *Behavioural Psychotherapy*, *1*, 147–172.

Mutrie, N., & Faulkner, G. (2004). Physical activity: Positive psychology in motion. In P. A. Linley & S. Joseph (Eds.), *Positive psychology in practice* (pp. 146–164). Hoboken, NJ: Wiley.

Needles, D. J., & Abramson, L. Y. (1990). Positive life events, attributional style, and hopelessness: Testing a model of recovery from depression. *Journal of Abnormal Psychology*, *99*, 156–165.

Nicholaichuk, T., Gordon, A., Gu, D., & Wong, S. (2000). Outcome of an institutional sexual offender treatment program: A comparison between treated and matched untreated offenders. *Sexual Abuse: A Journal of Research and Treatment*, *12*, 139–153.

Norcross, J. C. (2002). Empirically supported therapy relationships. In J. C. Norcross (Ed.), *Psychotherapy relationships that work: Therapist contributions and responsiveness to patient needs* (pp. 3–10). New York, NY: Oxford University Press.

Persons, J. B. (1991). Psychotherapy outcome studies do not accurately represent current models of psychotherapy: A proposed remedy. *American Psychologist*, *46*, 99–106.

Persons, J. B., & Silberschaltz, G. (1998). Are the results of randomized controlled trials useful to psychotherapists? *Journal of Consulting and Clinical Psychology*, *66*, 126–135.

Peterson, C. (2000). The future of optimism. *American Psychologist*, *55*, 44–55.

Peterson, C. (2006). *A Primer in positive psychology*. New York, NY: Oxford University Press.

Peterson, C., & Bossio, L. M. (1991). *Health and optimism*. New York, NY: Free Press.

Quinsey, V. L., Harris, G. T., Rice, M. E., & Lalumière, M. L. (1993). Assessing treatment efficacy in outcome studies of sex offenders. *Journal of Interpersonal Violence*, *8*, 512–523.

Redondo, S., Garrido, V., & Sanchez-Meca, J. (1999). The influence of treatment programs on the recidivism of juvenile and adult offenders: A European meta-analytic review. *Psychology, Crime, and Law*, *5*, 251–278.

Rice, M. E. (2010, September). Treatment for adult sex offenders: May we reject the null hypothesis? Paper presented at the 11th Conference of the International Association for the Treatment of Sexual Offenders, Oslo.

Rice, M. E., & Harris, G. T. (2003). The size and sign of treatment effects in sex offender therapy. *Annals of the New York Academy of Sciences*, *989*, 428–440.

Salter, A. C. (1988). *Treating child sex offenders and victims? Assessment and treatment of child sex offenders: A practical guide.* Beverly Hills, CA: Sage.

Seager, J. A., Jellicoe, D., & Dhaliwal, G. K. (2004). Refusers, dropouts, and completers: Measuring sex offender treatment efficacy. *International Journal of Offender Therapy and Comparative Criminology*, *48*, 600–612.

Seligman, M. E. P. (1991). *Learned optimism*. New York, NY: Knopf.

Seligman, M. E. P. (1995). The effectiveness of psychotherapy: The Consumer Reports Study. *American Psychologist*, *50*, 965–974.

Seligman, M. E. P. (1996). Science as an ally of practice. *American Psychologist*, *51*, 1072–1079.

Seligman, M. E. P., & Levant, R. F. (1998). Managed care policies rely on inadequate science. *Professional Psychology: Research and Practice*, *29*, 211–212.

Seto, M. C. (2011, March). Is there a way forward? Paper presented at advancing our understanding of treatment change among high risk sex offenders. Carleton University, Ottawa.

Seto, M. C., Marques, J. K., Harris, G. T., Chaffin, M., Lalumière, M. L., Miner, M. H., … Quinsey, V. L. (2008). Good science and progress in sex offender treatment are intertwined: A response to Marshall & Marshall (2009). *Sexual Abuse: A Journal of Research and Treatment*, *20*, 247–255.

Shaw, T. A., Herkov, J. M., & Greer, R. A. (1995). Examination of treatment completion and predicted outcome among incarcerated sex offenders. *The Bulletin of the American Academy of Psychiatry and the Law*, *23*, 35–41.

Smith, E. (2006). The strength-based counseling model. *The Counseling Psychologist*, *34*, 13–79.

Snyder, C. R. (2000). The past and possible futures of hope. *Journal of Social and Clinical Psychology*, *19*, 11–28.

Snyder, C. R., Ilardi, S., Cheavens, J., Michael, S. T., Yamhure, L., & Sympson, S. (2000). The role of hope in cognitive behavior therapies. *Cognitive Therapy and Research*, *24*, 747–762.

Snyder, C. R., & Lopez, S. J. (Eds.). (2005). *Handbook of positive psychology*. New York, NY: Oxford University Press.

Tangney, J. P., & Dearing, R. O. (2002). *Shame and guilt*. New York, NY: Guilford Press.

Taylor, A. H., & Faulkner, G. (2007). Inaugural editorial. *Mental Health and Physical Activity*, *1*, 1–8.

Taylor, F. G., & Marshall, W. L. (1977). Experimental analysis of a cognitive/behavioral therapy for depression. *Cognitive Therapy and Research*, *1*, 59–72.

Walborn, F. S. (1996). Process variables: Four common elements of counseling with male pedophiles. *Journal of Homosexuality*, *20*, 189–198.

Ward, T. (2002). Good lives and the rehabilitation of offenders: Promises and problems. *Aggerssion and Violent Behavior*, *7*, 513–528.

Ward, T., & Gannon, T. A. (2006). Rehabilitation, etiology, and self-regulation: The good lives model of sexual offender treatment. *Aggression and Violent Behavior*, *11*, 77–94.

Ward, T., & Mann, R. E. (2004). Good lives and the rehabilitation of offenders: A positive approach to sex offender treatment. In P. A. Linley & S. Joseph (Eds.), *Positive psychology in practice* (pp. 598–616). Hoboken, NJ: Wiley.

Ward, T., & Marshall, W. L. (2004). Good lives, aetiology and the rehabilitation of sex offenders: A bridging theory. *Journal of Sexual Aggression*, *10*, 153–169.

Ward, T., & Stewart, C. (2003). Good lives and the rehabilitation of sexual offenders. In T. Ward, D. R. Laws & S. M. Hudson (Eds.), *Sexual deviance: Issues and controversies* (pp. 21–44). Thousand Oaks, CA: Sage.

Whitehead, J. T., & Lab, S. P. (1989). A meta-analysis of juvenile correctional treatment. *Journal of Research in Crime and Delinquency*, *26*, 276–295.

Wilson, G. T. (1996). Manual-based treatments: The clinical application of research findings. *Behaviour Research and Therapy*, *34*, 295–314.

Yates, P. M., & Ward, T. (2009). Yes, relapse prevention should be abandoned: A reply to Carich, Dobkowski, and Delehanty (2008). *ATSA Forum*, *21*, 9–21.

RESOLVING ETHICAL ISSUES IN RANDOMISED CONTROLLED TRIALS

Robert F. Boruch, Joe S. Cecil,
Herb Turner III, Timothy Victor
and Jordan M. Hyatt

ABSTRACT

The chapter considers the ethical problems engendered by random assignment and privacy concerns in randomised controlled experiments and cluster randomised trials. The particular focus is on procedural, legislative and technical approaches to reducing or avoiding the problems. Examples are given from a variety of disciplines including health and education, though the main emphasis is on research in crime and delinquency.

INTRODUCTION

Randomised trials, like all experiments in the social sciences, 'are exposed to epistemological, social and ethical threats to their validity and, in turn, that the outcomes of any experiment are open to more than one interpretation'.

Perspectives on Evaluating Criminal Justice and Corrections
Advances in Program Evaluation, Volume 13, 95–127

ISSN: 1474-7863/doi:10.1108/S1474-7863(2012)0000013009

However, they offer the best chance, given the current state of experimental design and statistical know-how, to isolate the causal influences from exogenous noise. In affirmation, Tukey declared that 'the only source of reliable evidence about the usefulness of almost any sort of therapy or surgical intervention is that obtained from well-planned and carefully conducted randomised ... clinical trial'. Despite decades of research spent refining the statistical methodologies that underlie randomised trials, ethical issues persist.

Learning about the ethics of randomised controlled trials (RCTs) is not always easy. For instance, a recent Google search using the phrase 'randomized controlled trial ethics' yielded 1,800,000 results in 0.07 seconds. This chapter is intended to make it a bit easier for experimenters, trial participants, research policy people and the thoughtful citizen to understand the topic.

The focus here is on ethical issues encountered in RCTs and especially on how the issues can be or might be resolved. Boundary conditions such as law, local culture, institutional rules and government regulations are important, of course, and considered here. This is partly because they may embody ethical standards. Some ingredients of this chapter are dedicated to the future. This is because the interpretation of ethics can change with time and with new kinds of research just as the boundary conditions may.

In generating good evidence through RCTs, the main ethical issues usually emerge in two areas. The first concerns the random assignment feature that is common to any randomised trial. Put simply, individual people or entities, such as villages, crime hot spots or schools, that are randomly allocated to different interventions might be put at a disadvantage as a consequence of the attempt to compare interventions in a randomised trial. The ethical and legal issues engendered by such trials, real or ostensible, occur in many disciplines. Examples in research on crime and delinquency, education, health, welfare and other areas are included in what follows.

The second issue area concerns individual privacy. Here, we regard the two arms of a randomised trial as parallel surveys. The privacy imperative affects researchers' efforts to elicit information in probability sample surveys and ethnographic research, as well as in randomised trials. Privacy issues are also pertinent in efforts to linking research records on individuals who participate in experiments (or surveys) with administrative records from different sources on the same individuals, a form of integrated data system.

The issue areas and approaches to resolutions are discussed seriatim. The discussion depends heavily on actual trials. We also identify topics that deserve more attention from people who want to advance understanding of the topic based on empirical research at the interstices of ethics, law and RCTs.

THE RCT

The power of experimental trials to do certain things well has been clearly established. While the label may be something of a misnomer or misguided, randomised experiments are often referred to as the 'gold standard' of research methods within criminology, in medicine, education and other scientific disciplines. RCTs have provided evidence regarding the effectiveness of significant scientific advances.

Randomly assigning individuals or entities, such as organisations, to one of two or more interventions is a key element of a randomised trial. From this ostensibly simple process, a number of significant advantages are derived; we speak of only two here. First, RCTs allow for the elimination of bias in the sample by eliminating *all* potential systematic differences between the groups that are involved in the interventions being compared. This ensures that all known and unknown variables have the same expected values and that any post-experiment differences can be attributed to the interventions. Second, randomisation permits the measurement of uncertainty within a study.

In particular, random assignment of people or entities to different programmes avoids the need to depend on assumptions, sometimes heroic ones, about what would have happened to people or entities in the absence of the intervention they actually received. The random allocation to the two or more interventions, one of which may be a control, assures fairness in the sense of generating groups that do not differ systematically. It also permits legitimate probabilistic statements about confidence intervals for the differences in outcomes. Both products are important in science and, at times, in legislative and judicial settings (Boruch & Cecil, 1979; Kaye & Freedman, 1994).

The thoughtful ethicist might construe at least two basic types of randomised trials, classifying them by their intention: experimental trials are designed to test an intervention for which the outcome is unknown; and demonstration trials are designed to illustrate the benefits of a treatment, either in relation to an absence of treatment, or some other standard of care.

While the statistical methodologies behind the trial remain the same, the ethical implications of the trial vary significantly. A demonstration RCT, as the impact of the treatment is known, is of questionable ethical value, as the design may require denying some participants a treatment that is known a priori to be beneficial. Though a utilitarian approach would suggest that this is the cost of replicating findings – and a necessary step for the greater good – it also, Royall argues, violates the ethical obligations doctors, and perhaps other practitioners, have to those *individuals* under their supervision.

Experiments in which the impact of the treatment is unknown carry a different set of ethical concerns. One of the most frequently cited relates to the ideal of equipoise. Under this principle, an RCT is only appropriate when there is a genuine question as to the most beneficial treatment for the participant. When it becomes apparent, regardless of the state of the trial, the directionality of the outcomes, the experiment should cease. Failing to do so exposes participants to risk unnecessarily or denies them due treatment. This also lends itself to a tension between researchers and clinicians, each with a different perception of the benefits to be gained through the trial.

The nature and characteristics of the unit being randomly assigned also gives rise to a set of ethical concerns. The random assignment of individuals to different interventions at times engenders unique ethical problems. In many cases, but not all, the problem involves the professional's beliefs that a particular intervention is effective, on the one hand, coupled to the professional's ethic that requires delivery of the intervention on the other hand. This is in contrast, on the other hand, to another professional's belief that the evidence on the intervention's effectiveness is ambiguous or not scientifically defensible, and this professional's ethic then calls for a controlled randomised trial on the intervention. This kind of conflict is fundamental in many arguments about the propriety of randomisation.

A trial in which entire villages, police hot spots, emergency care units, schools or other entities are assigned by lottery to different interventions may also engender ethical issues. Some issues are similar to those in trials involving individuals as the units of random assignment. Some are not. Who, indeed, is the 'human subject' in a controlled trial in which schools or crime hot spots are the units of random allocation? The students or teachers? The criminal or the cops? See Boruch, Weisburd, and Berk (2010) on crime hot spots and Taljaard et al. (2009) on health-related cluster trials for instance and the other material in this chapter.

BOUNDARY CONDITIONS: LAW, REGULATIONS AND INSTITUTIONAL REVIEW BOARDS

Informed Consent, Law and Regulations

Generally speaking, a consent to participate is 'informed' when it is obtained after the participant has been adequately instructed about the ratio of risk and benefit involved in the procedure, as compared to alternative procedures or no treatment at all. As the Supreme Court of Kansas noted in *Williams v. Menehan* (1963):

> It is the duty of the doctor to make a reasonable disclosure to his patient of the nature and probable consequences of the suggested or recommended treatment and to make a knowledgeable disclosure of the dangers within his knowledge which are incident or possible in the treatment he proposes to administer.

The same logic and protections should arguably apply when the context is not medical, but rather social or educational. More complex considerations emerge, however, when competency, comprehension, outside influences and voluntariness are at issue.

The main boundary conditions, notably governmental rules in the United States and other countries, pertain to informed consent and demand consideration of (a) what information is provided, (b) the person (or groups) from whom consent may be sought, (c) how the information is provided, (d) how consent is affirmed and (e) how consent is monitored. Pertinent requirements have been laid out in U.S. Federal regulations and in government regulations of many developed countries. See U.S. Department of Health and Human Services (DHHS) (2005) and Marshall's (2006) review of international work on informed consent.

As Szabo and Britt (2007) further point out, U.S. regulations specify that U.S. researchers working in other countries should take the other countries' ethics and rules of law into account. Especially in developing countries, this is not always easy. Muslim law differs in character from U.S. law, for instance. Szabo and Britt (2007) have done the research community a service in determining whether and how 16 West African countries provide internet (and other) access to their guidelines on human subjects research, and in providing web and other addresses for those who seek information.

Depending on websites is a risky way of determining whether policies exist. Nonetheless they are a beginning. From Szabo and Britt's paper, the researcher may learn about conducting medical trials in Benin, Burkina

Faso, Senegal, Nigeria and Cote d'Ivoire. But the trialist will have to work harder to learn about roles in Cape Verde, Guine-Bissau, Liberia, Niger or Tago. The international organisations, such as WHO and international conferences that deal with health-related and pharmaceutical trials are also identified in the article.

The fact that '[i]nformed consent is universally recognized as a central component of ethical conduct in scientific research' (Marshall, 2006) is accepted in many social science communities. Nonetheless, there are limits in this as in other such declarations. The phrase 'informed consent', for instance, applies now only to scientific experiments, not to efforts that can be construed as 'experiments' with no scientific controls.

For example, politicians promulgate policies at times, and declare that the policy will be tried out. The politician does not declare that trying out is equivalent to research, though indeed it can be construed as such. The politician does not know the intervention will work; this 'trying out' is de facto a social experiment. Similarly, the physician may try out a drug on a patient. But the patient signs no consent form for 'research' per se, though does sign a form that informs the patient about other matters perhaps such as risk and liability for it. See, for instance, Evans, Thornton, and Chalmers (2006). The social worker who assigns services to a client may have no dependable evidence that the services work. This 'experiment', in the sense of 'trying something out', entails no informed consent.

Informed consent is a context-specific matter, as the issues that are faced in medicine vary significantly from those faced by people who do randomised trials in the social sciences. For example, informed consent becomes almost intractable when dealing with incarcerated persons and juvenile delinquents, two subpopulations not known for cooperative behaviour. Unlike some other research settings, obtaining informed consent poses a problem, not for the researcher, but for the subject. Offenders, where the only link to their participation in a study is the informed consent form, could be subject to a subpoena to collect data on self-reported criminal conduct, for example (Roberts & Indermauer, 2003). Informed consent forms also identify the individual's participation in research, an activity that may be seen in a less than positive light in some peer groups. It may also be the case that it is the informed consent procedure, not the research itself, which deters participation (Rowe, 2007).

The ethics of informed consent become more complicated when considering cluster randomised trials, regardless of the subject matter. In these experiments, groups of participants are assigned to receive a treatment, but there is some latitude, within the groups, as to which participants will receive it. What matters is that a significant proportion of each group receives the treatment, not if any individual does. However, as Sabin notes, this requires the appointment of a 'guardian' to ensure the protection of the individuals within the cluster. Since each individual, as an individual, did not agree to participate, the ethical complications are clear – there is no consent, let alone that of an informed variety.

Institutional Review Boards, Law, Regulations and the History of Randomised Trials

Oakes' (2002) article is a concise handling of the topic of Institutional Review Boards (IRBs) in the context of applied social research. Detailed discussions of IRBs and their processes, the regulatory frameworks and history, and some review of empirical data are available in specialised areas. The Institute of Medicine's *Ethical Conduct of Clinical Research involving Children* (Field & Behrman, 2004), for instance, covers these topics as well as legal interpretation of how the rights of minors or their representatives (e.g. parents) or both, are handled.

IRBs and Their Purview

In the United States, IRBs are, as a matter of federal law and regulations, responsible for overseeing the ethical propriety of studies in institutions to which federal funds are provided. The Board's membership, procedures and rules are determined by regulation governing research sponsored by the U.S. DHHS and 14–16 other federal agencies. Though the Department of Defense is among these, the Central Intelligence Agency, Department of Homeland Security, and others are not, to our knowledge. For the intelligence agencies, recent initiatives by the National Research Council with intelligence community support may help to clarify matters in this sector. See Pool (2010) for instance, and see Moreno (2006) for background.

National law in Canada, the United Kingdom, Sweden and other countries requires entities that are analogous to IRBs in the United States to review the ethics of a study. As is the case in the United States, the distinction between research and efforts to generate evidence on the effectiveness of better programmes (which can be construed as 'research' or 'evaluation') often is not clear. The latter will be discussed later.

IRBs, despite the specific legislation creating them, may be ill-equipped to manage, or to understand, the specific hurdles faced by those seeking to run RCTs in the field. For example, all interventions involving prisoners are also focused to undergo additional scrutiny from their outset: randomisation cannot protect researchers from IRBs. Under 45 CFR 46, Subpart C, all research that includes any individual who is or becomes a prisoner while participating in a research study must undergo this increased scrutiny before any protocol can be allowed to proceed.[1] At the very least, this secondary review delays the approval of protocols and the implementation of experiments. In an environment where 'time is money' (and the funding available is so often capped from the outset), this presents difficulties for those seeking to initiate a randomised trial.

IRBs per se do not exist in some countries. Indeed, some countries may have no laws that are stable and understood, much less understood in the narrow context of conducting randomised trials. See Szabo and Britt (2007), for instance, on West African countries that do and do not have relevant statutes or procedures.

Evolutionary Character of Ethics, Case Law and Areas of Agreement

Lois-ellin Datta (2002) likened the statements of ethical principles enunciated by the American Evaluation Association to the U.S. constitution and its interpretation:

> (It) is no feasible document, but it has required two centuries of debate as precedents develop. It needs continual reinterpretation as times change and as individual cases present complex nuances. Even after debates, unanimous conclusions are not typical .... (Datta, 2002, p. 195)

Her engaging article suggests ways to better inform the use of, and changes to, ethics standards. Datta (2002) also observed that in the ethics cases she considered, in the context of the *American Journal of Evaluation*, 'most agreement tended to involve design and data collection ...' as opposed to some evaluator's construal of their role, for example as 'social avengers'. In this chapter, we stick to task of making fair comparisons based on randomised trials, including issues of design, data collection, analysis and reporting.

The growth in randomised trials in which entire jurisdictions are the units of random allocation are a case in point, and illustrates part of the evolution to which Datta referred. In particular, contemporary ethical frameworks and government regulations focus on individuals as the targets of research. Few, as of this writing, focus on organisations, places, clusters of people, etc. as the randomised units. Taljaard et al. (2009) in Canada have taken a lead role in understanding the ethics of such trials, this initiative is considered below. In regard to the evolutionary character of codes of ethic and empirical underpinnings, see Sieber (2006), Blustein (2010) and American Institutes for Research (2011).

Vernacular

The language of U.S. law on ethics in research and many societies' statements on professional ethics refer to 'human subjects'. This characterisation can be construed as misleading and out of date in many ways, despite the conscientious attorney's adherence to the phrase in a legal context (Kilpatrick, personal communication, 2008). In this chapter, we use the phrase 'research participants' instead. This is because the individuals or entities engaged in randomised trials can no longer be regarded merely as 'subjects'. Their agreement to engage, or their representatives' engagement, in the design, conduct and even analysis of data makes them 'participants' (see Field & Behrman, 2004, p. 396, for a justification of this in the context of the Institute of Medicine and Boruch, 1997 and Fantuzzo, McWayne, & Childs, 2006 on the idea of partnerships in randomised trials).

The idea of random allocation is fundamental in assuring fair comparisons in a trial and in a statistical statement of confidence in one's results. The idea, however, is not handled uniformly in the scientific literature and is not part of a uniform vernacular in research ethics. The Institute of Medicine's report on clinical research on children, for instance, refers to control groups in the index. But no index entry, or chapter, refers to randomised trials or randomised experiments. Nor is there a reference to 'lottery' allocation. Many randomised trials are nonetheless recognised in the body of the report (Field & Behrman, 2004).

The phrase 'randomized experiment' has been used often to good effect, at times, in the social sector since the 1970s (Riecken & Boruch, 1974). But this phrase carries unnecessary and misleading connotations. For instance, consenting for my child to 'participate in a randomised controlled trial of a curriculum' is more tolerable than consenting to an 'experiment on my child'. Mosteller and Boruch (2002) used the phrase 'randomized controlled trial' in their book's title and text and others have adopted similar vernacular to reduce the misleading connotations and to inform the prospective study participant. Others have used the phrase 'pilot test', 'research study', which are usually tied to other vernacular such as 'lottery' to convey the meanings without unnecessary connotation.

APPROACHES TO RESOLVING ETHICAL AND LEGAL PROBLEMS THROUGH THE RANDOMISED TRIAL'S DESIGN

Certain features of any randomised trial's design can be altered at times so as to make the trial acceptable relative to local ethical or legal standards. A productive alteration is such that scientific standards for the fairness of a comparison can be met and a legitimate statement about statistical (chance level) error can be made, and it is such that other ethical professional or legal standards are met. Any such alteration also influences, to a greater or lesser degree, the nature of the scientific comparison being made. That is, the specific scientific question that is addressed in the trial may have to change. The pertinent features of the trial's design include

- intervention and control conditions,
- units of random allocation and analysis,
- the level of supply of and demand for the intervention,
- eligibility of individuals,
- imbalance in random configurations,
- ratio of treated to untreated participants.

These features are considered in an interrogatory form in the following.

Which Interventions Are Deployed and When?

The ethical experimenter relies on a randomised trial *only* if the relative effectiveness of two or more interventions under scrutiny is unknown. One of the interventions may be a control condition. In the vernacular of the medical ethicist, the interventions expected effects are in 'equipoise'.

The arguments about evidence that precede the decision to rely on a randomised trial are important, of course. Some will claim that extant evidence about the effects of intervention A versus B is wrong or incomplete. Others will aver that the evidence is satisfactory, favouring intervention A rather than B. Still others will admit that they do not know. The implication is that it is only for those who admit they do not know which intervention will be more effective that the randomisation will be appropriate on equipoise grounds.

One approach to ethical compromise is the construction of a simple dose–response trial in which a 'strong' version of the new and purportedly effective intervention and a weaker version of the intervention are compared. At times, this satisfies the local professional ethics of some service programmes, which state that 'everyone who needs the service should get something'. For instance, in the Spouse Assault Replication Program, the main intervention of interest was mandatory arrest for a misdemeanour domestic assault (Garner, Fagin, & Maxwell, 1995). The control groups' members were handled as usual, that is, with occasional arrest by police. To satisfy the local ethical concerns in at least one site, Milwaukee, victims in both the control condition and in the intervention condition were provided with information on victim assistance services and shelters. The high-dose intervention involved mandatory arrest for misdemeanour domestic violence.

The research question, of course, is altered by designing the trial in this way. The question now is: 'What is the high-dose treatment's effect relative to a low-dose treatment?' rather than: 'What is the high-dose intervention's effect relative to a no-dose control group?' The main assumption is that the low-dose treatment really is low and that the high-dose treatment really is high. Both theory and prior empirical data are usually brought to bear in understanding the tenability of this assumption.

A second approach to reducing ethical conflicts in this scenario is to design the intervention's deployment so that (a) every person or entity gets the intervention at some point in time and (b) the intervention is delayed randomly for some recipients so as to form a temporary control group. In the simplest case, this is referred to as the 'waitlist group' approach in efficacy trials. In some vernaculars, this is a variation on a 'cross-over' design. This satisfies the scientific ethic, a fair comparison of treatment and control group. And it satisfies a local ethic that presumes the intervention is good for everyone even if evidence is absent.

This approach, for example, has been taken in a randomised trial on the effects of monetary scholarships paid to high-achieving students from low-income families (Spencer, 1997). The monetary payments were delayed for one year for equally eligible students in the control group. The outcome variables of interest included subsequent grades and dropping out of junior high school.

Creative generalisations of the simple delayed intervention trial have been invented by statisticians and biostatisticians. These trial designs aim to meet: (a) a political imperative or a social ethic, requiring that the intervention is provided to everyone eventually and (b) a scientific, political or social ethic that requires estimating the intervention's effect where possible and when it is important to do so. These approaches fall under the rubrics of 'step wedge' and 'dynamic wait list' designs. They involve random allocation of the interventions to individuals or places or clusters periodically over an extended period of time until all eligible candidates receive it. These designs are not yet in common use. The relevant statistical machinery is being built and interesting applications are at hand, for example Brown and Hendricks (2006) and Brown and Lifford (2006).

Nonetheless, the designs beg at least two ethical questions. First, suppose that the tested intervention A's effects at a given point in time do not differ discernibly from the control group that receives B. What then is the ethical justification for later providing intervention A to the control group? The second question assumes that the intervention is found to be more effective in the trial than what the control group experiences. In particular, assume that providing the intervention A to people or places at Time 1, in their status of need at Time 1, works relative to the control group's status at Time 1. The effects of an intervention A provided at time 1, of course, is no assurance that the intervention will work for people or places engaged later, for example at Time 2 in their state. In trauma surgery, for instance, a treatment (experimental or otherwise) that is effective at time 1 may be useless one hour later. If this scenario is plausible, then the ethical framework on equipoise seems to hold. That is, one ought to promise another trial, and one ought not to promise to deliver the initial intervention to the control group.

A third design-oriented approach to resolving ethical issues is to recognise that a real 'no-treatment' control condition does not exist in many settings. It is obvious that something always happens to the control group members, that is some services are delivered. This 'something' intervention is supposed to differ from the intervention that is of primary interest to the researcher and that warrants testing.

Consider, for instance, the testing of new federally supported employment and training programmes for youths at risk of joblessness, crime and so forth. It was recognised that communities provide some resources apart from such new programmes and that those resources may be as effective as any new programme. This helped to justify the ethical propriety of randomised experiments on the federal programmes.

Datta (2002) recognised an implicit trap in this line of thinking: a trial makes no sense when intervention and control groups receive the same services, as in trails on Head Start programmes for pre-school children. Of course, it is sometimes difficult to learn from reports on trials exactly which services or ordinarily available interventions are actually delivered to members of a control group. Most attention is given to the main intervention being evaluated rather than to the often disparate, complicated, and diffuse activities that constitute the control condition. This lacuna is obviously as important in social science, as it is in the ethics of research.

Are People or Entities Randomly Allocated to Interventions in the Randomised Trial?

In any given setting, the service provider (police officer, teacher, social welfare worker, etc.) may object on ethical grounds to randomly assigning *individuals* to an intervention versus control group, or to one of two or more intervention groups. For instance, a particular judge may object to randomly assigning juveniles to a certain counselling intervention or to a control condition, regardless of the fact that the evidence on effectiveness of the new intervention, relative to the conventional condition, is equivocal. Parents may object to their child being part of a lottery for scholarships based on grades.

One approach to resolving this issue hinges on the idea that assigning entire jurisdictions or organisations, rather than individuals, to alternative interventions is a more ethical way to advance understanding. In debates over the ethical propriety of testing interventions in Swedish juvenile facilities, for instance, the culture (a representation of ethical standards) is such that assigning individual juveniles at random to different interventions within a facility is, at times, objectionable. However, because there are many juvenile facilities in Sweden, and changes in these facilities are periodically made as part of ordinary government mandates, randomly assigning facilities to alternative interventions may be more ethically acceptable.

Consider another example, crime prevention. A conscientious criminologist might choose to test a programme of intensive police surveillance of possible crime perpetrators against normal surveillance, so as to understand the relative effect of this intensive surveillance on reducing crime. That is, the focus would be on individuals who might commit crimes. Some would argue, on legal and ethical grounds, that such a programme would violate the individual's rights (possible crime perpetrator). In many jurisdictions, such surveillance can be construed as harassment, deprivation of constitutional rights, 'profiling' and so on.

Sherman and Weisburd (1995) handled the ethical and legal problems engendered by focusing instead on randomising geographic areas. In particular, their police patrol experiments estimated the effect of intensive patrol of crime 'hot spots' on reducing criminal activity. The research team located about 300 geographic areas with high criminal activity and then randomly assigned some areas to a control condition and others to the intensive police patrol. The crime rates in each condition were then compared. There were no serious ethical challenges to this trial (Boruch et al., 2010).

The character of the scientific question is changed in a compromise that meets standard human ethics when the units of random allocation become jurisdictions, entities or groups, instead of individuals. The new question asks whether entities or assemblies are affected by the interventions rather than whether individuals are so affected (the latter being the original question).

At times, the scientific rationale for this kind of change in the question's focus is at least as strong as the ethical rationale. Criminologists, for example, have posited a theory of general deterrence, implying that entire communities ought to be the units of random allocation and analysis in trials on an intervention's effect. Criminologists have also posited a specific deterrence theory, implying that individuals ought to be the units of random allocation and analysis. The theory that entire housing projects must be engaged in building social capital invites one to think about randomly assigning multiple projects to purportedly effective social capital building intervention or to a control condition to assess the treatment's effect on employment, crime, delinquency and so on. Indeed, this has been done in the Rockefeller Foundation's Jobs Plus experiment (Riccio, 1999).

Randomised trials that use entities, geopolitical jurisdictions, organisations or other groups (instead of individuals) as the units of random allocation are not uncommon. No standards of professional societies and no governmental regulations have attended explicitly to the ethics of such trials. Taljaard et al. (2009) and Binik et al. (2011), with Canadian government sponsorship, have taken a lead role to understand the ethical issues engendered by cluster/place/group randomised trials and how to understand and, to the extent possible, inform the understanding based on empirical research and analysis by ethicists.

What Is the Need for the Purportedly More Effective Intervention and What Is the Supply?

Suppose that the resources for a purportedly more effective intervention for those in need of intervention are low. When intervention resources are scarce, the idea of a lottery allocation to eligible recipients is acceptable to some people, including ethicists. A random allocation scheme then becomes the device for equitable distribution of resources.

In this context, it is important for the trial's designer to understand that the demand for a purportedly effective intervention may be artificially low at times. For instance, the local demand for an intervention may not match its local supply only because many of the people who are eligible for an ostensibly desirable intervention are not aware of it, do not understand it well enough to seek it, or lack the resources to become engaged. An implication of this is that the trial's designer can increase demand for the intervention. This then can induce a situation in which demand exceeds supply, making the intervention a scarce resource. The lottery/fairness argument can then be applied.

For instance, Philadelphia's White Williams Foundation has, for more than 100 years, awarded monetary scholarships to poor children who achieved A and B grades in school. The foundation's stakeholders have thought that these scholarships would decrease school drop-out rates, reduce delinquency and have other beneficial effects. During the 1990s, the demand for these scholarships was indirectly controlled by school counsellors who influenced which students would be told about the fellowships, notified when money for scholarships became available, and identified individuals who might be worthy of the award. This made the demand for scholarships neatly match the supply of scholarships.

In 1996, Margaret Spencer (1997) proposed a randomised trial to understand whether the scholarships had the effect the Foundation claimed. Intensive efforts were made to ensure that *all* eligible children and their parents became aware of the availability of the scholarships. The demand increased. That is, individuals who had heretofore been favoured by school counsellors *and* other eligible individuals who had not been so favoured became part of the target population. Given the scarce supply of scholarship money and the demand for scholarships by an eligible population (beyond the subset of eligible students chosen earlier with favouritism), the lottery allocation was accepted by the foundation's board as a fair way to allocate the scholarships.

Which Kinds of Individuals or Entities Are Randomly Assigned to Alternative Interventions and Which Individuals or Entities Are Not So Assigned?

At least one ethical issue arises at times because some people confuse the idea of the *random allocation* of eligible individuals from a specified eligible sample to alternative interventions with the idea of *random selection* of possibly ineligible individuals from some sample of an undefined target population. Put this debate aside. It is easily clarified. The quarrel can be resolved with mutual education rather than discussions about ethics.

The more interesting and nuanced point is that, in a randomised trial there is indeed a pool of eligible and willing individuals (or entities) who might be randomly assigned to different interventions. In particular, consider the fact that the criteria for determining the eligibility of individuals or entities for a randomised trial are manipulable features in the design of an ethical trial.

The ethical dilemma in this scenario usually involves professional service providers who believe that there are some people who are truly in need of the purportedly effective treatment. There may be good evidence that helps to justify their position. They may also believe that there are some people who do not need or deserve the service. The thoughtful designer of a randomised trial can tentatively accept the professional's beliefs about both ends of the need/merit continuum.

In particular, one approach to resolving the ethical concerns uses a framework in which *marginally* needy or deserving individuals are assigned randomly to one of two interventions. That is, the trial's designer assumes a measurable continuum of need or merit. Individuals who clearly fall above some threshold for need or merit, this threshold using the ethical standard, receive the intervention. Those who clearly fall below the threshold do not receive the intervention. At the margin, there is a range that includes individuals for whom need or merit is ambiguous and for whom the effectiveness of the intervention is not understood well. This is the range in which randomisation can be done ethically, if one subscribes to the idea of equipoise in an ethics framework.

The Spouse Assault Replication Program illustrates a variation on this theme (Garner et al., 1995; Sherman, Schmidt, & Rogan, 1992). At one extreme, serious domestic assaults were handled by police as felonies: the perpetrator was arrested. At the other extreme, police call outs on shouting matches between couples were handled as disturbances; no arrest of anyone on any charge was justified. The middle range of cases, the marginal ones, involved those in which probable cause evidence for a misdemeanour crime was at hand. In this middle range, it was not clear that arrest would be any more effective in reducing recidivism than handling the case as usual that is, with the police restoring order and moving on to the next case. Misdemeanour offenders in this middle range were then the eligible target group for RCTs on whether arrest for domestic assault would lower the likelihood of subsequent assaults.

'Trap door' approaches in determining eligibility for a randomised trial can also be exploited. That is, local ethical standards may be satisfied by handling outliers in a special way. Individuals who appear in the experiment's pipeline and who are judged to be unusually needy, deserving or exceptional might be defined in advance of the trial as the top 5% of individuals who are eligible for the intervention. The remaining 95% are randomly assigned. In Breger's (1983) essay on trials in the judicial sector, he denominates this option as a safety valve. This option is valuable for gatekeepers, such as judges, whose cooperation is essential to randomised trials in this arena. Earlier experience, described by Conner (1977), suggests that access to this safety valve can be enlarged too easily into an uncontrollable leak in the pipeline and to the breakdown of the experiment. Breger acknowledges this, based on work by Ross and Blumenthal (1983, p. 136, note 158).

Another approach to altering eligibility requirements so as to meet ethics standards and standards of evidence in a trial recognises that particular subsets of eligible individuals might be randomised even if the main target population cannot. In Zhu's approach, for instance, all the people who called for assistance on a telephone hotline were provided with information and directions to call back with further information. Not all individuals did indeed call back. Individuals in the subset who did call back were randomly divided into two groups. One group was actively called back to re-establish contact. The remaining group was not called because the available resources were not sufficient to do so. Zhu's experiment permitted estimates of the programme's effect to be made for the subset of callers in the population.

How Is It Possible to Avoid Objectionable Imbalances in the Characteristics of Individuals Who Are Assigned to Different Interventions?

In any randomised trial, chance allocation can generate peculiar and awkward random configurations. For instance, over the short term of a randomised trial that involves mandatory versus no arrest for domestic violence, it is possible for most African Americans to be randomly assigned to being arrested and most Whites to 'not being arrested'. Similarly, Latino women may find themselves put more often into a control group, relative to Afro-Americans or others, in a trial on the effects of a trial on an employment/training and child care programme for assisting single mothers. Although these outcomes are due entirely to chance, they are likely to discomfort the politicians (ethicists), the scientists (ethicists) and the target participants (ethicists).

The ethical trial designed can employ a variety of approaches to reducing this problem. The first approach involves randomisation within blocks of individuals. For example, one may construct pairs (blocks) of two African Americans, two Whites and so on. Within pairs, an individual is selected with a probability of 0.5 to be put into the intervention group; the second becomes a member of the control group.

A second tactic, suitable for small sample sizes, is to layout all possible random configurations beforehand. 'Imbalance' in all possible random allocations is defined beforehand. Imbalanced configurations are then eliminated from the possible random configurations that would be randomly selected. That is, configuration that is used in the actual experiment's design is then randomly selected from the eligible configurations. This approach can be construed as a technical resolution to an ethical issue and a scientific one.

How Many People Are Randomly Assigned to Which Interventions in a Randomised Trial?

Conscientious trialists do a statistical power analysis prior to the experiment to understand how many people or entities are required in each arm of the trial, so as to reliably detect the difference in the effects of the intervention in each arm. In the simplest cases, splitting the eligible target population randomly into intervention groups of equal size maximises the statistical power of a trial.

This 50–50 split is usually the starting point for the scientifically ethical trialist. The starting point for the ethical service provider may be different. In particular, the service provider may take the position that as many people as possible should receive the intervention that seems most desirable. Often, there is room for compromise by each side without sacrificing the ethical objectives.

For the trial's designer, a simple basis for compromise lies in the fact that the fraction of people (or entities) that is randomly assigned to two interventions can differ from a 50:50 ratio without losing much statistical power in the randomised trial. For the ethical service provider, this manipulable feature of an experiment invites increasing the fraction of people served by what the provider believes to be the better intervention programme. For the ethical designer of the trial, the bottom line is that 60:40 splits do not differ much from 50:50 splits with respect to statistical power in randomised trials. A 70:30 split does make a difference in statistical power, and this means that overall larger sample sizes may be necessary to discern differences in the effects of the interventions. This then leads to further discussion and compromise on different ethical standards.

An increase in the quality and number of measures taken prior to the trial (pretests) and afterwards (as in longitudinal studies) can enhance statistical power of a trial in ways that help to compensate for uneven splits and small samples. These options may impose more burdens on the trial's participants however.

PROCEDURAL ASSURANCES TO RESOLVING ISSUES

In the United States, 17 federal agencies require that contractors and grantees at institutions receiving federal funding for research involving human participants abide by the *Code of Federal Regulations (CFR)* on ethics. This falls under the rubric of the 'Common Rule'. In particular, 45 *CFR* 46 requires that such institutions maintain and use IRBs to screen proposals to assure that the research meets local ethical standards. The regulations require that trialists: (a) minimise risks to participants in an experiment; (b) assure that risks are reasonable in relation to benefits; (c) assure that selection of individuals for study is equitable; (d) obtain informed consent; (e) provide for privacy and confidentiality; and, (f) protect vulnerable participants (Office of Human Subjects Research, 2000). The IRBs are empowered to approve or not approve research proposals that fall in their ambit under the regulations.

Governmental oversight of this kind is fundamental to assuring the ethical propriety of research, including randomised trials, in the United States. Others such as the United Kingdom, and Canada and the Nordic countries have similar rules.

A more general framework for assuring the ethical propriety of experiments is embodied in a monograph issued by the Federal Judicial Center (1981), the research arm of the U.S. courts. In effect, the Centre suggested that one may mount a randomised trial only if the following questions can be answered in the affirmative: (a) Does the present policy or practice need serious improvement? (b) Is there significant uncertainty about the value of the new approaches to solving a problem? (c) Are there no other scientifically defensible means to determine the effectiveness of the new approach? (d) Will the results of the experiment be used to change policy? (e) Will the rights of individuals be protected? This framework has no legal standing though its guidance pertains directly to randomised trials.

JUDICIAL AND LEGISLATIVE RESOLUTIONS

A law may embody ethical standards. As a consequence, a law may eliminate an ethical issue, or reduce the appearance of issues or help to resolve them. In the United States, for instance, federal statutes that explicitly require that randomised experiments be run are not common but they are easily identified. For example, Section 770 of Public Law 105-85 required that the Secretary of Defense and Secretary of Veterans' Affairs jointly establish a programme of cooperative clinical trials to evaluate the effectiveness of treatments for Persian Gulf War veterans with ill-defined or undiagnosed conditions. Public Law 100-175 authorised the director of the National Institute on Aging to provide for clinical trials on treating Alzheimer's disease. The Education Sciences Reform Act of 2002 (HR 3201) is explicit in calling for research that 'employs experimental designs using random assignment, when feasible, and other research methodologies that allow for the strongest possible causal inferences when random assignment is not feasible' (Section 102, Paragraph 19(D)). In a locally focused initiative, the U.S. Congress authorised evaluations of a voucher programme in the District of Columbia's public schools in which rigorous scientific standards were to be employed. The relevant federal agencies' interpretation of law led to a randomised trial.

Randomised trials may also be authorised indirectly through law that provides federal agencies with the mandate to improve programmes whose aims are in accord with law. The implicit assumption is that one cannot improve unless one evaluates, and one may evaluate a programme's effects, at times, by depending on a randomised trial. Most of the randomised experiments on revision of welfare programmes during the 1970s, for instance, were authorised through a federal waiver system that permitted states to depart from federal welfare regulations so as to test new ways to enhance the effectiveness of state welfare systems (see Gueron, 1985, for instance).

How laws, a form of political and social ethic, can be constructed so as to encourage the production of good evidence, a form of scientific ethic, through randomised trials is not well documented. In one exception, Ritter and Boruch (1999) undertook to understand how Tennessee's statewide randomised experiments on the effects of reduced school class size came about. A confluence of researchers and politicians, including a legislator who happened to also be a well-trained social scientist, and others who understood the idea of fair comparison and the ambiguity of extant evidence, led to a high-quality milestone trial. Such a confluence is not common. Understanding how to frame law so as to enhance the likelihood of producing good evidence in this and other settings requires considerable skill.

For the federal sector, Lind, Shapard, and Cecil (1994) summarised the topic of randomisation in the following way:

'The essence of true experimentation is that some people are treated differently than other people and that randomization determines who gets which treatment. This has sometimes been thought to conflict directly with the Fourteenth Amendment's guarantee of equal protection. However, virtually all scholarly analysis and case law has concluded that "if the proposed research is not otherwise constitutionally impermissible, random assignment of research subjects, with limited exceptions, should not be considered to violate equal protection"' (Winick, 1981, p. 359). See also *Department of Motor Vehicles v. Hardin*, 58 Cal. App.3d 936, 130 Cal. Rptr. 311 (1976). Proponents of well-controlled experiments in this context are fond of citing Justice Brandeis' dissent in *New State Lee Co. v. Liebmann*, 285 U.S. 262, 52 S.Ct. 371, 76 L.Ed. 747 (1932). He stated, 285 U.S. at 310, 311, 52 S.Ct. at 386, 387:

> [A]dvances in the exact sciences and the achievements in invention [i]n large measure [h]ave been due to experimentation. [I]t is one of the happy incidents of the federal system that a single courageous state may, if its citizens choose, serve as a laboratory; and try novel social and economic experiments without risk to the rest of the country. This Court has the power to prevent an experiment. [B]ut in the exercise of this high power we must be ever on our guard, lest we erect our prejudices into legal principles. If we would guide by the light of reason, we must let our minds be bold.

In the United States, there have been few court challenges to randomised trials that have met procedural standards of the kinds discussed here.

In those cases brought to federal court, the judicial decisions that permitted mounting randomised field experiments in the interest of understanding the effects of welfare reform include *Aguoyo v. Richardson* and *California Welfare Rights Organization v. Richardson* (Breger, 1983). Between 2002 and this writing, over 80 large-scale cluster randomised trials and perhaps hundreds of smaller scale was mounted with support of the Institute for Education Sciences under authorisation of the Education Sciences Reform Act of 2002. The IES encountered no challenge brought in the courts to the conduct of the trials (Whitehurst, personal communication, 2008).

INDIVIDUAL PRIVACY AND CONFIDENTIALITY OF RESEARCH RECORDS

The individual's right to privacy is an important ingredient in professional codes of ethics in research. For instance, the International Statistical Institute's *Declaration on Professional Ethics* (1985) required that members 'take appropriate measures to prevent their data from being published or otherwise released in a form that would allow any participant's identity to be disclosed or inferred'. Assuring that the research records on individuals who have agreed to participate in research are used only for research and are not used for other purposes is important in this context.

In what follows, *privacy* is defined as an attribute of the individual. *Confidentiality* is regarded as an attribute of records. *Security* refers to the technical handling of records on identifiable individuals so as to eliminate accidental or unauthorised disclosure of the records. *Research* refers here to acquiring information so as to understand the effectiveness of programmes, notably in randomised experiments.

A variety of approaches can be employed to ensure that individual privacy is not seriously abridged or is preserved, and that the research records on the research participant remain confidential. In what follows, we summarise statistical and statutory tactics.

Statistical Approaches to Ensuring Privacy and Confidentiality

A variety of statistical approaches have been developed to ensure privacy mainly in social surveys and that can be used at times in randomised trials. These include randomised response, micro-aggregation of response to multiple direct questions, network-based estimation and others. We discuss only randomised response in what follows.

In personal interviews using randomised response, for instance, the interviewer presents two questions to a respondent, one which is sensitive and one which is not sensitive, in one of two randomly split samples. A sensitive question, with a Yes/No response might ask about having committed a felony, used a drug and so on. The second question is innocuous and might ask about having had breakfast that day (Yes/No). The respondent rolls a die to randomly choose the question to be answered. The interviewer is *not* told which question was chosen. In the second randomly split sample, only the innocuous question is asked. With two large randomly split samples and relatively simple probability equations, it is an easy matter to estimate the percentage of people who acknowledge the sensitive activity without anyone, including the interviewer, knowing what the respondent's status is. That is, individual privacy is protected. But this is at the cost of large samples. See Boruch and Cecil (1979), for the basics, early examples and references.

As of this writing, these approaches, though used at times in survey research, appear not to have been used in randomised trials. There may be several reasons for this. A first reason is that such methods usually require larger sample sizes than are common in surveys; they would require larger samples than are ordinarily used in RCTs.

A second reason why such statistical methods for ensuring privacy might not be used in randomised trials in criminal and juvenile research, education and other studies on effects of programmes is that preserving the confidentiality of individual records can be more directly achieved at times by depending on federal shield laws. That is, acquiring information by the trialists about individuals is regarded by the respondent or others as a tolerable diminution of the individual's privacy. Federal shield laws assure the respondent that the information will remain confidential. Moreover, such laws require no special increases in sample size or specialised statistical analyses. Of course, they do require time and effort in explaining the shield to respondents.

These reasons for the non-use of statistical privacy protection in randomised field trials are informed and plausible. But they are speculative. Researchers' ignorance about the statistical methods is also a plausible reason for the methods not being used.

Statutory Approaches to Ensuring Confidentiality of Research Records on Identifiable Individuals

In the absence of any explicit statutory assurance that records on identifiable research participants will be used only for research purposes, researchers and the individuals from whom they elicit information are vulnerable. That is, the courts, prosecutorial agencies or legislatures can appropriate identifiable records on research participants, through subpoena for instance.

To be sure, the appropriation of social research records on identifiable individuals, by the courts or administrative agencies, is rare in the United States. Appropriation is not rare, however, in high-stakes litigation on research on drugs, tobacco and auto safety, among other areas. Cecil and Wetherington (1996), for instance, brought together informative articles on the topic by judges, lawyers and legal scholars. From these articles, it is obvious that the confidentiality of research records on individuals who participate in research in a variety of commercially important arenas has no special guarantee in law. Indeed, if guarantees are necessary, then a special law has to be created to provide it.

In the United States, certain federal statutes ensure that particular kinds of research records on identifiable individuals *cannot* be disclosed to and exploited by non-research entities that seek to make institutional judgments about these individuals or to extract information from them. The Omnibus Crime Control Act and revisions of it (42USCPar3789g), and related regulations (28CFR Part 22), does so for research in the criminal justice area. The Public Health Services Act (Section 301(d), 42USC Section 241(d)) and revisions of it do so in health-related areas.

Consider, as an example, the Public Health Services Act. The 1970 amendment to the original Act authorised the researcher's withholding of information concerning the identity of people who are participants in research on the use and effect of drugs. This withholding authority is actualised through the issuance of Certificates of Confidentiality by the Secretary of the DHHS. The Act was amended in 1988 to broaden its reach. The amendment included provisions that authorised the secretary to issue Certificates to institutions in which specific researchers are engaged in a specific mental health, biomedical, clinical or behavioural research project. The authority to issue certificates is lodged with the National Institutes of Health within the DHHS. See, for instance, http://grants.nih/grants/policy/coc/.

The purpose of a Certificate of Confidentiality is to protect the records of people who participate in research by insulating researchers against involuntary disclosure of the participant's identity. Certificates are issued to an institution for a single project as opposed to a class of projects. The researcher whose institution is armed with a Certificate can then provide the assurance of confidentiality to the prospective research participant.

The position of the DHHS is that the federal Certificate's protection supersedes any state law appears not to have been challenged in the courts.

The relevant statutes and early challenges to aspects of the statutes are given in Boruch and Cecil (1979) and led to modification in statutes, but they led to no remarkable breaches in which research records on identifiable research participants was disclosed.

Challenges occur periodically. One emerged in a North Carolina case in which the judge was completely unaware of the Certificate and ordered disclosure of a research record on a research participant who happened not to be involved directly in the case itself. National Institute of Mental Health (NIMH) and the institutional recipient of the Certificate, Duke University, informed the court of the matter. The court retracted its order to disclose. Indeed, the judge is quoted as saying that he had not realised 'what kind of egg (he) was cracking open ... obviously it had lit a fire under somebody' (Breskow, Dame, & Costello, 2008, p. 1054). On further appeal, limited sealed disclosure was permitted to the defence attorney so as to determine whether indeed the research record on an identifiable research participant was material. It was not. Breskow et al. (2008) describe the episode succinctly, and provides an opinion of issues from a legal perspective.

A federal Certificate of Confidentiality provides some protection for the research participant, but there are limits to any such statutory shield of course. The protection provided for in the Certificate is nullified for a particular research participant, for instance, if the individual voluntarily consents to disclosure of his or her research record or waives the protection. A Certificate does not preclude a researcher from divulging the identity of a participant who may harm himself or others.

Researchers are responsible for telling research participants that a Certificate of Confidentiality will be employed to protect their privacy, and to give a clear explanation of the protection it affords including its limitations. This information may be included in the informed consent document or provided to the research participant, for instance. Furthermore, researchers need not have federal funding for their projects to be eligible for certificates. The project for which the certificate is being sought normally must also be approved by an IRB in the United States.

The federal shield laws that have just been described seem plain on the surface. However, their legislative history and implementation by agencies to which they pertain have not been the subjects of much serious research, as far as we can tell. Understanding how such shield laws have been developed and can be developed further is a fine challenge. The challenge is compatible with any attempt to understand how to improve evidence that is produced in the public interest and do so in an environment characterised by diverse ethical and legal standards.

RECORD LINKAGE, RECORD ACCESS AND INTEGRATED DATA SYSTEMS

Randomised trials often involve linking records from different sources on the same individuals or organisations so as to estimate the effect of an intervention on the individuals or on entities to which the interventions are directed. Access to each source of records may be governed by an ethical code or standard, and the access will usually be influenced by different government statutes or regulations that identify the trialists' responsibility for protection of the records. The ethical codes of the kinds identified earlier try to make clear what constitutes virtue in this area. The laws and regulations drive deeper of course. They are often not uniform, often unclear, and they certainly require attention to local laws as embodiments of local ethics.

For instance, one may wish to link: (a) police reports on alcohol-related traffic accidents; (b) hospital records on the individuals who were involved in the accident; (c) court records on the defendants; and (d) records of the fact that the individual was involved in a randomised trial designed to learn about the effects of an intervention that is designed to reduce such incidents. Each record system is governed by a different set of disclosure rules, hospital records being covered by the Health Insurance and Portibility and Accountibility Act of 1996 (HIPAA), police and court records being covered by municipal and state laws and so on. One might further wish to link these records with the simple research record on whether the individuals were assigned to Treatment A, B or C in a randomised trial on handling alcohol-related accidents; the rules governing access to research records can differ from those governing the administrative records. Understanding whether and how to link records on individually identified research participants in this scenario, and in survey research and randomised field trials more generally, is complicated.

A remarkable early example of efforts to solve the problem of linking research records with administrative records without breaching law or regulations on privacy appears in an experiment on tax compliance reported by Schwartz and Orleans (1967). In this study, individuals were randomly assigned to various interventions that were thought to influence their taxpaying behaviours. Some people, randomly assigned to Intervention A, were told that they ought to pay the proper amount; otherwise, they would get tied up with lawyers. In Intervention B, people were told to pay the right amount because it was their moral, civic and social responsibility to do so. Intervention C involved telling people that they would be publicly embarrassed if they failed to pay the proper amount.

To discern the effects of treatments on actual tax returns, the names of individuals and the intervention group to which they were assigned were supplied to the Internal Revenue Service (IRS). No research records, apart from names of individuals, were provided to the IRS. The IRS then computed *aggregate* data, not records on individuals, on tax payments for the members of each intervention group. The aggregate statistics were then supplied to the trialists. That is, the mean reported income for each group in each arm of the randomised trial was supplied. The average adjusted gross income declared in each group constituted the only information necessary for formal statistical tests of hypotheses about differences in the influence of the interventions. This approach is likely to be appropriate in some small-scale work nowadays, despite its age and apart from deductive disclosure issues.

More generally, there are numerous examples of the need to link administrative records on outcomes of a trial with the trial's records on who received which intervention. Many randomised trials on improving education, welfare reform, training and employment programmes in the United States involve joining wage rate data from unemployment insurance records with research records on the programmes to which individuals are assigned and on the characteristics of individuals at programme entry. Randomised trials in criminology often involve linking the researchers' records on which intervention is assigned to police records on arrest or to court records on adjudication. Randomised trials in education often involve linking each student's achievement test scores with information about the intervention programme in which the student is engaged, research data on the student's familial and neighbourhood characteristics and other administrative school records. Such linkages are rarely recognised explicitly but are embedded in the research process.

The relevant record systems and linkage and disclosure rules also vary. Consequently, it is difficult to make general statements about resolving privacy problems that are engendered by the need to link different kinds of records in a randomised trial. Moreover, it is difficult to make general statements for such activity in the broader context of integrated data systems designed to produce records that inform decisions about individuals and the use of such records in research. As of this writing, Culhane and Fantuzzo (2010) and their colleagues are working, with MacArthur Foundation support, to understand how to accomplish research in this complex setting at local, regional and federal levels. In what follows, we first describe approaches that might be used in linking the local trial's records with the records of national statistical agencies. We begin with this scenario because rules governing federal statistical agencies are more uniform than rules governing state, county and municipal agencies in the United States.

Current federal approaches to permitting record linkage without breaching privacy laws involve both legal and procedural elements. One approach is to create secure data enclaves in which linkage is permitted under the law. For instance, the National Center for Health Statistics (NCHS) maintains a secure centre that permits outside researchers to link their data with data from non-public NCHS records on the same entities or individuals (Hom, 1999). The arrangement is such that the researcher must agree not to carry away private information on individuals or entities. A second approach to linking local information to the data that is maintained by a federal statistical agency is exemplified by the National Center for Educational Statistics (NCES) and also used by NCHS. NCES has developed licensing arrangements to permit analyses of non-public use statistical records (from which clear identifiers are deleted) at the licensee's site (McMillen, 1999). Federal provisions are such that penalties can be employed to punish researchers who disclose information on identifiable individuals or entities or publish data that permits deductive disclosure.

In principle, it seems possible to link external research records on identifiable individuals who participate in randomised trials on, for example, prevention of risky behaviour with records from these non-public administrative records files. Such records might, for example, augment research data with data on statistical characteristics of schools that the individuals attend or other contextual information. A general rationale and strategy for coupling local randomised experiments with records from administrative and survey systems is given by Boruch and Terhanian.

Consider the topic of linking the trialist's research records with local administrative records maintained by state or municipal data systems. How might we arrange our thinking about ethics and law in this setting? To its credit, the Bureau of Justice Statistics in 1984 began to issue compendiums that help researchers to understand what criminal history information is accessible to researchers and others in what states of the United States. In the Bureau of Justice Statistics 2002 Compendium of State Privacy and Security Legislation, for example, each State's pertinent laws the matters are identified, listed and categorised. One of the categories concerns whether the law or regulation provides researchers with access to identifiable information. That is, the Compendium includes an item for 'Research Access'. The conscientious trialist in California, Connecticut, Delaware, and elsewhere, for instance, can then discover which statutes and which paragraphs (citations) in the state statutes provide access to which records for research purposes and under what conditions. Despite the fact that the Compendiums do not include reference to court cases beyond the citation, this is a remarkable resource in the United States. The trialist can get to the statute and read it to understand what it says if indeed the statute is intelligible. The BJS Compendium is unique. We are aware of no similar thorough compendium of state laws on privacy of administrative records in welfare and education for instance. Regardless of state of national statue, however, the interpretation of the laws by state's attorneys and other government officials can vary. It is partly on account of the unnecessary and even stupid variations that efforts have been made to achieve clear and balanced views, for example Hilton (2009) for the case of FERPA. Another approach to building an empirical knowledge base in this regard is to develop and publicise models a 'memorandum of agreement', covering rights of access and responsibilities of the trialist and the entities that provide access to identifiable records. Actual agreements exist, of course. But their quasi-public nature and idiosyncratic character make them less useful than models. Moreover, experience with and commentaries on the models can help to build case law of a kind that would be in the interest of balancing privacy rights with the societal need to share information in trials and in other kinds of legitimate social research.

SUMMARY

Two broad classes of ethical issues are at times engendered by RCTs. The first class concerns the random assignment of individuals or entities to alternative interventions. Randomisation is a characteristic of all randomised experiments in the social sector and in medicine. The second class of issues concerns the privacy of individuals to whom the interventions are provided and the confidentiality of the research records on these identifiable participants in a trial. This second class of issues appears in probability sample surveys, as well as in randomised experiments, ethnographic studies and in other social research efforts that involve record linkage.

The specific character of the ethical or legal problem varies from one randomised trial to another. Nonetheless, at least three broad approaches to resolving or reducing ethical issues. The first broad approach involves depending on statistical methods. In resolving conflicts over randomisation in experiments, for example, the trial's designer can capitalise on the manipulability of certain features of the trial's design to do so. These manipulable features include ratios of the sample sizes allocated to different treatment intervention (including control groups), units of random allocation and analysis individuals or groups or organisations, blocking and restricted randomisation (to prevent politically uncomfortable imbalances), eligibility criteria for including certain people in the experiment and excluding others, and influencing the demand for interventions when the supply is limited.

In survey research, as in randomised experiments, minimising sample size reduces the ethical problem of burdening participants in a crude sense, and this minimisation is based on a well-understood technology. Beyond this, survey researchers and experimenters might, at times, be able to exploit indirect estimation approaches such as randomised response and related statistical techniques.

A second kind of approach to avoiding or reducing ethical and legal problems is procedural. In the United States, one vehicle for the approach is required under law and involves the use of IRBs to judge the ethical propriety of research. The use of IRBs helps to ensure that some local standards of ethics are met, whether the ethical problem concerns randomisation or individual privacy. Another vehicle is routinely employing ethics standards of the kind enunciated by the Federal Judicial Center in deciding when to do a randomised trial.

A third kind of approach depends on statues which have been enacted to ensure that randomised trials are permitted and even required under law. Usually, this is in the larger context of the public's and its government's need to generate good evidence about which programmes work and for whom. Similarly, federal statutes have been created to ensure the privacy of individuals who participate in research in the sense that these statutes prohibit the disclosure of research records on identifiable individuals for non-research purposes. Laws have also been enacted to ensure that administrative records on individuals that are maintained by state or federal government and that are normally not accessible can be accessed by experimenters under certain conditions. These laws, enacted at the state level and federal level, actualise local and regional ethical standards that might otherwise remain vague and debatable.

Each kind of approach to resolving the ethical and legal problems engendered by randomised experiments invites research and development. Statistical approaches to the design of randomised experiments and nonrandomised quasi-experiments ought to be explored partly because they offer a technological fix, or a compromise, to an ethical conflict. More important, the technology advances more quickly than, for example law.

Procedural approaches to ensuring ethical propriety in experiments appear more transparent. But they too deserve research attention. How to enhance the quality of IRB procedures or the effectiveness of any advisory group in the business of enhancing evidence in a way that meets good ethical standards is not yet clear.

We have an imperfect understanding of how laws can be constructed so as to permit the production of good evidence in the public's interest and ensure that individual's rights are met, which is also in the public's interest. Research on the ways that laws have been constructed to do so, based on precedent in the arenas of RCTs, is essential. Research on ethics in this arena, empirical and theoretical, is no less essential.

NOTE

1. For a more complete explanation of the roles and increased responsibilities involved in reviewing and conducting federally funded research, or research at an institution receiving federal funding, see http://grants.nih.gov/grants/policy/hs/prisoners.htm#Roles_of_Staff

REFERENCES

American Institutes of Research. (2011). *Code of Conduct*. Retrieved from http://www.air.org/files/AIR_Code_of_Conduct.pdf. Accessed on July 5, 2011.

Binik, A., Weijer, C., McRae, A. D., Grimshaw, J. M., Boruch, R., Brehaut, J. C., … Zwarenstein, M. (2011). Does clinical equipoise apply to cluster randomized trials in health research? *Trials*, *12*, 118. doi:10.1186/1745-6215-12-118

Blustein, J. (2010). Toward more public discussion of the ethics of federal social program evaluation. *Journal of Policy Analysis and Management*, *24*(4), 824–852.

Boruch, R., Weisburd, D., & Berk, R. (2010). Place randomized trials. In A. Piquero & D. Weisburd (Eds.), *Handbook of quantitative criminology*. New York, NY: Springer.

Boruch, R. F. (1997). *Randomized experiments for planning and evaluation: A practical guide*. Thousand Oaks, CA: Sage.

Boruch, R. F., & Cecil, J. S. (1979). *Assuring the confidentiality of social research data*. Philadelphia, PA: University of Pennsylvania.

Breger, M. J. (1983). Randomized experiments and the law. In R. F. Boruch & J. S. Cecil (Eds.), *Solutions to ethical and legal problems in social research* (pp. 97–144). New York, NY: Academic Press.

Breskow, L. M., Dame, L., & Costello, E. J. (2008). Certificates of confidentiality and compelled disclosure of data. *Science*, *322*, 1054–1055.

Brown, C., & Hendricks. (2006). Dynamic wait list designs for randomized trials: New designs for suicide prevention. *Clinical Trials*, *3*, 259–271.

Brown, C., & Lifford, R. (2006). The step wedge trial design: A systematic review. *BMC Medical Research Methodology*, *6*(54). Retrieved from http://www.biomedcentral.com/info/1471-2288/6/54

Bureau of Justice Statistics. (2002). *Compendium of state privacy and security legislation*. Washington, DC: Author. Retrieved from http://bjs.ojp.usdoj.gov

Cecil, J. S., & Wetherington, G. T. (Eds.). (1996). Court ordered disclosure of academic research: A clash of values of science and law. *Law and Contemporary Problems*, *59*(3), (Entire Issue).

Conner, R. F. (1977). Selecting a control group: An analysis of the randomization process in twelve social reform programs. *Evaluation Quarterly*, *1*(2), 195–243.

Culhane, D., & Fantuzzo, J. (2010). *Integrated data systems: Intelligence for social policy*. Available at http://www.ispc.upenn.edu/documents/. Retrieved on 16 April 2012.

Datta, L.-E. (2002). The case of the uncertain bridge. *American Journal of Evaluation*, *23*(2), 187–198.

Evans, I., Thornton, H., & Chalmers, I. (2006). *Testing treatments: Better research for healthcare*. London: The British Library.

Fantuzzo, J., McWayne, C., & Childs, S. (2006). Scientist-community collaborations: A dynamic tension between rights and responsibilities. In J. Trimble & C. B. Fisher (Eds.), *The handbook of ethical research with ethnocultural populations and communities* (pp. 27–50). Thousand Oaks, CA: Sage.

Federal Judicial Center. (1981). *Social experimentation and the law*. Washington, DC: Author.

Field, M. J., & Behrman, R. E. (2004). *Ethical conduct of clinical research involving children*. Washington, DC: National Academies Press. Retrieved from http://www.napedu.

Garner, J., Fagin, J., & Maxwell, C. (1995). Published findings from the spouse assault replication program: A critical review. *Journal of Quantitative Criminology*, *11*(10), 3–28.

Gueron, J. M. (1985). The demonstration of state work/welfare initiatives. In R. F. Boruch & W. Wothke (Eds.), Randomization and field experimentation [Special issue]. *New Directions for Program Evaluation* (28), 5–14.

Hilton, M. (2009). *Protecting student records and facilitating educational research*. Washington, DC: National Academies Press.

Hom, J. (1999, October). National Center for Health Statistics approaches to the release of micro-data: Perturbation and the Research Data Center. Paper presented at the workshop on confidentiality of and access to research data files, National Academy of Sciences, Washington, DC.

International Statistical Institute. (2000). *Declaration on professional ethics*. Retrieved from http://www.cbs.nl.isi.ethics.htm

Kaye, D. H., & Freedman, D. A. (1994). Reference guide on statistics. In Federal Judicial Center (Ed.), *Reference manual on scientific evidence* (pp. 331–414). Washington, DC: Federal Judicial Center.

Lind, E. A., Shapard, J. E., & Cecil, J. S. (1994). Methods for empirical evaluation of innovations in the justice system. In J. Monahan & L. Walker (Eds.), *Social science in law: Cases and materials* (pp. 57–61). Westbury, NY: Foundation Press.

Marshall, P. (2006). Informed consent to research in international settings. *Journal of Empirical Research on Human Research Ethics*, *1*(1), 25–42.

McMillen, M. (1999, October). National Center for Education Statistics: Data licensing agreements. Paper presented at the workshop on confidentiality of and access to research data files, National Academy of Sciences, Washington, DC.

Moreno, J. D. (2006). *Mind wars: Ethics, brain research, and defense*. Washington, DC: Dana Press.

Mosteller, F., & Boruch, R. (Eds.). (2002). *Evidence matters: Randomized trials in education research*. Washington, DC: Brookings Institution Press.

Oakes, J. M. (2002). Risks and wrongs in social science research: An evaluator's guide to the IRB. *Evaluation Review*, *26*(5), 443–479.

Office of Human Subjects Research. (2000). *Human subjects protections*. Retrieved from http://helix.nih.gov:8001.ohsr/

Pool, R. (2010). *Field evaluation in the intelligence and counterintelligence context*. Washington, DC: National Academies Press.

Riccio, J. A. (1999). *Mobilizing public housing communities' for work: Origins and early accomplishments on the jobs plus demonstration*. New York, NY: Manpower Demonstration Research Corporation.

Riecken, H., & Boruch, R. (Eds.). (1974). *Social experimentation*. New York, NY: Academic Press.

Ritter, G., & Boruch, R. F. (1999). The political and institutional origins of Tennessee's experiment on class size. *Educational Evaluation and Policy analysis*, *21*, 111–125.

Roberts, L., & Indermauer, D. (2003). Signed consent forms in criminological research: Protection for researchers and ethics committees but a threat to research participants? *Psychiatry, Psychology and Law*, *10*(2), 289–299.

Rowe, M. (2007). Tripping over molehills: Ethics and the ethnography of police work. *International Journal of Social Research Methodology*, *10*(1), 37–48.

Schwartz, R. D., & Orleans, S. (1967). On legal sanctions. *University of Chicago Law Review*, *34*, 282–300.

Sherman, L., Schmidt, J. D., & Rogan, D. P. (1992). *Policing domestic violence: Experiments and dilemmas*. New York, NY: Free Press.

Sherman, L., & Weisburd, D. (1995). General deterrent effects of police patrol in crime "hot spots": A randomized controlled trial. *Justice Quarterly*, *12*(4), 635–648.

Sieber, J. E. (2006). Editorial: The evolution of best ethical practices in human research. *Journal of Empirical Research on Human Research Ethics*, *1*(1), 2.

Spencer, M. (1997). *Proposal for a randomized experiment on the effects of scholarships awards to high achieving students from low income families*. Philadelphia, PA: University of Pennsylvania.

Szabo, L. M., & Britt, T. J. (2007). Guide to researching human research subject laws in West Africa. *Journal of Empirical Research on Human Research Ethics*, *2*(4), 93–105.

Taljaard, M., Weijer, C., Grimshaw, J., Brown, J., Binik, A., Boruch, R., … Donner, A. (2009). Ethical and policy issues in cluster randomized trials: Rationale and design of a mixed methods research study. *Trials*, *10*, 61Retrieved from http://trialsjournal.com/content/10/1/61

U.S. Department of Health and Human Services. (2005). *45 CFR 46 (Code of federal regulations) protection of human subjects*. Retrieved from http://hhs.gov.ohrp/human subjects/guidance/45cfr46

Williams v. Menehan, 191 Kan. 6, 379P.2d 292 (1963).

Winick, B. (1981). A preliminary analysis of legal limitations on rehabilitative alternatives in corrections and correctional research. In S. Martin, L. Sechrest & R. Redner (Eds.), *New directions in the rehabilitation of criminal offenders*. Washington, DC: National Academy.

CRITICAL QUALITATIVE THEORY: OPENING UP THE BLACK BOX OF CRIMINAL JUSTICE INTERVENTIONS

Matt Barnard

ABSTRACT

There has been an increasing realisation within government circles that gaining insight into how and why an intervention works or does not is as important as measuring any change that it brings about. Without understanding the mechanisms for change, ensuring that the intervention is effective when transposed to different contexts can be highly challenging. However, while the need for high-quality, robust qualitative research is recognised, the theoretical and methodological tools available to researchers within the field have not kept up. Government-commissioned evaluation requires a methodology that provides genuine insight into how policy and interventions work on the ground and findings that can be generalised beyond the specific samples upon which they are based. In order to fill this conceptual gap, NatCen Social Research has developed an approach to qualitative research that draws on a wide range of existing traditions but that is robust and coherent enough to meet the needs of CJS evaluations. Recent work has led to a new articulation of this approach and a new

Perspectives on Evaluating Criminal Justice and Corrections
Advances in Program Evaluation, Volume 13, 129–141

ISSN: 1474-7863/doi:10.1108/S1474-7863(2012)0000013010

moniker, 'critical qualitative theory' or CQT. This chapter describes the key tenets of CQT and draws on three of published studies of interventions that are focused on or relate to the criminal justice system to illustrate the methodological advantages the approach brings. In particular, the chapter explores the different approaches taken by the authors to the issues of generalisability, the balance between inductive and deductive procedures and how they have approached analysing the data at a case and a theme level. The implication of the different theoretical and methodological choices made by the authors is then discussed in terms of the nature and quality of the authors' analysis.

INTRODUCTION

There has been an increasing appreciation within UK government circles that gaining insight into how and why an intervention works is as important as measuring the change that it brings about. Without understanding the mechanisms for change, ensuring that the intervention is effective when it is expanded or transposed to different contexts can be challenging. Similarly, understanding why it has less impact than expected can also be crucial in deciding whether to try and modify it or look to other interventions. This realisation is indicated by the fact that a substantial number of recent and current evaluations commissioned by the Home Office and Ministry of Justice are holistic in design, incorporating impact and process evaluations and often cost–benefit elements as well. Ongoing examples include the evaluation of the Drug System Change Pilots, the evaluation of the Social Impact Bond, the evaluation of the Integrated Drug Treatment Service and the Offender Management Community Cohort Study.

However, while the need for high-quality, robust qualitative research is recognised, the theoretical and methodological tools available to researchers within the field have not kept up with demand. Government-commissioned evaluation requires a methodology that provides genuine insight into how policy and interventions work on the ground and findings that can be generalised beyond the specific samples upon which they are based. These requirements are compromised by the available approaches to qualitative enquiry, which either operate using a constructionist framework, within which it is hard to judge whether individual perspectives of those studied can be made relevant to the wider population, or are based on a positivist paradigm that undermines the key advantage of a qualitative approach, which is to go beyond pre-conceived concepts and understanding.

In order to fill this conceptual gap, the National Centre for Social Research has developed an approach to qualitative research that draws on a wide range of existing traditions but that is robust and coherent enough to meet the needs of criminal justice system evaluations. Recent work has led to a new articulation of this approach and a new moniker, 'critical qualitative theory' or CQT (Barnard, 2012; Snape, Spencer, & Barnard, in press). The authors of CQT argue that the approach is relevant to a wide range of research challenges and substantive fields, but it is particularly useful within criminal justice evaluations as it meets the stringent requirements that commissioners demand. This chapter describes the key tenets of CQT and, drawing on a number of recent publications, illustrates the methodological advantages the approach brings to understanding complex interventions.

CRITICAL QUALITATIVE THEORY

As its name suggests, CQT is placed within the broad philosophical school of thought generally known as 'critical realism' (Robson, 2002). This means that ontologically, reality is seen as something that exists independently of those who observe it (in opposition to social constructionism, which holds that there is no fixed reality but instead many different individual constructions of it none of which are more 'accurate' than any other) but epistemologically that reality is only accessible through the perceptions of people and is therefore necessarily affected by their interpretations (in opposition to positivism, which argues that reality can be simple and directly observed). Within this middle ground, the theory emphasises the crucial importance of respondents' own experiences of the relevant research issues and accepts that their different perspectives will help researchers build a more complex nuanced understanding of the phenomena. Underlying this approach, however, is the assumption that an external reality exits which can be 'captured'.

This philosophical approach leads directly to the *first tenet* of CQT, which is a belief in the theoretical compatibility of qualitative and quantitative methods. In contrast to a pragmatic or toolkit approach, combining qualitative and quantitative approaches within CQT is not only seen as useful in order to answers different research questions, but also seen as methodologically and theoretically coherent, as both are seen as operating within a critical realist paradigm. This has clear advantages in terms of presentational coherence, but it also had practical implications in terms of the design and conduct of mixed method studies and in how the quality and robustness of those studies are judged.

The philosophical basis for CQT also leads to the *second tenet* of the approach, which is that an inductive–deductive balance should be maintained during the research process. At the start, existing research and theory is used to design and plan a study, develop a sampling approach and design fieldwork tools. In the field and during early analysis the focus is on understanding and exploring participants' views and experiences from their point of view and in the context of the conditions and circumstances of their lives, reflecting the theory's use of the interpretivist tradition, which emphasises the importance of individual beliefs and perceptions of the social world. The goal during this phase is therefore to seek to obtain thick description and as much detailed information as possible about people's lives. Then, towards the end of the analysis, the findings of the research are put back into the context of theory and existing research. However, throughout the process meta-concepts, such as 'impact', 'trigger', 'mechanism' and 'foundations', are used to help order and make sense of the data, but in a reflexive way.

A *third tenet* of CQT, which has profound implications throughout the research process, is that qualitative research is generalisable in terms of the range and diversity of the findings, though not the prevalence. As such, its aim is to produce findings that are meaningful without enumeration. This does not exclude the fact that it may be desirable to do further (quantitative) research to determine the prevalence of views or experiences. Instead, it is argued that the aim of qualitative research is to produce findings that do not need enumerating to be meaningful and that it is not possible to enumerate these findings using a purely qualitative approach. This means that the concepts of 'reliability' and 'validity' are relevant, but they need to be applied appropriately to qualitative research, otherwise they undermine rigour rather than enhancing it.

The *fourth tenet* of CQT is that the process of data collection provides the bedrock for the formal analytical stage. The aim of an interview within CQT is to map the full range of opinions and experiences of an individual and to probe fully to gain a rich understanding of a participant's perspective. Unlike some other approaches, within CQT there is a strong requirement for interpretation to be heavily grounded in, and supported by, the data and means that a core element of the analysis is seen as being conducted during the interview.

The *fifth tenet* of CQT is that there is a distinction between data management and interpretation. Data management is a process of coding that involves using pre-defined conceptual boxes that are then applied to the data. Interpretation involves using the data to create meaningful categories based on judgements of the 'essence' and 'similarity' of individual aspects of the data. Where interpretations move beyond the explicit data provided by individual respondents, great importance is placed on ensuring that the building blocks used by researchers in arriving at their interpretations are clearly visible to the reader. This means that in reporting the analysis, care is taken to show how more abstract interpretations relate to the data provided by study participants.

This leads on to the *sixth tenet* of CQT, which is that it is possible and desirable to do both thematic- and case-based analysis. That is, the process of analysis should involve looking at themes that are common across the data set but also looking at individual cases and comparing cases to search for typologies and explanations. As simple as this sounds, other approaches to qualitative research and the analysis of qualitative data mitigate against this kind of analysis, in part as a result of the procedures and data management tools that they advocate.

CQT IN PRACTICE

In order to illustrate the advantages of CQT over other approaches to qualitative enquiry, this section compares three UK-based studies on related topics. The first is a study of the views and experiences of a sample of 15 offenders' engagement with drug treatment and testing orders (DTTOs), conducted by researchers at the University of Sheffield. The study, which was reported in an article for the journal *Addiction Research and Theory* (Ricketts, Bliss, Murphy, & Brooker, 2005), used a grounded theory approach. In this chapter, the study is referred to as the 'DTTO study'. The second piece of research explored the views and experiences of a sample of 25 probation officers and 16 offenders of the Community Order and the Suspended Sentence. The study, conducted by researchers at the Centre for Crime and Justice Studies at King's College London, was written up in the form of a report published by the University (Mair & Mills, 2009). There is little explicit discussion about the methodology, other than comments about the small number of interviews carried out and the fact that they were transcribed. However, this detail along with an examination of the interview schedules in the appendix indicates that a qualitative approach was used, but very much within a quantitative or positivist paradigm. This study will be referred to as the 'Community Orders study' in the rest of this chapter.

The final study that will be used for comparison purposes is the qualitative component of the Drug Treatment Outcomes Research Study, conducted by the author along with colleagues at the National Centre for Social Research. Published as a Home Office Research Report (Barnard, Webster, O'Connor, Jones, & Donmall, 2009), it explored the factors influencing the outcome of treatment seekers contact with drug treatment providers (including those mandated into treatment as part of a Community Order) by interviewing 44 drug treatment seekers and 32 frontline treatment workers. The study was conducted using CQT but before it was named as a theoretical approach. This study will be referred to as the 'DTORS study' subsequently. These studies will be compared on three key issues for qualitative research: generalisability; the balance between induction and deduction; and the use of case-and-theme, versus solely theme-based, analysis. All of the studies represent good quality work and provide considerable insight into the topics they address. However, it will be argued below that the first two have limits that are a direct result of the methodological approach, and that the third, while not faultless, largely avoids these pitfalls by following a CQT approach.

Generalisability

CQT makes a very strong statement about the generalisability of qualitative research, both as a matter of principle and because of the practical impact this has on the way in which the research is carried out. The DTORS study included the following statement about generalisability:

> The findings reflect the range and diversity of drug treatment, and so this research will give a good sense of the variety of experiences that are present in the wider population. However, as is the case with all qualitative research, the numbers of participants expressing particular views or exhibiting particular behaviours is not reported as this has no statistical significance and no conclusions about the wider population can be drawn. (Barnard et al., 2009, p. 2)

The statement is short (as a result of the Home Office reporting requirements) but makes it clear that the way the findings can be generalised is in terms of range and diversity and that to a large extent this is based on the thoroughness of the sampling (which was purposive). It also indicates that the findings cannot be generalised in terms of prevalence. As such, the report includes minimal use of quantitative or quasi-quantitative language ('most', 'many', the 'majority') to report participants' views or experiences and instead focuses on displaying the richness and diversity, for example the range of pressures reinforcing dependency (*ibid.*, p. 3), and in providing explanations for views and behaviours, such as why trust was important in relationships with key workers.

> Treatment seekers indicated that a relationship based on trust enabled key workers to fully assess their needs and therefore refer them to appropriate services and also to encourage and provide emotional support through the treatment journey. (*ibid.*, p. 9)

The DTTO study includes a statement on generalisability that is similar, but which in fact indicates a number of weaknesses of the approach. The statement is as follows:

> Theoretical sampling has ensured that informants at varied stages of the [Community] Order, with varying service experiences, and with varying degrees of engagement have been selected. This enhances the ability to generalize from the findings ... Saturation was reached in the later interviews, as evidenced by the absence of new concepts being identified from the latter three interviews, although the definition of saturation is always contentious. (Ricketts et al., 2005, p. 77)

There is an inherent problem with theoretical sampling in that it is overly dependent on the point at which it begins and therefore can lead to a sampling 'silo'. This can mean that although saturation may be achieved, it is saturation within that particular silo rather than across the population; given that only 15 interviews were undertaken, practical experience of qualitative research indicates that this is too few interviews to achieve saturation across the whole population. The suspicion, therefore, is that there are kinds of offenders that the study has not interviewed. There is also the problem, as the statement indicates, that it is difficult to say when saturation has occurred. As such, the commitment to generalisability within this approach is weaker, and has a limited impact on how the research and analysis is carried out. This can be seen in the way the findings are reported, with frequent use of quasi-quantitative language ('for many informants ...' (*ibid.*, p. 69), 'a common experience was ...' (*ibid.*, p. 70), 'Generally, somewhat later in the Order ...' (*ibid.*, p. 72) and a concomitant reduction in the richness and diversity that is displayed and in the explanations that are reported. An example is the following statement:

> Clear direction from staff members with regard to expectations within the DTTO was valued highly by *many* informants. (*Ibid*, p. 70, emphasis added)

What is not described is *why* the direction is valued highly, nor why some informants *do not* value it. The problem is that it is content to say that this is the view of many participants, despite the fact that the findings are based on a sample of 15 offenders and therefore cannot tell the reader anything about prevalence of this view in the general population.

The Community Order study is even more contradictory in terms of its stance on generalisability:

> These samples cannot be taken as representative of probation officers or offenders on orders in any way ... [However] while it is important to acknowledge the limitations of the samples of probation staff and offenders ... it is equally important to point out that this is the first time that offenders have been questioned about their views of the new orders. During the course of the project we interviewed representatives of the three key stakeholders in the new orders – sentencers, probation officers and offenders – and the material from these interviews allows a fairly full picture of the new arrangements to emerge. (Mair & Mills, 2009, p. 7)

It is hard to square the circle this statement makes. On the one hand the samples are not representative in 'any way'; on the other hand they provide 'a fairly full picture of the new arrangements to emerge'. This equivocation about generalisation has very concrete implications, with the report using quantitative language as a matter of course: 'in all three-quarters of respondents stated that not all requirements were available' (*ibid.*, p18); 'most respondents thought that all of the 12 requirements were relevant' (*ibid.*, p. 19); 'around half of those interviewed thought that the SSO was working well' (*ibid.*, p. 20); 'most respondents thought that all of the requirements were helpful' (*ibid.*, p. 21). And because the prevalence is presented as a significant finding, the report does not go on to discuss why those officers thought all the requirements were helpful, nor why some officers did not think they were all helpful. In other words, the emphasis on quantification has meant that the range and diversity within the sample has not been displayed, and the explanations for the different views have not been explored.

Inductive/Deductive Balance

The second point of comparison will be on the balance between induction and deduction with the studies. The Community Order study takes a very deductive approach, as can been seen by the way in which the report is structured. The first half of the report focuses on the views of probation officers, reporting on 'the Community Order and use of requirements', 'the Suspended Sentence Order', 'the Orders as Alternatives to Custody', etc. The second half reports the views of offenders, with chapters on 'Being Subject to an Order', 'Views and Experiences of Requirements', 'Comparing Current Orders to Previous Community Sentences', etc. These are all entirely pre-conceived categories that closely match the questions that formed the topic guide, and as a result, restrict the freedom to analyse or report emerging concepts. It also means that the views of probation officers and offenders on the same subject have not being compared or used to provide a more complete, nuanced picture or how the orders are working. The DTTO study goes to the opposite extreme, presenting the material in terms of wholly inductive categories. The authors describe the identification of four main themes – 'outcomes', 'organisation', 'being kept active' and 'relationships' – that all sit within a core category of 'the Order having a life-course' (the final one referring to the fact that offenders views and experiences of it change through its course). The kind of questions the reader has, though, are how do the categories relate to each other, what factors influence the 'outcomes', is 'being kept active' the only benefit of a DTTO? In fact, there are answers to some of these questions within the text, but the sort of meta-concepts implied by those questions (i.e. 'cause', 'effect', 'barriers', 'facilitators') have not been explicitly used to analyse and structure the material with a resultant lack of clarity.

In contrast, the DTORS study attempts to tell a coherent analytical story that seeks to understand why treatment seekers experience different outcomes from their contact with treatment services. To some extent this can be seen from the chapter titles, 'Treatment seekers: needs from drug treatment', 'Treatment seekers: factors influencing recovery', 'Factors influencing the delivery of treatment', and 'Outcomes of contact with treatment services'. It is even more obvious from the detail of the text, which uses evidence from both treatment users and those providing it to identify what the pressures reinforcing drug users dependency and therefore the kind of help they need, the nature of the response of treatment providers and the factors influencing it, and then a section looking at the range of outcomes and drawing together the material in the rest of the report to provide explanations for the different outcomes. The key to this kind of analytical approach is to keep a balance between induction and deduction through using established conceptual frameworks to help design the study, paying close attention to participants' views and experiences from their perspective during data collection and analysis but then returning to existing conceptual frameworks when reporting to ensure that the material is relevant and comprehensible to the reader.

Case-and-Theme Based Analysis

The final aspect on which the three studies will be compared is in terms of whether the material has been analysed in a purely thematic way, or whether a case-based approach has also been used. These two ways of analysing qualitative data are conceptualised within CQT using the Framework approach to data management. Framework (Ritchie & Lewis, 2003), which was developed by Jane Ritchie Liz Spencer at NatCen (Pope, Ziebland, & Mays, 2006) in the 1980s, uses a matrix format, with each row assigned to an individual case (often a single participant) and each column assigned a theme. The matrix is not unlike the kind of spreadsheet that is used in statistical software programs such as SPSS, which has cases going across (as rows) and variables going down (as columns), but instead of numbers or fixed codes, the cells contain data that needs to be interpreted. Within this approach to data management, thematic analysis is conducted by looking down a column (i.e. by looking at the material on a single theme for lots of different participants), and case-based analysis is conducted by looking across a row (i.e. by looking at lots of themes for a single case or participant). Case-and-theme based analysis is conducted by doing both these things at the same time, that is by paying to attention to a number of different themes within a case but comparing cases with each other within the same piece of analysis. The importance of this is that it allows for the development of sophisticated typologies – ones which are defined using more than one characteristic – and it facilitates complex explanatory analysis of phenomena, such as the outcomes of an intervention.

The analysis for both the DTTO study and the Community Order study is exclusively theme-based. In neither study are there any typologies of participants nor any case-based explanation. The DTTO study, for example, does not explore how the individual themes of 'outcomes', 'organisation', 'being kept active' and 'relationships' relate to each other for different offenders. So it does not answer the question, what different outcomes exist for offenders who feel they are kept active but have poor relationships, for example? Similarly, the Community Order study does not ask whether there are offenders who find the requirements useful but do not like their supervising officer, and vice versa, and what impact does this have on their perception of the impact of the order? Yet these are surely crucial questions for anyone wanting to understand why either DTTOs or Community Orders are effective for some offenders and not for others, or how the system can be improved to increase its effectiveness. In contrast, case-and-theme based analysis is central to the DTORS study. The final chapter does not just summarise the preceding material but presents a typology of the outcomes of contact with drug treatment services that is based on three dimensions (the level and nature of participants' drug taking, the nature of participants' mental states and whether they were moving 'forward' in their lives in terms of relationships, education and employment). The chapter then goes on to explain why participants ended up in each of those categories. For example, for those in the 'recovering' category the following explanation is given.

> Treatment seekers in this category were characterised either by feeling that their needs were being met by treatment, or that they had sufficient motivation and capacity to address the pressures reinforcing addiction without the help of treatment. Where they felt their needs had been met, this could either be because they had high needs and received a lot of help or that they received a limited amount of help but had low needs. (Barnard et al., 2009, p. 12)

Although this may seem as if it is a fairly straightforward piece of analysis, it took considerable time and effort to do and was only possible using a case-and-theme based approach. It required the analysts to examine cases in terms of individuals' needs and capacities, the responses of treatment providers, the environments in which the individuals were living and receiving the intervention, and their outcomes. Having done this for each individual case, all the cases then need to be compared and contrasted with each other to build a comprehensive set of explanations for *all* outcomes and for *all* cases within the sample.

CONCLUSION

This chapter has argued that there is an increasing recognition that qualitative components are crucial to evaluations within the criminal justice system but that the exiting tools for carrying them out lack the methodological robustness that is required. It has been further argued that CQT, an approach developed by the National Centre for Social Research and recently named and defined by the author and his colleagues, is able to provide a coherent theoretical base and practical procedure for generating the level of detail and sophistication that is required by commissioners. The chapter has then gone on to illustrate, using three studies, the ways in which different approaches lead to different kinds of outputs.

Moving away from the detail of the comparison, it is useful to make a number of further points about CQT and the implications of using it for criminal justice evaluations. The first is that it has stringent requirements and this means that it is difficult to learn to do well and it requires substantial time and effort to undertake. As with other methodologies, CQT is a craft as well as a science, and there is no alternative to experience in learning how to do it effectively. It should also be recognised that learning to work within a CQT approach will be as much an emotional journey as an intellectual one. Research within the field of social research is dominated by quantitative approaches and this had led to a belief – often only barely perceived – that prevalence is synonymous with importance. In order to carry out CQT it is necessary to break free of the bonds of this axiom, as only then can qualitative data be properly explored with the aim of displaying diversity and identifying explanations. However, this can involve a genuine emotional struggle and this should not be underestimated by anyone wishing to learn about or adopt the approach.

While this chapter has made a case for using CQT as an approach to qualitative research, the broader message is less partisan. Whether one is convinced by the arguments for using CQT or not, it is hoped that the chapter has illustrated the fact that theoretical debates have practical implications. The issues that qualitative researchers grapple with, such as how generalisable the research is and to what extent existing concepts and theories should be used, have a real impact on what is actually done on a day-to-day basis. Commissioners of evaluations are not interested in the niceties of methodology but the utility of the findings, and whether they are better informed at the end of an evaluation than they were at the beginning and are therefore able to make better decisions. It is hoped that this chapter, whatever else it achieves, will encourage researchers to consider carefully the implications of adopting a particular theoretical or philosophical stance. Ultimately, this will have an impact beyond the conference hall and the pages of academic journals because it will affect the lives of those who may or may not receive an intervention because of the research evidence produced.

REFERENCES

Barnard, M. (2012). Critical qualitative theory and 'framework' analysis. In S. Becker, A. Bryman & H. Ferguson (Eds.), *Understanding research: Themes, methods and approaches for social policy and social work* (2nd ed.). Policy Press.

Barnard, M., Webster, S., O'Connor, W., with Jones, A., & Donmall, M. (2009). *The drug treatment outcomes research study (DTORS): Qualitative study*. London: Home Office.

Mair, G., & Mills, H. (2009). *The community order and the suspended sentence order three years on: The views and experiences of probation officers and offenders*. London: Centre for Crime and Justice Studies.

Pope, C., Ziebland, S., & Mays, N. (2006). Analysing qualitative data. In C. Pope & N. May (Eds.), *Qualitative research in health care*. Oxford, UK: BMJ Books, Blackwell Publishing.

Ricketts, T., Bliss, P., Murphy, K., & Brooker, C. (2005). Engagement with drug treatment testing orders: A qualitative study. *Addiction Research and Theory*, *13*(1), 65–78.

Ritchie, J., & Lewis, J. (2003). *Qualitative research practice: A guide for social science students and researchers.* London: Sage.

Robson, C. (2002). *Real world research: A resource for social scientists and practitioner-researchers.* Oxford: Wiley-Blackwell.

Snape, D., Spencer, L., & Barnard, M. (in press). The foundations of qualitative research. In C. McNaughton Nicholls, J. Ritchie, & J. Lewis (Eds.), *Qualitative research practice* (2nd ed.)., London: Sage.

SECTION 3
EVALUATION METHODS AND PRACTICE

WITHIN-TREATMENT CHANGE: FINDING THE INDIVIDUAL IN GROUP OUTCOMES

Erica Bowen

ABSTRACT

Traditionally evaluators of offending behaviour programmes have examined group-level mean change in treatment targets without acknowledging the potential variability of change at an individual level. Clinically significant change, although used widely in the therapy literature generally, has only recently been examined within forensic therapeutic contexts. This chapter provides an overview of key concepts, and the published literature in which clinically significant change has been examined within forensic samples is reviewed. It is concluded that although this technique has the potential to validate programme theory, it is yet to be used to its full potential within a forensic context.

INTRODUCTION

In England and Wales, as elsewhere, emphasis has been placed on implementing evidence-based policies through the development and accreditation of offending behaviour programmes, which are adopted nationally

Perspectives on Evaluating Criminal Justice and Corrections
Advances in Program Evaluation, Volume 13, 145–171

ISSN: 1474-7863/doi:10.1108/S1474-7863(2012)0000013011

Table 1. Summary of Accreditation Criteria for Offending Behaviour Programmes in England and Wales.

Criteria	Definition
1. Clear model of change	There must be an explicit model to explain how the programme is intended to bring about relevant change in offenders.
2. Selection of offenders	It must be specified clearly the types of offender for whom the programme is intended and how such offenders will be selected.
3. Targeting a range of dynamic risk factors	A range of dynamic risk factors known to be associated with reoffending must be addressed in an integrated manner within the programme.
4. Effective methods	There must be evidence to show that the treatment methods used are likely to have an impact on the targeted dynamic risk factors.
5. Skills oriented	The programme must facilitate the learning of skills that will assist participants in avoiding criminal activities and enable their involvement in legitimate pursuits.
6. Sequencing, intensity, duration	The amount of treatment provided must be linked to the needs of programme participants, with the introduction of different treatment components timed so that they complement each other.
7. Engagement and motivation	The programme must be structured to maximise the engagement of participants and to sustain their motivation throughout.
8. Continuity of programmes and service	There must be clear links between the programme and the overall management of the offender, both during a prison sentence and in the context of community supervision.
9. Maintaining integrity	There must be provision to monitor how well the programme functions and a system to modify aspects of it that do not perform as expected.
10. Ongoing evaluation	There must be provision to evaluate the efficacy of the programme.

after a period of design, implementation and evaluation (Hollin & Palmer, 2006). Based on the 'What works' (McGuire, 1995) philosophy, such programmes in England and Wales are required to meet 10 strict criteria in terms of approach, implementation and evaluation (HM Prison Service, 2004, Prison Service Order 4360). The 10 criteria are briefly summarised in Table 1.

The introduction of the accreditation policy constituted a significant policy shift and along with this came a requirement to identify the effectiveness of these programmes. According to the Prison Service Order (4360), the evaluation criteria:

> … in the long term means a reconviction study with relevant comparison data, as soon as reasonably feasible … a decrease in recidivism is intended to be achieved through change in … dynamic risk factors, improvement in these risk factors is an important … measure of efficacy.

This mandate highlights the importance placed on examining both impact and process within the accreditation criteria, bridging both sides of the 'paradigm wars' (Mark, Henry, & Julnes, 1999). Despite this, the focus of evaluation efforts has been on the impact of programmes on behaviour – that is, determining to what extent attendance at, and/or completion of, such programmes lead to a reduction in reoffending. This line of enquiry is fuelled inevitably by both public safety and efficiency concerns: Do the programmes reduce reoffending and how much do they cost?

Such an approach to evaluation can be considered atheoretical (see chapters by Astbury and Smith, this volume), as no appraisal of the mechanisms through which any identified 'impact' occurs is undertaken. A number of authors have argued that whilst identifying the impact of programmes is necessary, it is not sufficient for understanding how such programmes bring about change, and for whom expected change is achieved (Bowen, 2011; Bowen & Gilchrist, 2004; Friendship, Falshaw, & Beech, 2003; Pawson & Tilley, 1997).

It is particularly clear from the accreditation criteria that all therapeutic programmes are based on a programme theory that should be explicit. Regardless of the theory of human behaviour upon which such programmes are forged, there is a basic knowledge – attitude-behaviour meta-theoretical assumption (Weiss, 1997) shared by all approaches to intervention. From this it should be possible to identify the (typically, but not exclusively) psychological treatment targets deemed to be associated with offending. Consequently, the criteria above reiterate the importance of examining the impact of the programme on intermediary, dynamic risk factors or criminogenic needs (Andrews & Bonta, 2006) that are theoretically linked to the offending behaviour of importance. Moreover, as Astbury (this volume) and Bowen (2011) argue, by evaluating the appropriateness of programme theory, we may also be able to contribute directly to understanding offending behaviour. That is, if we can show that change in the intermediary criminogenic needs is associated with change in offending behaviour, we can validate the theoretical assumptions of the programme and the treatment targets. However, others argue that simply identifying group-level change and associations with reoffending is insufficient. Hanson and Wallace-Capretta (2000), for instance, suggested that in order to determine the criminogenic nature of a psychological factor, treatment-induced psychological change must be found to be associated with change in offending behaviour. Further, that if clients present at pre-treatment with clinical-level symptoms (e.g. anger), and at post-treatment the symptoms are still reported as being within a clinical range, albeit significantly reduced from pre-treatment, behavioural change associated with psychological change should not be expected (Hanson & Wallace-Capretta, 2000). Therefore, outcome studies need to determine the proportion of offenders who achieve 'clinically significant change' (Jacobson & Truax, 1991) and relate this change to the proportion of offenders who also achieve behavioural change in order to validate the 'criminogenic' status of the targeted need. This means that in order for treatment to be deemed to have had a meaningful impact, at the end of treatment the client group should be indistinguishable from the 'normal' group on a psychological measure of relevance (Kazdin, 1999; Kendall, Marrs-Garcia, Nath, & Sheldrick, 1999), and such change should be associated with behavioural change in the expected direction.

CLINICALLY SIGNIFICANT CHANGE: THEORY AND METHODS

The notion of clinical significance is not new within the field of psychotherapy, but is by comparison, new to the field of corrections, despite the obvious therapeutic ethos of the commonly adopted group-based offending behaviour programmes. The development of this concept marked an important advance in therapeutic evaluation (Kazdin, 1999) and therefore it is surprising that it has not been widely used within the evaluation of correctional programmes.

Basic to the concept of clinical significance are two limitations of traditional pre–post intervention statistical comparisons (Jacobson & Revenstorf, 1988; Jacobson, Roberts, Berns, & McGlinchey, 1999). First, group-based comparisons are not sensitive to individual variability in treatment responses. Whilst at an aggregate level change may be statistically significant, that is, the change in mean scores did not occur due to natural temporal variation, it is not possible to determine the proportion of clients who improved or recovered, or deteriorated as a consequence of treatment (Jacobson et al., 1999). This is important as it is likely that at pre-treatment, individuals will present with different levels of the trait to be targeted by intervention. Indeed, there is considerable evidence that offender populations identified on the basis of index offences (e.g. sexual offenders, domestic violence offenders) are heterogeneous in clinically meaningful dimensions (e.g. Huss & Ralstone, 2008; Tweed & Dutton, 1998). Moreover, it is likely that responses to treatment will vary within populations, so that some individuals may evidence considerable change, whilst others may evidence little change. Group-level pre–post statistical significance tests are mute on these issues.

Second, statistical comparisons typically do not enable an appraisal of the practical importance of the impact of change and the associated treatment effects. Even if the mean scores on a given measure are changed such that the level of significance is below the chosen significance level (e.g. $p<0.05$), this provides no information on whether the change has any practical meaning for individuals (Wise, 2004). Jacobson and Truax (1991) stated that 'the clinical significance of a treatment refers to its ability to meet standards of efficacy set by consumers, clinicians and researchers' (p. 12). Clinical significance was more clearly operationalised by Jacobson, Follette, and Revestorf (1984) as 'a change ... when the client moves from the dysfunctional to the functional range during the course of therapy' (p. 340). Expanding on this further Jacobson et al. (1984) defined the dysfunctional–functional continuum on the basis of three criteria:

1. Does the level of functioning at post-test fall outside the range of the dysfunctional population, where range is defined as extending to two standard deviations above (in the direction of functionality) the mean for that population?
2. Does the level of functioning at post-test fall within the range of the functional or normal population, where range is defined as beginning at two standard deviations below the mean for the normal population?
3. Does the level of functioning at post-test suggest that the subject is statistically more likely to be in the functional than in the dysfunctional population; that is, is the post-test score statistically more likely to be drawn from the functional than the dysfunctional distribution? (p. 340).

Consequently, 'dysfunctionality' is identified by a cutoff two standard deviations above (or below depending on the direction of functionality) the mean for a normative population. This does assume that distributions from both populations are not overlapping (Wise, 2004). If the normative distributions are adjacent then a normative cutoff (C) between these two distributions is derived from the following equation.

$$C = \frac{(\text{SD1})\,(\text{MEAN2}) + (\text{SD2})\,(\text{MEAN1})}{\text{SD1} + \text{SD2}}$$

where SD1 refers to the standard deviation of the non-offender population and MEAN1 refers to the mean non-offender score. SD2 refers to the standard deviation of the offender population and MEAN2 refers to the offender group mean score. This calculation would then lead to a critical value that would indicate that the individual had moved from one population to the other. However, this alone would not necessarily indicate that the change was reliable (in a statistical sense), that is, that it had not occurred by chance alone, or as a function of measurement error. Consequently, Jacobson et al. (1984) introduced an additional statistical standard, the Reliable Change Index (RCI), for data to be tested against, to ensure that the change reported was indeed both clinically meaningful and statistically reliable. The RCI is derived from the following equation:

$$\mathrm{RCI} = \frac{\text{(post-treatment score)} - \text{(pre-treatment score)}}{\mathrm{SE}}$$

where SE refers to the standard error of the measure used. The standard error is calculated from the following equation:

$$\mathrm{SE} = \mathrm{SD}\sqrt{(1 - \mathrm{rxx})}$$

SD is the standard deviation of the control group, normal population or pre-treatment group (Wise, 2004); rxx is the test–re-test reliability (or internal consistency; Jacobson et al., 1984) of the measure used. In order for any pre–post change to be classified as significant, the RCI has to exceed 1.64 for a one-tailed test (Beech, Fisher, & Beckett, 1999) or 1.96 for a two-tailed test. Consequently, the less reliable the measure used (e.g. the measure has a low test–re-test coefficient) is, the greater the required change in scores, for the change to be considered statistically reliable (Wise, 2004). This approach enables the magnitude of change to be more sensitively characterised in both wanted and unwanted directions. At pre-treat individuals can 'score' in a number of positions on a particular measure (e.g. in the normal population range or in a dysfunctional range) and this is also the case at post-treatment. Hence, there are a number of categories offenders can be located in on the basis of their pre-treatment and post-treatment scores, as listed in Table 2 (cf. Jacobson et al., 1999).

These concepts and the associated proposed procedures are not without controversy or critics (e.g. Speer, 1999); yet despite these concerns, this method has been the most widely used as a method of assessing treatment change in both general psychotherapy (Ogles, Lunnen, & Bonesteel, 2001) and forensic therapy contexts. It is deemed to provide a modest estimate of

Table 2. Categories of Change Based on the CS and RCI Indices.

Category	Definition
Normal[a]/Always okay[b]	Individual scores start and remain in functional population.
Recovered	Clinically significant reliable change, scores changing from dysfunctional to functional.
Improved	Reliable expected change that is not clinically significant, scores starting and ending in the dysfunctional group albeit closer to the functional distribution.
Deteriorated	Statistically reliable change in the opposite direction to that intended with initial scores in the normal population.
Regressed	Statistically reliable change in the opposite direction to that intended from scores originating in the normal population but changing to within the dysfunctional population.
Unreliable[a]/ Unchanged[c]	Statistically unreliable change regardless of starting point and relation to clinical cutoff.

[a]Additional categories added by Bowen et al. (2008).
[b]Alternative category identified by Barnett (2011).
[c]Alternative category identified by Nunes et al. (2011).

treatment-based improvement (Bauer, Lambert, & Nielsen, 2004) and is as valid as alternative methods (McGlinchey, Atkins, & Jacobson, 2002).

CLINICALLY SIGNIFICANT CHANGE: REVIEW OF EVIDENCE OF ITS USE WITH CORRECTIONS POPULATIONS

Although these concepts were introduced into the clinical literature in the mid-1980s, it took fifteen years for these methods to be used with any level of consistency within the evaluation of forensic therapeutic programmes, led in the United Kingdom by Professor Tony Beech in his evaluation of sexual offender treatment programmes. A search of the peer-reviewed published literature in which clinically significant change in forensic therapeutic contexts is examined yielded only 11 studies, which are summarised in Table 3. These studies reflect three different strains of research that have examined clinically significant change: in-treatment change only ($n = 7$ studies); therapeutic environment and in-treatment change ($n = 2$ studies) and in-treatment change and recidivism ($n = 2$ studies). This section of the chapter will critically review these studies in order to determine the impact

Table 3. Summary of Empirical Papers in Which Clinical Significance Is Examined Within Forensic Settings.

Authors (Date)	Country of Origin	Programme	Sample	Measures	Main Findings
Greeven and de Ruiter (2004)	Netherlands	Hospital for forensic psychiatric patients	59 patients (54 men)	Personality Diagnostic Questionnaire-Revised (Hyler & Rieder, 1987)	• 27% of patients achieved clinically significant improvement in personality disorder traits. • Patients with schizoid, dependent and passive–aggressive personality disorders had better prognosis. • Patients with narcissistic, antisocial, histrionic and avoidant personality disorders achieved little or no reliable change.
Beech and Hamilton-Giachritsis (2005)	United Kingdom	Prison-Based Sexual Offender Treatment Programme (SOTP)	76 adult male sexual offenders who attended 12 treatment groups	• Victim Empathy Distortions Scale (Beckett & Fisher, 1994) • Cognitive Distortions Scale (Beckett, 1987) • Emotional Identification with Children Scale (Beckett, 1987) • Group Environment Scale (Moos, 1986)	• Considerable variation in the proportion of members of each treatment group whose psychometric scores were 'normal' at the end of treatment: 29–80% range for short groups; 56–75% for long groups; no relationship between group length and change. • Perceptions of group cohesion and expressiveness positively correlated with impact.

Beech and Ford (2006)	United Kingdom	Residential sex offender treatment setting	51 male sex offenders	• Children and Sex Questionnaire (cognitive distortions and emotional identification with children subscales; Beckett, 1987) • Victim Empathy Distortions (Beckett & Fisher, 1994) • Short Self Esteem Scale (Webster, Mann, Thornton, & Wakeling, 2006) • UCLA Emotional Loneliness Scale (Russell et al., 1980) • Social Response Inventory (Keltner et al., 1981) • Interpersonal Reactivity Index (Davis, 1983) • Nowicki-Strickland Locus of Control Scale (Nowicki & Duke, 1976)	• Percentage of individuals achieving 'treated' profile varied by risk category: 19% very high risk; 21% high risk; 50% medium risk; 44% low risk. • Percentage of individuals achieving 'treated' profile varied by deviance category: 25% high deviance; 48% low deviance. • None of the 'treated' individuals reoffended, 14% of those judged as not responding to treatment reoffended.
Bowen et al. (2008)	United Kingdom	Probation-based non-accredited domestic violence perpetrator programme	52 male domestic violence offenders; 37 for whom police data available	• Inventory of Beliefs about Wife Beating (Saunders et al., 1987) • Novaco Anger Scale (Novaco, 1994) • Interpersonal Dependency Inventory (Hirschfield et al., 1977) • Multidimensional Locus of Control (Levenson, 1974) • Police call out data	• 27% of offenders did not achieve reliable change across measures. • Rate of 'recovery' different across measures; most likely (30%) for IBWB; least likely (11%) cognitive domain of the NAS. • Extent of change not associated with reoffending.

Table 3. *(Continued)*

Authors (Date)	Country of Origin	Programme	Sample	Measures	Main Findings
Mandeville-Norden et al. (2008)	United Kingdom	Probation-based accredited sexual offender treatment programmes	341 sexual offenders convicted of sexual offences against a child (under 14 years)	• Children and Sex Questionnaire (cognitive distortions and emotional identification with children subscales; Beckett, 1987) • Victim Empathy Distortions (Beckett & Fisher, 1994) • Short Self Esteem Scale (Webster, Mann, Thornton, & Wakeling, 2006) • UCLA Emotional Loneliness Scale (Russell et al., 1980) • Social Response Inventory (Keltner et al., 1981) • Interpersonal Reactivity Index (Davis, 1983) • Nowicki-Strickland Locus of Control Scale (Nowicki & Duke, 1976)	• 7–33% achieved clinically significant change across measures. • Greater proportion of clinically significant change for those in longer term treatment (16–59% across measures) than those in short-term treatment (5–30% across measures).
Shuker and Newton (2008)	United Kingdom	Prison-based therapeutic community	172 male prisoners	• Eysenck Personality Scales (Eysenck & Eysenck, 1991) • Culture Free Self Esteem Inventory (Battle, 1992) • The Hostility and Direction of Hostility Questionnaire (Caine et al., 1967)	• 24–38% of participants achieved clinically significant change across measures. • Individuals who resided for 12 months or less evidenced change in mental health indices.

				• Parole board outcome	• Individuals who resided for more than 12 months clinically significant change seen on all measures. • Men granted parole ($n = 20$) evidenced greater than average expected change than those transferred or not granted parole.
Nolan and Thompson (2009)	Australia	Benelong Haven residential alcohol and drug rehabilitation centre	38 voluntary and 42 legally coerced clients at T1; 26 voluntary and 30 coerced at T2	• Opiate Treatment Index (Darke, Ward, Hall, Heather, & Wodak, 1991) • Brief Symptom Inventory-53 (Derogatis, 1993) • Depression Anxiety and Stress Scale-21 (Lovibond & Lovibond, 1995) • Stages of Change Scales (McConnaughy et al., 1983) • Interpersonal Reactivity Index (Davis, 1983)	• 55% GSI; 94% DASS depression; 68% DASS anxiety; 89% DASS stress achieved clinically significant change.
Tapp et al. (2009)	United Kingdom	Prison-based Enhanced Thinking Skills programme	83 mentally disordered offenders	• Clinical Outcomes in Routine Evaluation – Outcome Measure (Evans et al., 2002) • The Psychological Inventory of Criminal Thinking Styles (Walters, 1995) • Social Problem Solving Inventory (Freedman, Rosenthal, Donahoe, Sclundt, & McFall, 1978)	• 20–40% of participants achieved clinically significant change on CORE-OM subscales. • Only 6% of clients achieved clinically significant change on SPSI subscales.

Table 3. (*Continued*)

Authors (Date)	Country of Origin	Programme	Sample	Measures	Main Findings
Bowen (2010)	United Kingdom	Probation-based non-accredited domestic violence perpetrator programme	77 male domestic violence perpetrators	• Inventory of Beliefs about Wife Beating (Saunders et al., 1987) • Novaco Anger Scale (Novaco, 1994) • Interpersonal Dependency Inventory (Hirschfield et al., 1977) • Multidimensional Locus of Control (Levenson, 1974) • Group Environment Scale (Moos, 1996)	• Perceptions of group leaders as supportive were associated with the number of scales on which clinically significant change was achieved.
Barnett (2011)	United Kingdom	Extended Sex Offender Treatment Programme	322 male incarcerated offenders	• The Revised Dissipation-Rumination Scale (Caprara, 1986) • The 'My Life' Questionnaire (Mann, 2005) • Self-Esteem Questionnaire (Thornton, Beech, & Marshall, 2004)	• 6.8% 'recovered'; 9.3% 'improved'; 3.1% 'deteriorated' 60.2% 'unchanged'; 20.5% 'always ok' on Dominance scale. • 2.4% 'recovered'; 8.4% 'improved'; 2.4% 'deteriorated'; 67.1% 'unchanged'; 19.6% 'always ok' on Ruminations scale.

Nunes et al. (2011)	Canada	Low or Moderate intensity National Sex Offender Program	439 adult male sex offenders	• MOLEST and RAPE scales (Bumby, 1996) • Miller Social Intimacy Scale (Miller & Lefcourt, 1982) • Revised UCLA Loneliness Scale (Russell et al., 1980) • STABLE 2000 (Hanson & Thornton, 1999, 2000)	• 21–44% of clients 'recovered' across measures; 1–17% deteriorated across measures; 42–66% no reliable change across measures for offenders who started off with scores in 'dysfunctional' range. • 1–21% deteriorated for those offenders who started off with scores in functional range.

of examining clinically significant change on our understanding of the process of rehabilitation.

In-Treatment Change

The majority of the available peer-reviewed studies have focused solely on identifying and characterising in-treatment change across a range of settings including: prison-based sex offender treatment programmes (Barnett, 2011; Nunes, Babchishin, & Cortoni, 2011); community-based sex offender treatment programmes (Mandeville-Norden, Beech, & Hayes, 2008; Nunes et al., 2011); a prison-based cognitive skills programme (Tapp, Fellowes, Wallis, Blud, & Moore, 2009); a forensic psychiatric hospital (Greeven & de Ruiter, 2004); a residential drug rehabilitation interventions (Nolan & Thompson, 2009); and a prison-based therapeutic community (Shuker & Newton, 2008).

Mandeville-Norden et al. (2008) examined individual change in a sample of 341 adult male sex offenders who had completed treatment programmes offered across probation areas in England and Wales. Rather than using the standard method for calculating clinically significant change described previously (Jacobson & Truax, 1991), the researchers used the approach adopted by Beech and Ford (2006), which is a more conservative method initially proposed by Christensen and Mendoza (1986). In this variation it was proposed that in order to reflect the expected difference between two scores obtained on the same test by the same individuals as a function of measurement error alone, the reliable change index should be calculated by replacing S_E with $\sqrt{2(S_E)^2}$. This means that a greater level of change is required for it to be deemed statistically reliable.

Initially pre-treatment scores on the measures adopted (see Table 3) were cluster analysed in order to derive a psychometric typology of offenders based on their 'treatment need' profiles. Three groups emerged – Low need ($n = 224$), Medium need ($n = 92$) and High need ($n = 25$). The Low need group evidenced markedly low self-esteem, but otherwise reported no difficulties on the other socio-affective measures assessed, and no problems on the offence-specific measures used. In contrast to non-offender means, the Medium need offenders' scores were lower on measures of cognitive distortions, victim empathy, self-esteem, emotional loneliness, under-assertiveness, personal distress and locus of control (p. 503). The High need group evidenced global deficits across measures on both domains (social-affective and offence).

Although a more conservative method was used from which to derive RCI cutoff scores, Mandeville-Norden et al. determined clinically significant change on the basis that post-test scores fell within the normal range, regardless of the relative pre-treatment scores. Consequently, offenders who were in the functional and dysfunctional group at pre-treatment were not discriminated against in this analysis. As Nunes et al. (2011) observe, however, combining these two groups of offenders may result in misleading effects; for example, the inclusion of offenders in the functional range at pre-treatment may lead to inflated rates of treatment success. In addition, the reliable change analysis would miscalculate the effectiveness of treatment, as those who were already functional are less likely to exhibit marked improvement (i.e. creating ceiling effects). Nevertheless, the Mandeville-Norden et al. (2008) study established that the extent of individual change varied as a function of level of need (see Table 3). Specifically 50–81% of the Low need group scored within the normal range at post-treatment, although it is likely that a high proportion of these individuals started treatment within this range. Indeed only between 3% and 26% had shifted to a clinically significant degree. In the Medium need group, 34–75% were in the normal range at post-treatment (9–100% had changed to a clinically significant level) and between 16% and 50% of the High need sample scored within the cutoff at post-treatment (15–80% of those who scored in the normal range post-treatment, had achieved clinically significant change).

Based on their critique of this study, Nunes et al. (2011) examined group-level change, effect size estimates and individual-level change in their evaluation of a Canadian sex offender treatment programme that was delivered in both prison and community settings. In their sample of 313 offenders, when group-level analyses were conducted, it was found that statistically significant improvement was achieved on four out of the five measures employed (all except social intimacy) (see Table 3 for the measures used). Moreover, effect sizes were in the moderate range (−.41 to .75). In contrast to the study by Mandeville-Norden et al. (2008), Nunes et al. examined both positive and negative individual change. Depending on the direction and magnitude of change achieved, offenders were classified post-treatment as either 'recovered', 'improved', 'unchanged' or 'deteriorated' (see Table 2 for definitions of these terms in relation to the reliability and clinical significance of change achieved).

As expected, the results indicated substantial heterogeneity in individual treatment responses. Approximately 70% of offenders scored in the dysfunctional region on the Stable-2000 at pre-treatment and of these, 21.3% were identified as recovered at post-treatment. On the MOLEST scale, 59.1% were classified in the dysfunctional range at pre-treatment, and of these 29.9% 'recovered'. On the RAPE scale, 54.7% were dysfunctional at pre-treatment, and of these 44.4% 'recovered'. On the MSIS, 37.8% were dysfunctional at pre-treatment and of these, 27.3% 'recovered', and on the revised UCLA Loneliness Scale, 53.7% were dysfunctional to begin with and 37.7% of these 'recovered'. Only one moderator of treatment impact was found: on the MOLEST scale, participants whose victims had been children were significantly more likely to have either improved or recovered than those whose victims had not been children.

Barnett (2011) examined both group mean and individual-level change in the context of validating two new measures of grievance thinking. A sample of 322 imprisoned high-risk sex offenders who had completed treatment as part of their sentences participated in the study, and it was anticipated that the programme would directly challenge and modify this type of thinking. Due to the lack of control group, the pre-treatment standard deviation was used in the calculation of the RCI. Moreover, a change in the expected direction of one rather than two standard deviations away from the pre-treatment mean was deemed to indicate clinically significant change. This is due to its representation of a large effect size (cf. Wise, 2004).

At a group level it was found that in general scores improved on the Need for Respect and Vengeance scales and on the Dominance scale (see Table 3 for measures used). Scores also improved on the Ruminations scale, although as with the improvement on the Dominance scale, only small effect sizes were recorded. When clinically significant change was examined, it was found that 18.3% of the sample achieved clinically significant change on the Dominance scale and 16.1% achieved such change on the Ruminations scale. A further 16.1% and 10.9% achieved reliable change in the desired direction. Examination of positive and negative change categories (see Table 3) indicated that the majority of scores were unchanged across both measures.

Further analyses were conducted by splitting the pre-treatment sample into high and low scorers. On this basis, 55.8% of the high scorers and 8.9% of the low scorers on the Dominance scale achieved clinically significant change. In addition, 57.5% of the high and 6.1% of the low scorers on the Ruminations scale achieved this change. Finally, the prevalence of different change categorisations in both positive and negative directions was examined in relation to pre-treatment score categories. This analysis found that on the Dominance scale, 50% of high scorers achieved clinically significant change (in contrast to only 8.9% of low scorers), whereas 57% of the low scorers were unchanged (in contrast to 34.4% of high scorers). Similarly, on the Ruminations scale, 57.5% of high scorers achieved clinically significant change (in contrast to 6.1% of low scorers), and 49.8% of the low scorers were unchanged (in contrast to 30% of high scorers).

Tapp et al. (2009) evaluated the Enhanced Thinking Skills (ETS) programme in a sample of 83 mentally disordered offenders. The programme targets interpersonal problem solving, self-control, cognitive style, social perspective taking, moral values and critical reasoning (p. 202). Both group and individual change analyses were examined across the measures adopted (see Table 3). At group level it was found that statistically significant pre–post change occurred on four of the eight PICTS subscales (mollification, cutoff, power orientation and cognitive indolence). No significant differences were obtained on the CORE-OM scales. On the SPSI, significant change was achieved on subscales of passivity and aggression.

Analyses of clinically significant change on the CORE-OM and SPSI subscales indicated that the greatest degree of change was achieved on scales measuring problems/symptoms (40%), with considerably less change demonstrated on scales measuring subjective well-being (20%). On the SPSI, the majority (70%) achieved change in the undesired direction on the passivity scale. Reliable change analyses indicated that across the PICTS subscales between 10% and 21% of participants achieved reliable change, whereas across CORE-OM and SPSI subscales between 2% and 9% achieved reliable change.

Greeven and de Ruiter (2004) examined change in personality disorder traits arising from residence in a forensic hospital therapeutic community for personality disordered offenders. The therapeutic approach combined the community model and social skills training with a view to increasing personal responsibility for behaviour. Group therapy approaches designed to train social skills, reduce impulsivity and increase the management of aggression were offered as part of the therapeutic context. The sample comprised 59 inpatients who did not have a diagnosis of schizophrenia or 'mental retardation', but were diagnosed with some form of personality disorder. Analyses examined both group-level and individual change in the prevalence of personality disorder features across a two-year intervention period.

It was found that across the two-year time period, the prevalence of personality disorder diagnoses reduced significantly. Specifically, at Time 1, patients met the diagnostic criteria for on average 3.8 personality disorders. At Time 2, 23 patients no longer met the criteria for any personality disorder and 36 met the criteria for only one diagnosable personality disorder. In addition, the mean number of DSM criteria met reduced significantly from pre- to post-treatment (43.8 at pre-treatment; 31.6 at post-treatment).

An analysis of individual clinically significant and reliable change indicated that 27% of patients achieved clinically significant change on the PDQ-R total score, which represents total number of DSM criteria met. When individual personality disorder criteria were examined, it was found that patients with certain diagnoses at the start of the intervention were more likely to achieve reliable and/or clinically significant change. Specifically, patients with Schizoid, Dependent and Passive-Aggressive personality disorders achieved clinically significant change, whereas patients with Antisocial, Histrionic, Narcissistic and Avoidant personality disorders achieved little change.

Nolan and Thompson (2009) examined psychological change resulting from residence in a community-based therapeutic community designed to treat the needs of both self-referred and legally coerced (solicitor referral, Magistrate's early referral or Supreme Court bail) drug-addicted clients. Psychometric data were collected at three time points. Time 1 represented 15 days into treatment; Time 2 at 35–40 days and Time 3 at 70–75 days. Of the initial 80 participants assessed at Time 1, only 56 participants remained at Time 2. At a group level it was found that there was a statistically significant effect of time on scores for the Brief Symptom Inventory (BSI) and DASS subscales (see Table 3 for measures used) in the expected direction. In relation to motivation to change, it was found that scores on the Maintenance subscale decreased over time. No group-level change on empathy (IRI) was found. At Time 3, only 38 participants remained. The Time 2 and Time 3 analyses broadly replicated those reported in the earlier phase, although scores on the Somatisation and Depression scales of the BSI did not change significantly. There were no statistically significant changes on the IRI subscales.

Examination of clinically significant change was conducted on the data from the 38 clients who remained in treatment until Time 3. Analyses were conducted on the Global Severity Index (GSI), BSI and DASS scales using change between Time 1 and Time 3. Due to a lack of normative data, test–re-test reliabilities were used to calculate the RCI for the GSI and DASS subscales. It was found that the majority of clients achieved reliable change on the GSI (89%) and on the DASS (68% Depression; 70% Anxiety; 56% Stress). In addition, more than half of participants who achieved reliable change also achieved clinically significant change across these measures too (55% GSI; 94% Depression; 68% Anxiety; 89% Stress).

Shuker and Newton (2008) focused on the extent of psychological change resulting from residence in a prison therapeutic community. The philosophy of the community is underpinned by cognitive, social learning and psychodynamic principles which are drawn upon to address offence-related risk factors and also psychiatric symptoms characteristic of personality disorder.

The approach differs to traditional group work programmes, in that whilst programmes are offered, the broader living context is also designed to have therapeutic effects. In order to validate the clinical significance of any change identified, associations with parole board outcome were also assessed.

Group-level change was assessed and it was found that change on all subscales (see Table 3) at the end of residence was statistically significantly reduced. In general, the effect sizes were moderate to large (0.5 Psychoticism and HDHQ Extrapunitive hostility; 0.6 Impulsiveness, Neuroticism; 0.8 HDHQ Intropunitive hostility; 0.9 Self-esteem). Examination of individual change, however, found that only between 24% and 39% of offenders actually achieved clinically significant change across measures, although in keeping with the general trend the greater success was on the measure of self-esteem. Further analyses examined the extent to which clinically significant change was achieved in relation to length of treatment. It was found that time in treatment was associated with the extent of change achieved. Specifically, those offenders who stayed for less than 12 months were found to achieve change on mental health characteristics. Those who left after 12 months evidenced clinically significant change across all measures. Finally, it was found that men who were granted parole evidenced greater average expected change than those not granted parole. Statistically significant differences were found between these groups for neuroticism, impulsiveness and self-esteem.

Taken together the findings of these studies indicate that underlying group-level positive change is a range of individual change profiles, not all of which are in the expected direction. Moreover, such an analysis enables the identification of the differential impact of treatment, such that individuals who are high scorers to begin with are likely to evidence greater change, although not everyone belonging to these groups evidences consistently reliable and/or clinically significant change. What these studies fail to address, however, is the question of whether the change identified occurs on constructs that are actually criminogenic – that is, whether such change is associated with behavioural change. Such an approach requires behavioural follow up data, and as such studies are notoriously difficult to conduct and are expensive, it is perhaps not surprising that the majority of studies have focused on in-treatment change alone.

Therapeutic Environment and In-Treatment Change

Two studies (Beech & Hamilton-Giachritsis, 2005; Bowen, 2010) have examined how perceptions of the therapeutic environment link to in-treatment change within sexual offender and domestic violence perpetrator programmes (DVPPs) respectively. Both studies employed the Group Environment Scale (Moos, 1994) as a measure of therapeutic environment and used the same metric for assessing reliable and clinically significant change.

Beech and Hamilton-Giachritsis (2005) examined the data at both therapeutic group and individual levels in a sample of 88 male incarcerated offenders. For example, comparisons of group environment and the percentage of participants achieving clinically significant change were made across the 12 therapeutic groups. Treatment intensity also varied between 74 and 186 hours and groups comprised between 7 and 10 offenders. In calculating individual change, the authors focused purely on whether the post-treatment scores fell within the normal population range, regardless of the relative pre-treatment score. Consequently, whilst clinical change may have occurred, it may not always have been statistically reliable. Interestingly, this was justified on the basis that not all offenders at pre-treatment would have profiles substantially different from non-offenders. Considerable variation in the percentage of individual group members who achieved clinical change thus defined was identified (see Table 3). It was also found that perceptions of groups as cohesive and as fostering expressiveness was associated with the extent of psychological change achieved.

Bowen (2010) found that overall, the 77 participants of the 24-session DVPP psycho-educational programme perceived that it emphasised the discussion of personal problems, being well organised and focusing on skills training. Perceptions of leaders as supportive were more strongly associated with these therapeutic factors, than were perceptions of groups as cohesive. Indeed it was also found that perceptions of leaders as supportive was associated with the extent of clinically significant and reliable change achieved across the psychological characteristics targeted by the programme theory, whereas group cohesion was not. Therefore, the more supportive the leaders were rated by the subsample of 52 offenders who had complete datasets, the greater the extent of clinically significant and reliable change achieved across the measures.

The examination of therapeutic process variables along with psychological change in these two studies provides a unique insight into the process of meaningful psychological change. It is interesting to note that despite both programmes being based upon psycho-educational models, different therapeutic factors were associated with meaningful change. It is possible that this reflects some of the methodological differences in the calculation of clinically significant change between the studies. Obviously, with such a limited literature to draw from, more research is required in order to validate these associations. However, that such questions have been asked represents an important advance in evaluation research.

In-Treatment Change and Recidivism

Two studies (Beech & Ford, 2006; Bowen, Gilchrist, & Beech, 2008) have examined how in-treatment psychological change is associated with measures of recidivism post-treatment. Beech and Ford (2006) categorised their sample of 51 treatment completers based on their levels of risk and deviance. The sample consisted of men who had completed at least six months of treatment and whose exit from treatment was planned. In addition, participants had to have left treatment at least two years prior to the study date in order for reconviction data to be collated. On average, participants had resided at the clinic for 58.5 weeks, which amounted to approximately 877 hours of treatment on average. Sixteen participants were rated as Very high risk, 14 men as High risk, 12 men as High Deviance and 25 were deemed to be Low Deviance.

Beech and Ford adopted the more conservative method proposed by Christensen and Mendoza (1986) for the calculation of reliable change. It was found that the extent of clinically meaningful change varied across measures and also varied as a function of the risk and deviance levels that individuals presented with at pre-treatment (see Table 3). Three of the 26 High Deviance men achieved clinically significant and reliable change on all pro-offending measures and four out of five socio-affective measures, including both Self-Esteem and Emotional Loneliness (see Table 3 for measures used). Of the Low Deviance men, 10 showed change on at least three of the socio-affective measures. In addition, it was found that of those offenders who at the end of treatment were deemed to have been 'treated' based on the extent of clinically significant change achieved across measures, none had reoffended. In contrast, 14% of those who were identified as not having responded to treatment had reoffended within five years. However, no statistical analyses were conducted to determine whether change on individual scales or total change predicted reoffending. Moreover, there was no examination of broader profiles of change and their relation to behaviour.

Bowen et al. (2008) examined the nature of group mean and individual change achieved as a result of attending a DVPP in a sample of 52 male offenders. It was found that at a group-level, post-treatment scores on measures of pro-domestic violence attitudes, chance and powerful others locus of control were statistically significantly lower than pre-treatment. No group-level reductions in anger or interpersonal dependency were identified. When pre-treatment social desirability scores were controlled for, all pre–post treatment differences were rendered non-significant. When individual change was considered, however, a different picture of treatment impact emerged.

It was found that a substantial proportion of offenders (27.2%) did not achieve reliable change across measures. A further 26.5% were categorised as Normal, that is both pre- and post-treatment scores were within the range of the normal population. Of those offenders who did achieve reliable change, the most frequent categorisation on average was clinically significant change (Recovered), with 17.3% achieving this status. The least frequent categorisation was Regressed (5%). In general, at an individual level the data indicate a pattern of positive change where reliable change was achieved. The profile of change achieved within the sample also varied according to the construct assessed. For example, offenders were most likely to achieve unreliable change in levels of behavioural reactions to anger provocation, and were least likely to achieve unreliable change in pro-domestic-violence attitudes. Moreover, offenders were most likely to achieve clinically significant change and to be categorised as Improved on the IBWB and least likely to achieve clinically significant change in their reported cognitive mediation of anger responses, a scale for which offenders were most likely to be categorised as Normal.

Of the 37 offenders for whom alleged reoffending data were available, it was found that 4 (10.8%) reoffended within the observation period. Contrary to expectations, reoffending is neither associated with achieving clinically significant change on the Cognitive, Arousal, and Behavioural domains of the NAS, nor reductions in pro-domestic-violence attitudes and external locus of control. In addition there was no association between the number of scales on which clinically significant change was achieved and alleged reoffending based on police call-out data.

SUMMARY AND CONCLUSIONS

It is clear from the studies reviewed that the examination of reliable and clinically significant change has found its place within corrections evaluations and this represents a welcome advance in evaluation practice. However, there are a number of weaknesses in the studies which mean that so far there has been many missed opportunities to more directly evaluate the validity of programme theory, particularly with regard to the identification of criminogenic needs (cf. Hanson & Wallace-Capretta, 2000). Most notably, all the studies failed to include a control group – that is, an untreated comparison group of offenders matched to those in treatment. As a consequence, it is not possible to ascertain if the in-treatment change identified resulted from the treatment explicitly, or to other non-treatment factors. This is of particular concern for the studies that did not also include some form of behavioural outcome measure. Whilst there is clear evidence for reliable change across a range of psychological traits and offender populations, it is possible that other non-treatment factors contributed to this change (Nunes et al., 2011).

There are other considerations that may hamper the adoption of this methodology more widely. Firstly, the calculation of clinically significant and reliable change requires that evaluators understand the explicit theoretical premise upon which the programmes are based. Whilst accredited programmes in the United Kingdom afford evaluators this opportunity, it may be more difficult to specify these in other programmes, including those in the United Kingdom that are not part of the accreditation process. Even when the theoretical basis of programmes is clearly articulated, individual change analyses require that the measures used are of good quality and further that normative datasets are available (although test–re-test reliabilities and Cronbach's alphas may be used as substitutes; Jacobson et al., 1999). This means that measures should be both reliable and valid and conceptually matched to the theoretical basis of the programme being evaluated, thereby minimising measurement error. As Jacobson and Truax (1991) note, the cutoff score and the method of analysing individual-level change are only as good as the norms on which they are based.

Perhaps the greatest methodological challenge, however, comes from a feature of all good-quality evaluation studies, and that is the availability of large samples for whom some form of behavioural follow-up data are available. Only when such datasets become available will we be in a position to truly validate the clinical significance of individual change and embark on more nuanced analyses of offender subgroups for whom treatment appears to be either ineffective or indeed anti-therapeutic.

REFERENCES

Andrews, D. A., & Bonta, J. (2006). *Psychology of criminal conduct*. Cincinnati, OH: Anderson Publishing.

Astbury, B. (this volume). Using theory in criminal justice evaluation. In E. Bowen & S. Brown (Eds.), *Perspectives on evaluating criminal justice and corrections*. Advances in Program Evaluation (Vol. 13). Bingley, UK: Emerald Group Publishing.

Barnett, G. D. (2011). What is grievance thinking and how can we measure this in sexual offenders? *Legal and Criminological Psychology*, *16*, 37–61.

Battle, J. (1992). *Culture-free self-esteem inventories: Examiner's manual*. Austin, TX: Pro-Ed.

Bauer, S., Lambert, M. J., & Nielsen, S. L. (2004). Clinical significance methods: A comparison of statistical techniques. *Journal of Personality Assessment*, *82*, 60–70.

Beckett, R. C. (1987). *The children and sex questionnaire*. Unpublished Manual.

Beckett, R. C., & Fisher, D. (1994). *Assessing victim empathy: A new measure*. Paper presented at the 13th Annual Conference of the Association for the Treatment of Sexual Abusers, San Francisco, CA, November.

Beech, A. R., Fisher, D. D., & Beckett, R. C. (1999). *An evaluation of the prison sex offender treatment programme: UK home office occasional report*. London: Home Office.

Beech, A. R., & Ford, H. (2006). The relationship between risk, deviance, treatment outcome and sexual reconviction in a sample of child sexual abusers completing residential treatment for their offending. *Psychology, Crime & Law*, *12*, 685–701. doi:10.1080/10683160600558493

Beech, A. R., & Hamilton-Giachritsis, C. (2005). Relationship between therapeutic climate and treatment outcome in group-based sexual offender treatment program. *Sexual Abuse: A Journal of Research and Treatment*, *17*, 127–140.

Bowen, E. (2010). The association between therapeutic environment and outcomes in a U.K domestic violence perpetrator program. *Small Group Research*, *41*, 198–220.

Bowen, E. (2011). *The rehabilitation of partner-violent men*. Chichester: Wiley-Blackwell.

Bowen, E., & Gilchrist, E. A. (2004). Comprehensive evaluation: A holistic approach to evaluating domestic violence offender programs. *International Journal of Offender Therapy and Comparative Criminology*, *48*(2), 215–234.

Bowen, E., Gilchrist, E. A., & Beech, A. R. (2008). Change in treatment has no relationship with subsequent re-offending in U.K. domestic violence sample: A preliminary study. *International Journal of Offender Therapy and Comparative Criminology*, *52*, 598–614.

Bumby, K. M. (1996). Assessing the cognitive distortions of child molesters and rapists: Development and validation of the MOLEST and RAPE scales. *Sexual Abuse: A Journal of Research and Treatment*, *8*, 37–54.

Caine, T. M., Fould, G. A., & Hope, K. (1967). *Manual of the hostility-direction of hostility questionnaire*. London: London University Press.

Caprara, G. V. (1986). Indicators of aggression: The dissipation-rumination scale. *Personality and Individual Differences*, *7*, 763–769.

Christensen, I., & Mendoza, J. I. (1986). A method of addressing change in a single subject: An alteration of the RC index. *Behavior Therapy*, *17*, 305–308.

Darke, S., Ward, J., Hall, W., Heather, N., & Wodak, A. (1991). *The opiate treatment index (OTI) manual*. Technical Report No. 11, National Drug and Alcohol Research Centre, Sydney.

Davis, M. H. (1983). Measuring individual differences in empathy: Evidence for a multiple dimensional approach. *Journal of Personality and Social Psychology*, *44*, 113–120.

Derogatis, L. R. (1993). *Brief symptom inventory: Administration, scoring and procedures manual* (4th ed.). Minneapolis, MN: National Computer Systems.

Evans, C., Connell, J., Barkham, M., Margison, F., McGrath, G., Mellor-Clark, J., & Audin, K. (2002). Towards a standardised brief outcome measure: Psychometric properties and utility of the CORE-OM. *British Journal of Psychiatry*, *180*, 51–60.

Eysenck, H. J., & Eysenck, S. B. G. (1991). *Eysenck personality scales (EPX adult)*. London: Hodder & Stoughton.

Freedman, B. J., Rosenthal, L., Donahoe, C. P., Sclundt, D. G., & McFall, R. M. (1978). A social-behavioural analysis of skill deficits in delinquent and non-delinquent adolescent boys. *Journal of Consulting and Clinical Psychology*, *46*, 1448–1462.

Friendship, C., Falshaw, L., & Beech, A. R. (2003). Measuring the real impact of accredited offending behaviour programmes. *Legal and Criminological Psychology*, *8*, 115–127.

Greeven, P. G. J., & de Ruiter, C. (2004). Personality disorders in a Dutch forensic psychiatric sample: Changes with treatment. *Criminal Behaviour and Mental Health*, *14*, 280–290.

Hanson, R. K., & Thornton, D. (1999). *Static 99: Improving actuarial risk assessment for sex offenders*. User Report No. 99-02. Corrections Research, Department of the Solicitor General of Canada, Ottawa, ON.

Hanson, R. K., & Wallace-Capretta, S. (2000). *Predicting recidivism among male batterers*. Ottawa, Canada: Department of the Solicitor General.

Hirschfield, R. M. A., Klerman, G. L., Gough, H. G., Barrett, J., Krodin, S. J., & Chodoff, P. (1977). A measure of interpersonal dependency. *Journal of Personality Assessment*, *41*, 610–618.

HM Prison Service. (2004). *Correctional Services Accreditation Panel. Prison Service Order 4360*. London: HM Prison Service.

Hollin, C. R., & Palmer, E. J. (2006). Offending behaviour programmes: History and development. In C. R. Hollin & E. J. Palmer (Eds.), *Offending behaviour programmes: Development, application and controversies* (pp. 1–32). Chichester: Wiley.

Huss, M. T., & Ralstone, A. (2008). Do batterer subtypes actually matter? Treatment completion, treatment response and recidivism across a batterer typology. *Criminal Justice and Behavior*, *35*, 710–724. doi:10.1177/0093854808316218

Hyler, S. E., & Rieder, R. O. (1987). *Personality disorder questionnaire-revised*. New York, NY: New York State Psychiatric Institution.

Jacobson, N. S., Follette, W. C., & Revestorf, D. (1984). Psychotherapy outcome research: Methods for reporting variability and evaluating clinical significance. *Behavior Therapy*, *15*, 36–352.

Jacobson, N. S., & Revenstorf, D. (1988). Statistics for assessing the clinical significance of psychotherapy techniques: Issues, problems, and new developments. *Behavioral Assessment*, *10*, 133–145.

Jacobson, N. S., Roberts, L. J., Berns, S. B., & McGlinchey, J. B. (1999). Methods for detecting and determining the clinical significance of treatment effects: Description, application and alternatives. *Journal of Consulting and Clinical Psychology*, *67*, 300–307.

Jacobson, N. S., & Truax, P. (1991). Clinical significance: A statistical approach to defining meaningful change in psychotherapy research. *Journal of Consulting and Clinical Psychology*, *59*, 12–19.

Kazdin, A. E. (1999). The meanings and measurement of clinical significance. *Journal of Consulting and Clinical Psychology*, *67*, 332–339.

Keltner, A. A., Marshall, P. G., & Marshall, W. L. (1981). Measurement and correlation of assertiveness and social fear in a prison population. *Corrective and Social Psychiatry*, *27*, 41–47.

Kendall, P. C., Marrs-Garcia, A., Nath, S. R., & Sheldrick, R. C. (1999). Normative comparisons for the evaluation of clinical significance. *Journal of Consulting and Clinical Psychology*, *67*, 285–299.

Levenson, H. (1974). Activism and powerful others: Distinctions within the concept of internal-external control. *Journal of Personality Assessment*, *38*, 377–383.

Lovibond, S. H., & Lovibond, P. F. (1995). *Manual for the depression anxiety stress scales* (2nd ed.). Sydney: Psychology Foundation.

Mandeville-Norden, R., Beech, A. R., & Hayes, E. (2008). Examining the effectiveness of a UK community-based sexual offender treatment programme for child abusers. *Psychology, Crime & Law*, *14*, 493–512.

Mann, R. E. (2005). *An investigation of the nature, content and influence of schema in sexual offending*. Unpublished PhD thesis, University of Leicester, England.

Mark, M. M., Henry, G. T., & Julnes, G. (1999). Towards an integrative framework for evaluation practice. *American Journal of Evaluation*, *20*, 177–198.

McConnaughy, E. A., Prochaska, J. O., & Velicer, W. F. (1983). Stages of change in psychotherapy: Measurement and sample profiles. *Psychotherapy: Theory, Research and Practice*, *20*, 368–375.

McGlinchey, J. B., Atkins, D. C., & Jacobson, N. S. (2002). Clinical significance methods: Which one to use and how useful are they? *Behavior Therapy*, *33*, 529–550.

McGuire, J. (Ed.). (1995). *What works: Reducing reoffending*. Chichester: Wiley.

Miller, R. S., & Lefcourt, H. M. (1982). The assessment of social intimacy. *Journal of Personality Assessment*, *46*, 514–518.

Moos, R. H. (1986). *Group environment scale manual*. Palo Alto, CA: Consulting Psychologists Press.

Moos, R. H. (1994). *Group environment scale manual: Development, applications and research* (3rd ed.). Mountain View, CA: Consulting Psychologists Press.

Nolan, J., & Thompson, A. P. (2009). Psychological change in voluntary and legally coerced clients of a residential drug and alcohol treatment programme. *Psychiatry, Psychology and Law*, *16*, 458–472.

Novaco, R. W. (1994). Anger as a risk factor for violence among the mentally disordered. In J. Monahan & H. Steadman (Eds.), *Violence and mental disorder: Developments in risk assessment* (pp. 1–60). Chicago, IL: University of Chicago Press.

Nowicki, S., & Duke, M. P. (1976). *Adult Nowicki-Strickland Internal-External Lcus of Control*. Test manual. Unpublished manual. Emory University.

Nunes, K. L., Babchishin, K. M., & Cortoni, F. (2011). Measuring treatment change in sex offenders: Clinical and statistical significance. *Criminal Justice and Behavior*, *38*, 157–173.

Ogles, B. M., Lunnen, K. M., & Bonesteel, K. (2001). Clinical significance: History, application and current practice. *Clinical Psychology Review*, *21*, 421–446.

Pawson, R., & Tilley, N. (1997). *Realistic evaluation*. London: Sage.

Russell, D., Peplau, L. A., & Cutrona, C. A. (1980). The revised UCLA loneliness scale: Concurrent and discriminant validity evidence. *Journal of Personality and Social Psychology*, *39*, 472–780.

Saunders, D. G., Lynch, A. B., Grayson, M., & Linz, D. (1987). The inventory of beliefs about wife beating: The construction and initial validation of a measure of beliefs and attitudes. *Violence and Victims*, *2*, 39–57.

Shuker, R., & Newton, M. (2008). Treatment outcome following intervention in a prison-based therapeutic community: A study of the relationship between reduction in criminogenic risk and improved psychological well-being. *British Journal of Forensic Practice*, *10*, 33–44.

Smith, D. (this volume). Arguments about methods in criminal justice evaluation. In E. Bowen & S. Brown (Eds.), *Perspectives on evaluating criminal justice and corrections*. Advances in Program Evaluation (Vol. 13). Bingley, UK: Emerald Group Publishing.

Speer, D. C. (1999). What is the role of two-wave designs in clinical research? Comment on Hageman and Arrindell. *Behaviour Research and Therapy*, *37*, 1203–1210.

Tapp, J., Fellowes, E., Wallis, N., Blud, L., & Moore, E. (2009). An evaluation of the Enhanced Thinking Skills (ETS) programme with mentally disordered offenders in a high security hospital. *Legal and Criminological Psychology*, *14*, 201–212.

Thornton, D., Beech, A. R., & Marshall, W. L. (2004). Pretreatment self-esteem and posttreatment sexual recidivism. *International Journal of Offender Therapy and Comparative Criminology*, *48*, 587–599.

Tweed, R. G., & Dutton, D. G. (1998). A comparison of impulsive and instrumental subgroups of batterers. *Violence and Victims*, *13*, 217–231.

Walters, G. D. (1995). The psychological inventory of criminal thinking styles. Part 1: reliability and preliminary validity. *Criminal Justice and Behavior*, *22*, 307–325.

Webster, S. D., Mann, R. E., Thornton, D., & Wakeling, H. C. (2006). Further validation of the short self-esteem scale with sex offenders. *Legal and Criminological Psychology*, *12*, 207–216.

Weiss, C. H. (1997). How can theory-based evaluation make greater headway? *Evaluation Review*, *21*, 501–524.

Wise, E. A. (2004). Methods for analyzing psychotherapy outcomes: A review of clinical significance, reliable change, and recommendations for future directions. *Journal of Personality Assessment*, *82*, 50–59.

PROPENSITY SCORE ANALYSIS

Sarah Brown

ABSTRACT

In the evaluation of most interventions in criminal justice settings, evaluators have no control over assignment to treatment and control/comparison conditions, which means that the treated and comparison groups may have differences that lead to biased conclusions regarding treatment effectiveness. Propensity score analysis can be used to balance the differences in the groups, which can be used in a number of ways to reduce biased conclusions regarding effectiveness. A review of propensity scoring studies was conducted for this chapter, where the limited number of evaluations of criminal justice interventions using these methods was identified. Due to the small number of these studies, research was also reviewed if propensity scoring had been employed to evaluate interventions that are similar to those in criminal justice systems. These studies are used as examples to demonstrate how the methods can be used to evaluate criminal justice interventions, the different ways propensity scores can be used to analyse treatment and comparison group differences, and the strengths and limitations of this approach. It is concluded that, while not appropriate for all interventions/settings, propensity score analysis can be useful in criminal justice arenas, at least to investigate the comparability of treatment and comparison groups, with suspected non-comparability being a common weakness of traditional quasi-experimental studies and

Perspectives on Evaluating Criminal Justice and Corrections
Advances in Program Evaluation, Volume 13, 173–198

ISSN: 1474-7863/doi:10.1108/S1474-7863(2012)0000013012

frequently cited limitation in terms of drawing efficacy conclusions from such evaluations.

INTRODUCTION

Propensity scoring was developed by Rosenbaum and Rubin (1983), and propensity score methods are becoming standard techniques for controlling confounding variables in medicine and epidemiology (Brookhart et al., 2006). In the evaluation of many interventions, and most interventions in criminal justice settings, evaluators have no control over assignment to treatment and control/comparison conditions. This means that the treated and comparison groups may have differences that lead to biased conclusions regarding treatment effectiveness. Propensity scores can be used to balance the differences in the groups, which can be used in a number of ways to reduce biased conclusions regarding effectiveness. These methods involve collecting data on a range of variables that could be argued to be related to assignment to treatment and/or treatment outcome. These data are used to develop a model of 'assignment to treatment', which is employed to allocate each participant a propensity score. These scores can then be used in a range of ways to evaluate treatment outcome, as will be discussed in more detail below. These methods are less commonly used in criminal justice evaluations and for evaluations outwith the medical context, though they have been used more frequently in recent years.

A review of propensity scoring studies was conducted for this chapter.[1] Evaluations of criminal justice interventions using these methods were identified. Due to the small number of these studies (Berk & Newton, 1985; Berk, Newton, & Berk, 1986; Jones, D'Agostino, Gondolf, & Heckert, 2004), research was also reviewed if these methods had been employed to evaluate interventions that are similar to those in criminal justice systems (e.g. foster care, alcoholics anonymous), or targeted similar populations (at risk children, mothers) to criminal justice populations, and/or have a similar format to criminal justice interventions (welfare-to-work programmes). These studies were included as such interventions have similar problems/ difficulties employing randomised treatment control designs (for a more detailed discussion, see Chapters 3 and 4, this volume). These studies, which are discussed in more detail below, revealed that propensity scoring methods are more frequently used in the United States than elsewhere: all but one of the evaluation studies reviewed for this chapter were based in the United States, with the other based in Jamaica.

THE USE OF PROPENSITY SCORING FOR THE EVALUATION OF INTERVENTIONS

The propensity score is 'the conditional probability of assignment to a particular treatment given a vector of observed covariates'(Rosenbaum & Rubin, 1983, p. 41), that is, it is the 'conditional probability that a person will be in one condition rather than in another (e.g. get a treatment rather than be in the control group) given a set of observed covariates used to predict the person's condition' (Luellen, Shadish, & Clark, 2005, p. 531). Estimation of propensity scores using a range of variables allows researchers to assess the differences between treatment and comparison groups and to control for these, and/or balance them in statistical comparisons, avoiding, or reducing, the problems of non-equal groups that plague traditional quasi-experimental methods (which have been discussed in Chapters 3 and 4 in this volume and so will not be repeated here). The method also has the advantage over traditional methods in that factors associated with 'selection' to treatment can be identified (assuming appropriate variables are measured) and the impact of treatment on groups of participants with different levels of these variables (i.e. different propensities for treatment) can be established. Thus, additional information that can be useful in the consideration of who benefits from treatment, where resources should be targeted, etc., can be generated over and above the usual 'does it work?' assessment.

Propensity scoring provides a statistical method of matching treatment and comparison participants on a large number of variables. All known and measurable confound variables (e.g. motivation to change, distance from intervention, ethnicity, age, support network) where data can be collected for all offenders in the treatment and comparison groups can be used and there is no restriction – methodologically or practically – on the number of variables that can be used. Ye and Kaskutas (2009) explain that using large numbers of variables can be included in this method without compromising statistical power: usually large sample sizes are required to avoid Type II errors (failing to detect true differences) when a large number of predictor variables are included in regression analyses (which are used to estimate propensity scores). However, because variables are not being used as individual independent variables in propensity scoring methods, a large number of variables can be included in the computation of propensity scores without Type II errors/statistical power being a concern. This means that this method can be used to improve the methodological rigour of evaluations where random allocation to treatment and control groups is not possible but where data can be identified/measured for treatment and comparison groups (it is possible to use this method prospectively and retrospectively).

According to the Maryland Scale of Scientific Rigor (Sherman et al., 1997), methodological designs that apply procedures such as participant matching or statistical control to ensure equivalence between treatment and comparison groups are assigned the second highest score (4) on the scale (the highest score of 5 being awarded for uncompromised randomised control trials). Designs where offenders are incidentally assigned to treatment and non-treatment but where equivalence between the two groups can be assumed, for example when equivalence on a range of variables between the two groups can be statistically demonstrated, are assigned a score of 3. The more common but less methodologically rigorous method of using comparison groups where equivalence cannot be assumed is given a score of 2, and such studies routinely face criticism for not being able to demonstrate if it was the treatment/intervention being evaluated that caused any identified differences between treatment and comparison groups, or some other variable such as selection to treatment. The use of propensity scoring methods, therefore, can allow researchers to take a treatment and comparison quasi-experimental design (score of 2), and by demonstrating that the groups are equivalent raise the rigour score to 3; or use the propensity scores to match participants and increase the rigour score to 4. If more criminal justice evaluations were able to employ such designs, some of the debate around the effectiveness of interventions could perhaps be reduced.

In traditional matching designs, only a small number of variables are included and these tend to be demographic variables (age, race, sex, etc., that may have little relationship with assignment to treatment and/or treatment outcome). Moreover, it is extremely difficult to find matched pairs of participants on more than a couple of variables, or in order to find 'matches', they are made within 'bands' of a variable (no offences, 1–5 offences, 6+ offences, for example), rather than the exact values of the variable, which reduces the effectiveness of using a matched design. Nicholaichuk, Gordon, Gu, and Wong (2000) in their evaluation of a sex offender treatment programme, for example, were able to match only 283 offenders from a total sample of 2,600; and although offenders were only matched on age at index offence, date of index offence and prior criminal history, the researchers had difficulty in matching such that treated offenders often had more previous convictions than 'matched' offenders. Similarly, Looman, Abracen, and Nicholaichuk (2000) could not find matches for 63 offenders in their study leaving a sample of 89 matched offenders and previous criminal convictions were matched at a plus or minus 2 level. Propensity scoring allows these and other variables to be combined into a single variable, which can then be used to match treatment and comparison participants. Rosenbaum and Rubin (1983) show that individuals with the same propensity scores also have the same distribution of the full set of covariates: hence, matching can be performed using the propensity scores only, which is simpler than trying to match a number of variables – although calculating the propensity score is quite complex. Propensity scoring methods if employed well, then, can be more similar to a randomised control study than a traditional matched design, and given the difficulties in criminal justice settings of employing uncompromised randomisation methods (see Chapters 4 to 6, this volume), it might actually be preferable.

In comparison to more traditional methods of matching, the propensity score method has a number of advantages: it does not necessarily lead to a large reduction in the number of offenders that can be matched; matching can be done using a large number of variables; and because data is collected throughout the study and matching is done statistically at the end of the study, there is no requirement for lengthy analysis and selection procedures to identify matched comparison offenders to include in the study. As Jones et al. (2004) discuss, there is some evidence to suggest that propensity scores have superiority over other quasi-experimental methods (e.g. Dehejia & Wahba, 1999). Though there is some debate about this (see Smith & Todd, 2001), the key factor seems to be the number of variables and appropriateness of the variables employed to formulate the propensity scores. Jones et al. (2004, p. 1004) conclude that 'Rich data sets that contain information about previous outcomes as well as contemporaneous risk factors are … good candidates for this method.'

These methods, as all methods, are not 'perfect'. In assessments of the method, propensity scoring is most commonly compared to randomised control trials. The key issue is that it is not possible to identify (some variables may simply be unknown) and measure all variables that are linked to treatment selection, self-selection and treatment success, and some researchers may include a small number of variables that will limit the robustness of studies. Including large numbers of variables is likely to be dependent on a range of factors, such as the data available for use, the resources available for the study and the support of relevant groups/organisations. It is likely that it will be more difficult to collect data for non-treatment participants, though this depends on the dataset being used and whether existing datasets are being taken advantage of to evaluate an intervention, or whether data is being generated to conduct an evaluation. It is always possible, therefore, that some variables have not been taken into account and the groups are not as equal as randomisation to treatment and non-treatment groups should allow.

Randomised control studies do not always produce equal groups, however, as discussed elsewhere in this volume (see Chapter 4, this volume). In a school-based intervention in Jamaica (Lockheed, Harris, & Jayasundera, 2010), for example, programme schools (i.e. the treated schools) had larger numbers of children, perhaps because parents were more likely to choose schools that had been identified for inclusion in the project: a problem likely to occur in other randomised studies where it is possible to identify where the treatment has been assigned. When it is possible to identify that participants have not been allocated to treatment, and in criminal justice settings it is difficult to see how people could be allocated to a no-treatment condition and not recognise this (i.e. it is extremely difficult to create placebo treatments/interventions), the participants themselves and/or their 'supporters' (e.g. criminal justice staff/families) may seek the intervention, or a similar or replacement interventions, which means the no-treatment condition is 'contaminated'. In criminal justice settings, 'no-treatment' rarely means no treatment is provided and is often 'treatment as normal', which could include a variety of measures and variation within this group that also limits the reliability and validity of randomised designs. In addition, treatment can vary in the treatment conditions, which means that treated participants do not all get a 'uniform' treatment that is the basis of the robustness of randomised control designs. Comparing propensity scoring to randomised control trials where randomised control trials are not possible, or are likely to be compromised, then, is rather moot.

Compared to the treatment/comparison group quasi-experimental studies that are so frequently employed in criminal justice arenas, the use of propensity scoring should improve the robustness of the study, as discussed above. It could be argued that even if the number of variables included in the calculation of the propensity score model is not 'ideal', or as planned, it is better to do some assessment of the groups using this method, as the similarity of the groups can be tested. Dehejia and Wahba (1999, p. 1053) argue that propensity score methods 'quickly reveal the extent of overlap in the treatment and comparison groups in terms of preintervention variables'. This may reveal that the groups are too dissimilar to render comparison inappropriate or unreliable; or statistical adjustments can be made to statistical comparisons of group difference to take account of the dissimilarities in the groups. It is this potential dissimilarity in treatment and comparison groups that is the most often cited criticism of treatment/comparison group studies, and propensity score analysis would at least allow researchers to identify the extent to which this criticism is valid in their evaluations. Ye and Kaskutas (2009), for example, clearly demonstrated in their study that there were significant differences between Alcoholics Anonymous (AA) attenders and non-attenders on variables likely to be linked to treatment outcome (readiness to change, motivation, support, etc.) and when AA attenders and non-attenders were compared without adjustment for this, AA effectiveness was exaggerated. Similar findings are likely to be found in many criminal justice evaluations.

In an interesting paper, Falconer, Clark, and Parris (2011) used two methods, a 'traditional' multiple variable covariate adjustment (though this is rare in criminal justice evaluations) and propensity scoring to make statistical adjustments to quasi-experimental treatment and comparison groups in an evaluation of the Health Families Florida programme. The researchers argued that both methods were effective in reducing selection bias provided that the covariates selected sufficiently account for that bias. Slightly different results were observed across the different methods used and models generated throughout the study, and it is difficult to identify which results should be used/reported, as no one method was clearly superior. This will be problematic for funders/policymarkers, etc., who need clear results regarding the effectiveness of interventions.

STUDIES USING PROPENSITY SCORING METHODS

In their 1983 paper, Rosenbaum and Rubin showed that the propensity score is sufficient to remove bias from observed covariates. In their 1984 paper they explained the use of propensity score stratification and in 1985, propensity score matching; both of which reduced bias and allowed treatment effects to be adjusted with the propensity scores taken into account. Others then developed the method further (e.g. Dehejia & Wahba, 2002) and published papers giving more information on the selection of variables to include in the computation of propensity scores (Brookhart et al., 2009) and providing a 'tutorial' of the method (D'Agostino, 1998). This has led to an increase in the use of the method, though it is not common in non-medical/clinical research. A range of studies that have used propensity scoring methods are outlined below to provide examples of how the method has been used to evaluate a variety of interventions.

Ye and Kaskutas (2009) used propensity scoring to consider the effectiveness of attending AA on drinking abstinence. The paper clearly explains the issue of self-selection bias that would also be applicable to many criminal justice interventions, which would also have other selection biases to consider. It also provides a good explanation of the use of propensity scoring to both match and stratify participants. So, although the paper does not describe an evaluation of a criminal justice intervention, it is a good paper to read to understand how the use of propensity scoring can address some of the selection and group-difference issues of quasi-experimental studies, which is of relevance to criminal justice evaluations. Randomised control trials are difficult in the evaluation of AA as participants randomised to no treatment, can easily still attend AA groups that are readily accessible in the local community and as discussed elsewhere in this book (Chapters 3 and 4, this volume), randomisation to treatment and no treatment can be difficult, and some would argue unethical, in criminal justice settings. In their evaluation of AA, Ye and Kaskutas considered factors including motivation to change, pressure to seek treatment, problem severity, help-seeking behaviours, extent of social support network, social network pressures to drink and demographic characteristics, all of which would be relevant to many criminal justice evaluations. In total 21 potential confounders were included in the computation of the propensity scores.

Ye and Kaskutas concluded that AA is effective in increasing abstinence, though the difference between AA attenders' and non-attenders' levels of abstinence was less pronounced following propensity score adjusted analyses, demonstrating that 'self-selection' factors are important factors in drinking abstinence, and which may have inflated the effects of AA in studies that simply compared AA attenders and non-attenders using traditional quasi-experimental techniques. More importantly, perhaps, the use of propensity scoring, particularly the stratification method (see below for more detail on this method), allowed the researchers to identify that AA attendance was most effective in participants who had a lower propensity to attend AA. Although initially this may seem counter-intuitive, it is easy to understand on the basis that those who have a high propensity to attend, who do not actually attend, also have many factors that would support and encourage abstinence without the support of AA; that is, the difference that AA adds is less great for participants with a propensity to attend (e.g. they have more motivation to change, greater social support, etc.). Conversely, to participants with limited propensity to attend, AA provides the greatest benefit and might explain why a treatment intended to help participants engage with AA has also reported positive effects (Project MATCH Research Group, 1997; Timko & Debenedetti, 2007; both cited in Ye & Kaskutas, 2009). The approach also identified factors associated with AA attendance, such as age and marital status, which may help to target resources more effectively and/or encourage attendance in other participants, which could help to maximise the benefit of the intervention. Such findings would be relevant in criminal justice evaluations and would help identify more clearly for whom the interventions work and perhaps why; something that is not easily answered by traditional evaluation designs, nor often addressed in criminal justice evaluations, where the focus has just tended to be on whether the intervention works or not, as discussed elsewhere in this book.

Berzin (2010) explained why propensity scoring is an appropriate method to establish if youths who experience foster care have different outcomes to other youths (in the United States). Like many criminal justice interventions, random allocation to foster care is not possible. Furthermore, in the way that individuals are assessed/selected/assigned to criminal justice interventions based on the practices of the relevant practitioners/organisations, so there are practice decisions that affect whether youths are deemed to be suitable for foster care and presumably also resource and availability issues that would also be similar to many criminal justice interventions. Berzin (2010) argued that many studies of foster care outcome are problematic as children who are placed in foster care have many factors (e.g. poor parenting, abuse/neglect, poverty) that are associated with negative long-term outcomes. When studies compare children who experience foster care with the broader population, it appears that foster care causes negative outcomes. Some studies have attempted to match foster care children with children who are more similar; however, traditional matching studies tend to use demographic information to match children, and/or a limited number of variables, such that the full range of factors that affect long-term outcomes are rarely considered.

In her 2010 paper, Berzin provides a clear explanation of propensity scoring and how it can be applied to a study of foster care, which would be a useful paper to read for those who wish to investigate this method further.

To assess the value of propensity scoring, Berzin used traditional matching methods using previous studies as a guide and matching on variables including gender, race, age, poverty, parents' education and presence of a stepparent and propensity scoring methods. The National Longitudinal Survey of Youth 1997 conducted by the Bureau of Labor Statistics in the United States was used as the dataset: hence, the study investigated foster care outcomes for the whole of the United States.

Berzin's (2010) analysis clearly demonstrated that the foster care and non-foster care groups generated by traditional matching methods had significant differences in post-matching. Foster and non-foster care groups matched using propensity scoring were very similar post-matching, that is there were no significant differences in the groups apart from the numbers of youths who had a stepparent, which suggests that this is a better method of matching, assuming the appropriate data are available. Groups matched using propensity scoring showed no difference in long-term outcomes, suggesting that foster care in itself is not the cause of the long-term negative effects, as had been suggested in previous studies. Interestingly, when the groups matched using traditional methods were compared, differences in outcomes were identified. In a further analysis of housing experiences, with a smaller sample of 133 foster care individuals, each matched to five non-foster individuals, Berzin, Rhodes, and Curtis (2011) identified that foster care individuals struggled more than their matches. They experienced higher rates of homelessness, had less housing stability, relied on public housing assistance and lived in poorer communities.

Berger, Bruch, Johnson, James, and Rubin (2009) investigated whether out-of-home placements had an impact on short-term cognitive and behavioural characteristics of 4–17-year-old children. They used a national (United States) sample of children investigated by child protection agencies (National Survey of Child and Adolescent Well Being, NSCAW Research Group, 2003), which was a sample of 5,501 children 14 years or younger who had been randomly selected from families who entered the US Child Welfare Service between October 1999 and December 2000. Out-of-home placements have the same issues for evaluators as foster care and so quasi-experimental and statistical methods have to be used to investigate the impact of these placements. To investigate the impact of methodological designs on conclusions regarding the impact of placements, Berger et al. employed a number of different statistical techniques using the entire sample of children (342 children who experienced out-of-home placements and 2,111 children who remained in the home) and a smaller sample matched using propensity scores. Berger et al.'s sample of matched children (308 children who had experienced an out-of-home placement and 308 matched comparison children) was larger than Berzin's sample that had experienced foster care.

Berger et al. argued that their matching models took account of a greater number of background factors than Berzin's study, though essentially, they replicated Berzin's findings. When comparisons were conducted using the entire sample, outcomes were different for the placement and non-placement children. However, no matter what post-matching analyses were conducted, no differences (cognitive or behavioural) were identified in the matched samples. This provides further evidence that selection factors have an impact on the findings of comparison group studies. The findings also suggest that placements do not add to the difficulties experienced by already vulnerable children, though they do not demonstrate a positive effect of out-of-home placements (aside from the protection from harm that the placement itself might generate) either.

The NSCAW data was also used by Casanueva, Martin, Runyan, Barth, and Bradley (2008) to investigate the impact of parenting service support provided to mothers. Selection criteria were applied to the entire sample, leaving 1,340 cases, of which 325 had missing data. This resulted in a sample of 1,015 mothers, of whom 360 had received parenting services. Two hundred and ninety-four of these women could be matched with women in the sample who had not received parenting services. The authors concluded that some benefits had been demonstrated as a result of the intervention (particularly for mothers of 3–5-year-old children, though the benefits were not found in multivariate analyses when other variables were controlled for) and that spanking was not affected by parenting services.

In a study more directly relevant to criminal justice, Chiu, Ryan, and Herz (2011) used the administrative records of families involved with the Department of Probation and Department of Children and Family Services in Los Angeles to investigate the differences between youths for whom allegations of maltreatment against them was either substantiated or unsubstantiated. Delinquency records of the youths were assessed. The samples sizes were particularly large: In 2002, 57,906 youths were associated with their first allegation of maltreatment in Los Angeles County who had no prior arrests. Of these 12,273 were substantiated and 25,950 were unsubstantiated (19,683 were deemed inconclusive). All of the substantiated cases were matched with unsubstantiated cases. Youths associated with substantiated allegations of maltreatment, compared to those associated with unsubstantiated allegations, were significantly more likely to be involved with the juvenile justice system, a consistent finding across all gender and racial groups.

In an evaluation that focuses on schools rather than individuals, Lockheed et al. (2010) used propensity score matching to create post hoc control groups to independently examine the impact of Jamaica's 'New Horizons for Primary Schools' improvement programme. This intervention included needs assessments and school improvement plans and Lockheed et al. did find that the 72 programme schools had greater support and higher levels of provision, though a high proportion of the non-programme schools also had this too. Children in programme schools did not perform significantly better, however, than children in the propensity score matched non-programme schools on school average ratings of literacy and numeracy.

The only study that could be identified that used propensity scoring to stratify treatment and comparison groups (none could be found that used propensity scoring to match treatment and comparison participants) in an evaluation of a criminal justice intervention was conducted by Jones et al. (2004). These researchers argued that the use of propensity scoring could address the intention to treat (ITT) problem associated with evaluations: that is that all those who started treatment are included in treatment group, no matter how much treatment they actually received, and compared with non-treated comparison groups. In some designs, treatment drop-outs may be excluded from the treatment group and then this group is difficult to include in conclusions regarding treatment effectiveness. In their analyses, Jones et al. sub-divided their sample into men who completed treatment for domestic violence and those who dropped-out of treatment and stratified the sample on the basis of propensity scores. They used data from three different batterer programmes located in three different regions of the United States. Batterers were a self-selected sample, though a significant proportion (78%) were mandated to attend the programme. Just over half the sample (54%) completed the total number of sessions of their programme. A range of variables were included in the propensity score computation, including age, race, education, employment, marital status, number of children, non-domestic violence arrest prior to intake, use of drugs, severe domestic violence prior to intake and partners' use of domestic violence services prior to intake.

In their analysis of 233 programme completers and 202 drop-outs stratified by propensity score into quintiles, Jones et al. found that at all but one propensity level, programme completers were less likely to re-assault their partners at 15-month follow-up compared to treatment drop-outs. Using this stratified analysis, Jones et al. were also able to show that the largest differences between completers and drop-outs were found in men who were less likely to complete the treatment (lowest propensity score groups). Overall, treatment completion reduced the probability of re-assault by 33%. Further analyses also revealed that men who did not have severe psychopathy were most likely to benefit from treatment completion; a finding that was replicated in respect of court ordered attendance: men ordered by the courts to complete treatment benefited from treatment completion more than men who entered programmes voluntarily. Based on these findings, Jones et al. recommended screening for psychopathy and more efforts to increase treatment compliance. In relation to the use of propensity scoring, they argued that it 'presents a more nuanced picture of programme effect' (Jones et al., 2004, p. 1017).

In the final two studies identified in this review, propensity scores were used in a different way to all the studies previously discussed. Rather than using propensity scores to stratify or match groups (see below), Berk and his colleagues used propensity scores as a covariate in analyses to investigate the impact of arrest (Berk & Newton, 1985) and shelters (Berk et al., 1986) on future intimate partner violence. This method was adopted as it was not possible to use the stratification method (see below for more details). Berk and Newton utilised a sample of 783 'wife-battery incidents' that were attended by California police officers between June 1981 and October 1983. Officers made arrests in 207 (26%) incidents. Variables were collected from police files and offence and arrest forms and 14 variables were included in the propensity score computation, including perpetrator's age, perpetrator's drinking, past convictions, victim injured, victim employed, victim called and victim drinking. Berk and Newton concluded that among individuals who were not arrested, those who otherwise would have been more likely to have been arrested (i.e. based on the propensity score variable), were more likely to be involved in a future repeat incident. An arrest, they argued, deterred prospective batterers and eliminated the relationship between probability of arrest and probability of new violence. Put another way, 'there is a general tendency for individuals with a greater likelihood of being arrested to commit battery again. However, an arrest somehow inoculates the higher-risk offender against new violence' (Berk & Newton, 1985, p. 259).

Berk et al. (1986) analysed data collected during 1982 and 1983 in Santa Barbara, California, where face-to-face interviews were conducted at two time points with 155 intimate partner violence victims. In this analysis, 24 variables were used in the calculation of the propensity scores including prior shelter stay, victim and perpetrator live together, victim's property damaged, arrest of perpetrator made, prior counselling for victim, number of prior calls made to the police, victim feels family will disapprove of shelter stay and victim feels shelter stay will do no good. Berk et al. concluded that shelters had a positive impact; however, this impact was influenced by attributes of the victim: 'When she [victim] is actively taking control of her life, a shelter stay can dramatically reduce the likelihood of new violence. Otherwise, shelters may have no impact or perhaps even trigger retaliation for disobedience' (Berk et al., 1986, p. 488).

USING PROPENSITY SCORING IN EVALUATIONS

The main reason for using propensity scores is to balance, or more evenly distribute the variables that are associated with treatment assignment in each of the groups being compared, or to take account of these variables in statistical analyses. When the propensity scores are balanced in these ways, statistical calculations allow section/treatment allocation biases to be reduced (Rosenbaum & Rubin, 1983, 1984, 1985). The first step, therefore, is to obtain a score that represents the likelihood of receiving the intervention, or being placed in the intervention group.

In randomised experiments, each person has a 50% chance of being in the treatment group (and 50% chance of being in the control group) and hence, the 'true' propensity score is known (Luellen et al., 2005). In non-randomisation trials, placement or selection to interventions, the 'true' propensity score, is unknown: instead, propensity is estimated using a number of variables (as can be seen below, the number and type of variables used varies enormously across studies). The probability of receiving treatment is likely to vary from 0.5 (50%). If receiving treatment is coded as '1' and being in the comparison group coded as '0', a propensity score higher than 0.5 means the person was more likely to receive treatment; while a propensity score lower than 0.5 means that the person is more likely to be in the comparison group (Luellen et al., 2005). As propensity scores are probabilities, scores will range from 0 to 1. Most commonly logistic regressions are employed to predict these probabilities (see Luellen et al., 2005 for further discussion and for other methods that can be used, such as classification trees), where treatment assignment is dummy coded as 0 or 1 and the observed variables are predictors. The quality of these calculations is clearly dependent on the selection of variables and the measurement of them. Rubin and Thomas (1996) suggested that all variables related to treatment outcome should be included in the estimation of the propensity score and this was supported by Brookhart et al. (2006). Luellen et al. (2005) argue that potential relevant covariates are ones that can be expected to affect treatment selection and outcome and that consultation with experts and pilot studies should be used to identify relevant variables.

In Casanueva et al.'s (2008) study, propensity scores were calculated using a logistic regression model that included the predictor variables of maternal age, maternal substance abuse, maternal depression, mother abuse as a child, inter-partner violence, education, race, marital status, family stress, poverty level, trouble paying for basic amenities, social support, type of maltreatment at baseline, child age, number of children, prior involvement with child protection services, having an open child protection case, and mother's level of cooperation with child protection services. The variables were selected based on predictors of service use identified from the literature. Ye and Kaskuta (2009) used 21 variables across six domains: self-motivation and external coercion, alcohol problem severity, help-seeking, social influences and demographic characteristics. Berzin (2010) included 24 variables within the domains of parent characteristics (e.g. substance abuse, mental health problems), child characteristics (e.g. emotional and behavioural problems, physical health and disabilities), family or home environment (e.g. homelessness, domestic violence or increased conflict) and neighbourhood or community (e.g. overcrowded neighbourhood, high unemployment rates). Berger et al. (2009) included child age, race and gender; caregiver age, marital status, education and nativity; grandparent presence; family income-to-poverty ratio and risk score; types of maltreatment alleged; whether initial report was substantiated; prior out-of-home placement; and child's baseline vocabulary, matrices and behaviour problems.

Falconer et al. (2011) used participant characteristics obtained at intake into the programme: age, race, marital status, education, number of children at intake and the Healthy Families Assessment Tool score that determined the risk of child abuse and neglect and programme eligibility. To calculate the propensity scores, these variables were regressed into a dichotomous variable indicating type of group and the predicted probabilities from the regression were transformed using a log linear function (Rubin, 2001, cited in Falconer et al., 2011). Lockheed et al. (2010) used four criteria that were initially used to place schools in the programme and four other characteristics of teachers and schools that were important and could be obtained from administrative data.

In the intimate partner violence studies, Jones et al. (2004) employed perpetrator's age, race, education, employment, marital status, use of drugs, use of alcohol and psychopathy; number of children living with perpetrator, age of youngest child, court ordered attendance at programme, at least one re-assault at 15 months, programme completion, non-domestic violence arrest prior to intake, partner-used domestic violence services prior to intake, severe domestic violence prior to intake, programme length and whether perpetrator believes he will be jailed if he drops out of treatment. Berk et al. (1986) used 24 variables outlined above, which were obtained from interviews with the victims, while Berk and Newton included 14 variables, as discussed above, that were coded from police files and forms. Each of these studies employed a logistic regression to generate the propensity score model. It is interesting to note that even when studies investigate interventions aimed at similar problems/people, the range of variables included in the propensity score calculations vary greatly, which makes comparisons between studies difficult and challenges the reliability and validity of this method.

The result of the propensity model is then used to compute a 'score' for each individual (school, etc.), which is then used as a new variable to balance the samples, adjust the group difference analyses. Berzin (2010) explained that there are four methods that can be used: weighting, stratifying, exact matching and nearest-neighbour matching (see also Dehejia & Wahba, 1997 who describe weighting, stratifying and matching).

Weighting

The first method involves using the propensity scores as a weight to estimate the value of the treatment effect, that is the weight controls for selection bias in the treatment group. This method is not commonly used, however (none of the studies reviewed here used this method), as the estimate of treatment effect is sensitive to bias in the estimation of the propensity score (Berzin, 2010). It is also not used when there is an unequal distribution of propensity scores across intervention and non-intervention groups, nor when the samples of participants in each group are dissimilar (*ibid.*).

Stratification

Stratification divides the combined sample (treatment and non-treatment) into equal groups based on the frequency distribution of the propensity scores (see Luellen et al., 2005, for a detailed explanation of this method and Jones et al. (2004) for a criminal justice application of this method).

Rosenbaum and Rubin (1984) argued that based on Cochran's (1968) results, 90% of the reduction in bias that could have been achieved by matching can be achieved when the sample is divided into five equal groups (quintiles), which is the number of groups most frequently used in studies using these stratification techniques. 'To oversimplify, the idea is that people who have the same propensity score but who choose to be in different experimental conditions are nonetheless comparable because the distributions of the covariates are in balance' (Luellen et al., 2005, p. 532). Like matching (as describe above), stratifying on a single variable is simpler than stratifying on many variables (*ibid.*).

Berzin (2010) points out, however, that this method is not suitable in all cases, as it requires each quintile to have a similar distribution to the full sample and the sample needs to be large enough that it can be split into five and still have sufficient numbers in each group for the group comparison analyses. Berk and Newton (1985) were not able to use this method, as there was not enough overlap in the propensity scores between those who had been arrested and those had not been arrested. In Berzin's study, foster youth were underrepresented in the lower quintiles and overrepresented in the highest. Furthermore, the numbers of foster care individuals in each quintile was small.

When this method can be used, however, Luellen et al. (2005) argued that it is easier to use than matching and almost as efficient (and less sensitive to the problems associated with co-variance or weighting methods). This method has advantages in that the impact of treatment to groups of individuals with differencing propensities to treatment can be examined, although it is less commonly used in the studies reviewed here. Ye and Kaskutas (2009), for example, sorted the predicted probabilities from the fitted logistic regression for the whole sample in order of increasing magnitude, and divided the sample into quintiles, such that predicted probability of AA attendance was lowest in the first group, through to highest in the fifth group. From this analysis, as discussed above, it was possible to identify that AA was most effective for people with a lower propensity to attend AA. Jones et al. (2004) found the same in relation to the effects of the completion of batterer programmes.

Matching

Exact matching relies on each subject in the treatment sample having an identical propensity score as a subject in the non-treatment group, which is rare, meaning that this method is rarely used (Berzin, 2010; Rosenbaum & Rubin, 1985). Most studies, therefore, use nearest-neighbour matching where each subject in the treatment group is matched to a non-treatment subject (and sometimes each non-treatment subject is matched to a treated subject) that has the closest propensity score (nearest-neighbour matching), or has a propensity score within a certain range (calliper matching). There are several methods of matching within these approaches: in some methods, the matched subjects are removed from the 'matching pool' once matched, so that subjects are only used once. In other methods, matched subjects are not removed and some subjects may be included many times in the matched pairs. Another difference occurs in the way the matches are selected: some methods select the closest match and other randomly select a match from the total number of matches that fall within a range of propensity scores (calliper). Rosenbaum and Rubin (1985) compared three matching methods and concluded that nearest-neighbour matching, which required less computation than the other methods, was 'fairly successful in reducing bias' (p. 38) and that a within calliper method (with callipers defined by the estimated propensity score) 'appeared superior ... with respect to balancing the covariates' (*ibid.*).

This group of methods is the most commonly used in the studies reviewed in this chapter, though, as can be seen below, each study has a slightly different approach, which can make comparison between studies difficult. Some researchers employed a number of methods to produce the matches and conducted analyses for group differences on all the pairs of groups generated by the different procedures. It is most common to match one subject from the treatment group with that of the comparison group, though Berzin (2010) matched each foster care individual with five non-foster care individuals.

Ye and Kaskutas (2009) used the logit form of the estimated probabilities from the fitted logistic regression and used the STATA user-written command PSMATCH2 (Leuven & Sianesi, 2003) to locate nearest available matches, with the maximum distance (known as the calliper) limited to 0.1. Rosenbaum and Rubin (1985) recommend using a calliper with a maximum of 20% of the standard deviation of the logit propensity scores of the combined treated and untreated groups. Ye and Kaskutas used a calliper that was 7% of this standard deviation and therefore expected to remove even more of the bias. They performed two different matching procedures: matching 282 AA attenders with 102 AA non-attenders (many non-attenders were matched to more than one attender); and, matching 209 non-AA attenders to 104 AA attenders (as before many of the attenders were matched to more than one non-attender). This method of not using 'replacements', or not eliminating participants from the matching pool once matched, means that some participants are matched to the same participants in the other group and that some participants feature more than others. As noted by Ye and Kaskutas, this may mean that the results were sensitive to the individuals who were used many times during the matching processes. It also means that the matched groups more closely resemble the 'starting' group: that is the first analysis included more AA attenders than the second procedure and as the best matches only are selected from the non-attender group, the combined group of attenders and matched non-attenders is more similar to the overall AA attender group. The converse applies to the second procedure and means that the results, when these groups are used to compare treatment, vary as demonstrated in this study.

Falconer et al. (2011) matched participants using a paired calliper matching procedure written in C+ + with the maximum distance being allowed between the matched values of each group restricted to ensure a 95% reduction in selection bias (Cochran & Rubin, 1973, p. 421). Similarly, Casanueva et al.'s study used an algorithm that identified the nearest match within a calliper of the propensity score (one quarter of the standard deviation of the logit of the propensity score) and selected at random a match if several controls had the same matching score.

Chiu et al. (2011) used STATA/PMATCH2 to conduct nearest-neighbour matching within calliper with no replacement. This method randomly orders the treatment and control participants. The first treated participant is matched with the comparison participant with the closest propensity score within a predetermined region called a calliper. Both these participants are then removed from the 'matching pool' and the next matched is identified and so on. The same software was used by Berzin (2010) to conduct nearest-neighbour matching with a calliper of 25% of the standard deviation, where five matches were identified for each individual ($n = 158$) in the treatment group.

Lockheed et al. (2010) created three groups based on the methods used to match schools, in one group, for example, 58 matches were made when some programme schools were matched with the same non-programme schools and in another group 71 matches were made when each programme school was matched to a unique comparison school.

Differences in techniques and use of more than one matching technique by some researchers means that comparison across studies can be difficult and that interpretation of results is difficult, as slightly different treatment effects and effects sizes are produced by each variation used. Matching requires subjects in both treatment and comparison groups to have a similar range of propensity scores. Where matches cannot be found, subjects are excluded from the analysis. This is an important point to note. If, for example, higher risk offenders are selected for an intervention and lower risk offenders are in the comparison group, then only the overlap of risk level will be included, that is the higher risk comparison group offenders and the lower risk treatment group offenders. While this ensures that the outcome of the intervention is being compared between more similar offenders, the outcome is only being assessed on offenders with mid levels of risk. The evaluation will not, therefore, be valid for treated offenders with high or low levels of risk (and whatever other factors are included in the propensity score computation). However, such non-equal groups would not produce valid results using other designs/methods and if the starting groups are very unequal, the numbers included in the analysis will be small, rendering propensity scoring impossible, or unreliable. It could be argued, however, that propensity scoring makes this issue clear and as long as researchers make this limitation clear in their discussions of their results, propensity scoring at least allows the intervention to be assessed for a sub-set of offenders.

Once treatment/intervention participants have been matched with non-intervention participants, or stratified, then conducting group comparison analyses is fairly straightforward. Essentially, the same methods are used as in group comparison analyses used on quasi-experimental designs. So although it is fairly complex to create propensity scores and to do matching, or stratifying, it becomes more straightforward to compare the resulting groups. Rosenbaum and Rubin (1984, 1985) argue that an advantage of matching and stratification techniques is that although the calculations of the propensity scoring is complex and difficult for non-statisticians to understand, it is easy for non-statisticians to understand the matched or stratified comparisons, which can be presented in simple graphs/charts for ease of communication.

Co-varying

In some instances, as in the studies conducted by Berk and Newton (1985) and Berk et al. (1986), matching and stratification by propensity score is not possible, due to the nature of the samples being investigated. In this instance, propensity scores can be used as a covariate in group comparisons, or as a variable in regression analyses. These analyses require more statistical expertise than group comparison procedures; though given that these are the same skills that are required to compute propensity scores, this is not likely to be a significant problem. The results of such studies, however, can be difficult to interpret and explain clearly to non-statisticians.

POTENTIAL LIMITATIONS OF PROPENSITY SCORING METHODS

As discussed above, this method is not perfect and will not be possible in some evaluations. Data for a large number of variables to compute good, reliable propensity scores is a necessity. Furthermore, large samples are required, though exactly how large samples should be is not clear (Luellen et al., 2005). These methods are not therefore appropriate to evaluate small-scale, single-delivery interventions. They are most useful for organisations that are able to collect data on a large number of programmes, perhaps across multi-sites and across many deliveries of a programme. This means that the specific factors that make each site, each programme team, treatment group, etc., unique are not investigated: a problem that is evidenced in many criminal justice intervention evaluation studies, as discussed in Chapter 4 in this book.

Furthermore, this method requires a comparison group, which can be difficult to find in criminal justice settings. It is difficult to find comparison groups when interventions are routine, for example. Most sex offenders are assessed for suitability for treatment in the United Kingdom and so offenders who do not complete treatment are not comparable to treated offenders and they are likely to be so different that propensity scoring will not be possible on all but a small sub-section of offenders, which would greatly limit the generalisability of the findings of such an evaluation. In Casanueva et al.'s (2008) study, the mean propensity score of mothers who had received the parenting services was 0.41, but 0.29 in the mothers who had received this service, which meant that there was no match for 66 mothers. After matching, means of the groups included in the analysis was 0.35. If there, genuinely, is a difference between the comparison and intervention groups, then propensity scoring will not be appropriate – which would also mean that a traditional quasi-comparison study would have serious limitations too.

Casanueva et al.'s (2008) study is also a good example of how, even with a large database of data (5,501 cases), only a proportion (588) might be included in the eventual analysis, in this instance the greatest reduction in the sample size was due to the limited number of mothers who had received the intervention being evaluated. Similarly, the dataset that Berzin (2010) used to assess foster care was also large with data on over 8,000 individuals; however, only 171 had a history of foster care and 158 were matched with non-foster care individuals. Sample size issues are, therefore, not avoided using this type of methodology, though these issues would be relevant to most types of methodology and would be present in traditional matching designs. In fact, attrition is one of the factors associated with randomised control trials and very large pools of people are needed at the start of the study, all assessed as being in need of the intervention and appropriate for it, before random allocation can begin. It is not uncommon for those assigned to a no-treatment condition to drop out of the study and/or to seek the intervention, or a similar intervention independently affecting the validity of the study. As can be seen by the selection of studies reviewed for this chapter, this method is easier in organisation/places where a lot of data is routinely collected on all, or where datasets collected for another purpose can be employed. Otherwise, it can be difficult to collect data on a sufficient number of variables for comparison participants.

Choosing variables to include in propensity score calculations is likely to be difficult. This should be done using theory (see Chapter 1, this volume) and the empirical evidence base, though when using datasets collected for other purposes, the variables included will be limited to the available data. In studies where data is generated for the analysis, the number of variables may be restricted for other reasons: cost, practicality, feasibility, time, resources, access, etc. It is also unclear exactly which method of calculating propensity scores produces the most accurate estimates of treatment effect (Luellen et al., 2005). All the studies discussed here took a slightly different approach and even studies on the same issue, for example domestic violence, selected a different array of variables.

It is argued that due to the variable selection problem, and the fact that even with unlimited resources, etc., it may not be possible to know/identify all the variables that should be included, the use of propensity scoring is never quite good as randomisation. Although 18 variables were included in the development of the propensity score, Casanueva et al. argued that 'the omission of some unmeasured variables affecting treatment assignment could have produced noncomparable groups' (p. 874). Chiu et al. (2011) noted that there were some variables that they were not able to include in their analyses: mental health or behaviour problems, family factors and neighbourhood factors. Ye and Kaskutas (2009) included 21 variables in their study but the potential influence of unobserved variables was noted and they identified some factors that had been empirically linked to drinking abstinence since the collection of their data that had not been included in the study. Berzin (2010) also noted this issue as a limitation and identified variables that could have had an influence on long-term outcome, parent substance abuse and incarceration, which could not be included in the propensity score computations as these were not recorded/collected in the original survey.

As has been noted in some of the studies discussed here (e.g. Casanueva et al., 2008; Lockheed et al., 2010), large datasets can be used to evaluate an intervention but this may mean that the 'intervention' is actually a range of interventions. Lockheed et al. noted the each school varied, which applied to both programme schools and non-programme schools and so the programme was not the same throughout the study. Casanueva et al. noted that a potential limitation of their study (and perhaps a reason for the limited findings of parenting service effectiveness) was the potential variation in the services provided to all women in the sample. Berzin (2010) also noted a similar issue as a potential weakness in her paper: a national dataset was used and it is likely that foster care practices/experiences varied across the United States. Moreover, the type of foster care placement, duration of the placement, numbers of placements, etc., all vary across individuals, so it is unlikely that individuals would have received the same 'treatment'. The issue of treatment/interventions in criminal justice setting not being uniform is discussed in this volume in Chapters 2 and 6 and elsewhere, and is a major difficulty in evaluating criminal justice evaluations where large sample sizes are needed.

A related issue is that propensity scoring works best when conducted using locally matched samples (Michalopoulos, Bloom, & Hill, 2004; cited in Berzin, 2010) and in many of the studies referenced in this chapter, individuals or schools were matched nationally. This limits the studies' abilities to take account of local/regional contexts and characteristics. Lockheed et al. also noted that the non-programme schools obtained some of the 'programme activities' via other funding methods and that enrolments had increased in the programme schools (perhaps due to parents choosing these schools). In the Casanueva et al. study it is presumably possible that some mothers in the comparison group received the services but that this was not recorded/noted, or that mothers not provided with the services, sought help/advice from elsewhere. This issue of confounds being 'added' throughout the duration of an evaluation due to differing reactions/responses to both treatment and non-treatment groups has also been discussed in relation to other evaluation designs: Propensity scoring does not necessarily resolve such issues.

CONCLUSIONS

Propensity scoring has hitherto been rarely used to evaluate criminal justice evaluations; yet, in some instances where appropriate data are available the use of propensity scoring may allow evaluators to identify the similarity and differences between their treatment and comparison groups and to assess the reliability and validity of their results based on this. Moreover, statistical procedures and analyses may allow for the control of these differences such that more reliable and valid conclusions regarding effectiveness can be drawn. Randomised control trails are rarely possible in criminal justice settings and propensity scoring may provide the means to improve the scientific rigour of evaluations based on traditional quasi-experiment treatment/comparison group designs.

Luellen et al. (2005, p. 549) argued that the findings from published studies 'suggest a degree of unpredictability to the use of propensity scores that should caution researchers against relying on the technique to routinely improve estimates from quasi-experiments', though it is not clear if this conclusion was in comparison to randomised control trials. As well as being potentially very useful when randomised designs are not possible, Berzin (2010, p. 109) pointed out that propensity scoring 'increases our understanding of group differences beyond what we can ascertain through simple matching. This adds richness to our understanding of the relationship between intervention and outcomes.' This richness is unlikely to be achieved in randomised trials, which tend to focus exclusively on whether the interventions are effective or not. Furthermore, as Dehejia and Wahba (1999) concluded: 'The methods we suggest [propensity scoring] are not relevant in all situations. There may be important unobservable covariates, for which the propensity score method cannot account. However, rather than giving up, or relying on assumptions about the unobserved variables, there is substantial reward in exploring first the information contained in the variables that *are* observed. In this regard, propensity score methods can offer both a diagnostic on the quality of the comparison group and a means to estimate the treatment impact.' (p. 1052, *emphasis in original*).

NOTE

1. This review was not exhaustive, or systematic. It was conducted to identify a range of studies that could be used to provide examples and explain the utility of the method. It is likely, therefore, that additional studies using propensity scoring methods to evaluate criminal justice interventions can be identified in the literature.

REFERENCES

Berger, L. M., Bruch, S. K., Johnson, E. I., James, S., & Rubin, D. (2009). Estimating the 'impact' of out-of-home placement on child well-being: Approaching the problem of selection bias. *Child Development*, *80*(6), 1856–1876.

Berk, R. A., & Newton, P. J. (1985). Does arrest really deter wife battery? An effort to replicate the findings of the Minneapolis Spouse Abuse Project. *American Sociological Review*, *50*, 253–262.

Berk, R. A., Newton, P. J., & Berk, S. F. (1986). What a difference a day makes: An empirical study of the impact of shelters for battered women. *Journal of Marriage and the Family*, *48*, 481–490.

Berzin, S. C. (2010). Understanding foster youth outcomes: Is propensity scoring better than traditional methods? *Social Work Practice*, *20*(1), 100–111.

Berzin, S. C., Rhodes, A. M., & Curtis, M. A. (2011). Housing experiences of former foster youth: How do they fare in comparison to other youth? *Children and Youth Servcies Review*, *33*, 2119–2126.

Brookhart, M. A., Schneeweiss, S., Rothman, K. J., Glynn, R. J., Avron, J., & Stürmer, T. (2006). Variable selection for propensity score models. *American Journal of Epidemiology*, *163*(12), 1149–1156.

Casanueva, C., Martin, S. L., Runyan, D. K., Barth, R. P., & Bradley, R. H. (2008). Parenting services for mothers involved with child protective srvices: Do they change maternal and spanking behaviors with children? *Children and Youth Services Review*, *30*, 861–878.

Chiu, Y.-L., Ryan, J. P., & Herz, D. C. (2011). Allegations of maltreatment and delinquency: Does risk of juvenile arrest vary substantiation status? *Children and Youth Services Review*, *33*, 855–860.

Cochran, W. G. (1968). The effectiveness of adjustment by sub-classification in removing bias in observational studies. *Biometrics*, *24*, 205–213.

Cochran, W. G., & Rubin, D. B. (1973). Controlling bias in observational studies: A review. *SankhyaR, Series A, Indian Journal of Statistics*, *35*, 417–446.

D'Agostino, R. B. (1998). Propensity score methods for bias reduction in the comparison of a treatment to a non-randomized control group. *Statistics in Medicine*, *17*, 2265–2281.

Dehejia, R. H., & Wahba, S. (1997). Causal effects in non-experimental studies: Reevaluating the evaluation of training programs. In R. Dehejia (Ed.), *Econometric Methods for Program Evaluation*. PhD Dissertation, Harvard University (Chapter 1). Retrieved from http://www.nber.org/~rdehejia/papers/pscore_thesis

Dehejia, R. H., & Wahba, S. (1999). Causal effects in non-experimental studies: Reevaluating the evaluation of training programs. *Journal of the American Statistics Association*, *94*, 1053–1062.

Falconer, M. K., Clark, M. H., & Parris, D. (2011). Validity in an evaluation of Healthy Families Florida – A program to prevent child abuse and neglect. *Children and Youth Services Review*, *33*, 66–77.

Jones, A. S., D'Agostino, R. B., Gondolf, E. W., & Heckert, A. (2004). Assessing the effect of batterer program completion on reassault using propensity scores. *Journal of Interpersonal Violence*, *19*, 1002–1020.

Leuven, E., & Sianesi, B. (2003). PSMATCH: Strata module to perform full mahalanobis and propensity score matching, common support graphing, and covariate imbalance testing. Retrieved from http://ideas.repec.org/c/boc/bocode/s432001.html

Lockheed, M., Harris, A., & Jayasundera, T.. (2010). School improvement plans and student learning in Jamaica. *International Journal of Educational Development, 30*, 54–66.

Looman, J., Abracen, J., & Nicholaichuk, T. P. (2000). Recidivism among treated sexual offenders and matched controls: Data from the Regional Treatment Centre (Ontario). *Journal of Interpersonal Violence, 15*(3), 279–290.

Luellen, J. K., Shadish, W. R., & Clare, M. H. (2005). Propensity scores: An introduction and experimental test. *Evaluation Review, 29*(6), 530–558.

Michalopoulos, C., Bloom, H. S., & Hill, C. J. (2004). Can propensity-score methods match the findings from a random assignment evaluation of mandatory welfare-to-work programs? *The Review of Economics and Statistics, 86*(1), 156–179.

Nicholaichuk, T., Gordon, A., Gu, D., & Wong, S. (2000). Outcome of an institutional sexual offender treatment program: A comparison between treated and matched untreated offenders. *Sexual Abuse: A Journal of Research and Treatment, 12*(2), 139–153.

NSCAW Research Group. (2003). *National survey of child and adolescent well being: The characteristics of children and families entering child welfare services*. Washington, DC: U.S. Department of Health and Human Services, Administration for Children and Families.

Project MATCH Research Group. (1997). Matching alcoholism treatment to client heterogeneity: Project MATCH posttreatment drinking outcomes. *Journal of Studies in Alcohol, 58*, 7–29.

Rosenbaum, P. R., & Rubin, D. B. (1983). The central role of the propensity score in observational studies for causal effects. *Biometrika, 70*, 41–55.

Rosenbaum, P. R., & Rubin, D. B. (1984). Reducing bias in observational studies using sub-classification on the propensity score. *Journal of the American Statistical Association, 79*, 516–524.

Rosenbaum, P. R., & Rubin, D. B. (1985). Constructing a control group using multivariate matched sampling methods that incorporate the propensity score. *American Statistician, 39*, 33–38.

Rubin, D. B., & Thomas, N. (1996). Matching using estimated propensity score: Relating theory to practice. *Biometrics, 52*, 249–264.

Sherman, L., Gottfredson, D., MacKensie, D., Eck, J., Reuter, P., & Bushway, S. (1997). *Preventing crime: What works, what doesn't, what's promising*. Report to the U.S. Congress, Washington, DC.

Smith, J. A., & Todd, P. E. (2001). Reconciling conflicting evidence on the performance of propensity score matching methods. *American Economic Review, 91*, 112–118.

Timko, C., & Debenedetti, A. (2007). A randomized controlled trail of intensive referral to 12-step self-help groups: One year outcomes. *Drug and Alcohol Dependence, 90*, 270–279.

Ye, Y., & Kaskutas, L. A. (2009). Using propensity scores to adjust for selection bias when assessing the effectiveness of Alcoholics Anonymous in observational studies. *Drug and Alcohol Dependence, 104*, 56–64.

DEVELOPING OFFENDER ENGAGEMENT: EVALUATING PROBATION TRUST PILOTS

Sue Rex, Elaine Ellis, Nigel Hosking and Wendy Hyett

ABSTRACT

The Offender Engagement Programme (OEP) within National Offender Management Service (NOMS) has been built on our collaborative approach with probation trusts to develop approaches which can support more effective offender engagement. Drawing areas of potential practice development from our early fieldwork and literature review, events for trusts and reference groups with practitioners and middle managers, we identified where more focussed work with trusts would develop learning and evidence which could be shared. In response to an invitation to express an interest, 22 trusts committed themselves to taking forward an OEP pilot, starting between March and May 2011. External evaluation is planned for nine trusts in total and is being undertaken by our research partners: a team from the Institute of Criminal Policy Research (ICPR) Birkbeck College London and Leicester University, and a team based at Sheffield University which includes Fergus McNeill from Glasgow University.

Perspectives on Evaluating Criminal Justice and Corrections
Advances in Program Evaluation, Volume 13, 199–209

ISSN: 1474-7863/doi:10.1108/S1474-7863(2012)0000013013

This chapter looks at how we implemented pilot work on approaches to involving offenders in Sentence Planning; Developing Effective Engagement Skills through training and continuous professional development; and a model for Reflective Supervision by senior and middle managers to support effective engagement. It also examines how the methodology for the external and internal evaluation was developed, and what we are hoping to get out of the evaluation. In short, the purpose of this work is to investigate and test the core proposition that the relationship between the offender and the practitioner can be a powerful means of changing behaviour.

INTRODUCTION

This chapter reports on our experience so far of working on the Offender Engagement Programme (OEP) in the National Offender Management Service (NOMS) in England and Wales. In taking the programme forward, we have adopted a collaborative approach with probation trusts to develop models that can support more effective offender engagement. Drawing areas of potential practice development from our early fieldwork and review of existing research, as well as extensive engagement with trusts, we identified where more focussed initiatives would develop learning and evidence, which could be shared through pilot work.

In response to an invitation to express an interest, 22 trusts committed themselves to taking forward an OEP pilot, and the pilots started between March and May 2011. External evaluation is now taking place in nine trusts in total, and we are also conducting an internal evaluation. The pilots will continue to the end of March 2012, and we will be receiving reports on the evaluation throughout 2012 and into 2013. At the mid-way point of the pilots, we review in this chapter the rationale for the programme, how we worked with staff in trusts to set up the pilots, how we established the evaluation and the early pilot experience.

DEVELOPING OFFENDER ENGAGEMENT – WHY A NEW PROGRAMME

The OEP is a three-year programme that started in early 2010 with the core purpose of improving the effectiveness of one-to-one engagement between the probation practitioner and the offender in order to reduce reoffending. The hypothesis on which the OEP is based is that the one-to-one relationship between the offender and the practitioner can be a powerful means of changing behaviour and therefore reducing reoffending. The aim of the programme, as well as reducing reoffending, is to increase public confidence in community sentences and make best use of staff time, especially given current financial constraints.

Practitioners know that the relationship with the offender is critical to success and this is borne out by the research that tells us that the supervisory relationship between the offender and the case manager is important in rehabilitating offenders and reducing reoffending. Interventions have been found to be more effective when delivered by staff deploying core correctional practices, including working through warm, open and enthusiastic relationships (Dowden & Andrews, 2004). Skilled engagement has been related to lower rates of reconviction in studies in Australia, North America and Canada.[1] So why did we need a programme to develop offender engagement in England and Wales?

One reason was to address the gap in our knowledge about the effectiveness of supervision. Evaluation has focussed on interventions and programmes, and the evidence about the importance of the relationship between the practitioner and the offender is mostly from North America and Canada. There has not been a systematic study of supervision in England and Wales, nor have we collected evidence before on the quality of engagement and its potential impact.

Linked to that was the need to refocus community supervision to improve its effectiveness, using the research that was available. Analysis showed that over 178,000 offenders received one-to-one interactions with a probation professional in the community, the total cost of which was estimated to be around 150 million to NOMS. However, despite this high volume, NOMS had little way of measuring the effectiveness of one-to-one engagement with offenders in the community, or of using such information to inform the commissioning of offender services.[2]

Another aim of the programme is to reduce unnecessary prescription through process-based performance targets and national standards to enable practitioners to use their professional discretion and skills to reduce reoffending. Following a pilot on Professional Judgement (PJP) in Surrey and Sussex Probation Trust, NOMS issued new national standards and a practice framework in April 2011 for which trusts are planning a phased implementation. Evidence from the PJP pilot showed that staff had more purposeful and better focussed contact with offenders by being able to exercise their professional judgement in deciding how to work with each individual. The work of the OEP is to support that purposeful work by strengthening practitioner skills and management support for effective engagement with offenders.

Using the Desistance Research

A more recent area of research, on which we were able to build, was the desistance research that suggests that practitioners can help reduce reoffending and prevent future victims by working with offenders on the wider social factors associated with moving away from crime. The research on desistance tells us that the reduced criminal activity that is associated with greater maturity comes about through desisters' personal relationships, social networks and how they see themselves (Maruna, 2001). Early in the life of the OEP, we commissioned a review on the implications for NOMS of the desistance literature (McNeill & Weaver, 2010), which spelled out that practitioners should

- accommodate and exploit *identity* and *diversity*,
- create and maintain *hope* as well as motivation,
- encourage and respect offenders' *own determination to turn their lives around*,
- support and develop offenders' *skills and abilities* – as well as tackling risk and need,
- build on an understanding of the role of *human relations*,
- strengthen offenders' *social networks*.

This body of research provides key insights on which to focus practice: the importance of individual relations, both with offender manager and also with other people who can support non-offending choices, which includes intimate partners and parents and others who play a significant role in a desister's life – for example an aunt or a uncle, a teacher or a sports coach, an employer or a work supervisor. It points to the benefits of a forward-looking approach that builds on a person's strengths and resources and which is based on an individualised assessment of where the offender is and what he or she requires to move away from offending.

This does not mark a departure from the effectiveness research or NOMS' commitment to accredited programmes. Our interest in the desistance research is based on the need for NOMS to draw on the widest possible evidence base for a range of effective services for offenders, delivered by skilled practitioners ('who works', if you like). The desistance research refocuses attention on to the core correctional practices whose importance was recognised by the architects of 'What Works'.

Developing a Research Programme

An early step in the programme was to establish a research programme to provide evidence about the quality and impact of offender engagement, and evaluation of the OEP pilots. This was achieved by two research contracts negotiated following a competitive tender: one with Birkbeck College London (Institute for Criminal Policy Research (ICPR)) and Leicester University and a second with Sheffield University.

We have also pursued a wide range of other activities to capture and disseminate relevant academic expertise including establishing an academic reference group to act as a critical friend; preparing a series of short research bulletins aimed at a practitioner audience; and organising research seminars to learn about the latest research and thinking on offender engagement; as well as seek feedback on our own research activities.

We have a number of inter-related research projects. *Developing Offender Management Feedback Questionnaire* (*OMFQ*) is an investigation by ICPR and Leicester University of offenders' and their supervisors' views of supervision and how they relate to better outcomes and lower reconviction. *Quality in Probation Supervision* is an exploration by Sheffield University of practitioners' views, with the aim of producing quantitative ratings of dimensions of engagement. Both of these projects have informed the evaluation of the OEP pilots: skills for effective engagement and development (SEED); reflective supervision model (RSM); and sentence planning approaches (SPA). In the next section, we discuss the first two pilots before going on to explain our approach to the evaluation.

Establishing Pilot Initiatives

Our pilots, which started in the spring of 2011, developed from our early collaboration with probation trusts to look into practice initiatives that could support more effective offender engagement. We ran regional events in April to May 2010 attended by nearly 200 practitioners and managers from across England and Wales. These were followed up by engagement with trusts on specific initiatives and the establishment of our practitioner and middle managers reference groups to help maintain that engagement. It soon became clear that there were two main areas in which development was required.

Skills for Effective Engagement and Development

The origin to this pilot was that a lack of focus on engagement had left practitioners feeling insufficiently equipped with skills or supported to engage effectively with offenders whom they were supervising. During the evidence gathering stage of the OEP described above, staff told us they felt de-skilled and not in a position to use the skills in which they were trained. They also felt they had not been trained in appropriate engagement skills and that they have become technicians and process compliant, at the expense of building relationships with offenders. This feedback from staff and additional feedback from service users about their experiences of supervision influenced the development of the SEED model.

The training materials drew on by relevant research including the Canadian Strategic Training Initiative in Community Supervision (STICS) Project which set out to research the effectiveness of community supervision (see Bonta et al., 2010). This study found that it was the combination of relationship building and cognitive techniques that proved to be important in reducing reoffending. The SEED model also draws on recent research on desistance and seeks to merge evidence-based methods of working with offenders with a desistance-influenced approach, as described above.

Through training, the project aims to equip practitioners with *skills of engagement* and for those practitioners to receive follow-up training, coaching, action learning sets and observation (continuing professional development) to ensure that these skills are *continually refreshed and built upon*. The purpose of this will be to highlight the importance of 'engagement' between the practitioner and the offender in reducing risk of reoffending.

At this stage we can report on the early experiences of the pilot: the initial three-day training was well received by the majority of practitioners who found it useful to refresh their existing skills and learn new ones. The action learning sets, which provide a forum for practitioners to discuss cases, have proved to be popular with staff. The observation and feedback from line managers are a useful contribution to their professional development. Three months into the pilot, 82% of practitioners said that the training had made a real difference to their supervision sessions.

The Reflective Supervision Model

This pilot started with recognition that organisational culture can enable or inhibit effective engagement with offenders. It was seen that culture was in large part determined by the behaviours and activities of an organisation's managers and senior leaders. Our investigations started at the OEP regional events, where we looked at what managers and senior leaders could do practically to support offender engagement, and continued with engagement with practitioner and middle manager reference groups to ensure that our model was practical and likely to be effective.

A number of conclusions provided the principles for the model: firstly, that enabling culture change would require a whole system approach (White, 2000, p. 166), secondly, the need to focus on the middle manager role given its pivotal position linking strategic direction with the quality of operational practice, and thirdly, we found a wealth of high-quality materials already available and saw that our value lay in adapting these resources to secure a real and sustainable impact on practice.

The resulting model includes four key themes: pro-social modelling, reflective supervision, observed practice and action learning. Implementation included a manager's workshop, supporting resources and the implementation of a range of practice activities including reflective practice sessions for practitioners and middle managers, observed practice and feedback, middle manager action learning sets and senior manager practitioner engagement.

The workshop approach (including role and style of facilitators) involves a blended approach of different learning activities, mirroring the approach that the model itself is intended to promote. This is characterised by the creation of an honest and safe environment, strongly encouraging participants to take responsibility for their own learning and promoting learning as an ongoing process requiring a degree of letting go of control: 'we don't have all the answers'.

Early learning emerged from senior manager feedback that their involvement was crucial and they needed something tailored for them. Middle managers welcomed senior commitment but did not necessarily feel as 'safe' learning in the same environment. This reinforced the need for a whole system approach, further developed through a senior manager workshop and supporting resources, practitioner toolkit and revision of the model to be used across the organisation. Implementation also highlighted the value of transferrable skills and practice: whether working with offenders, practitioners or managers, many roles within the organisation rely on similar skills. This has been accommodated in the practitioner toolkit.

In both pilots, the observation of one-to-one practice has been one of the most successful aspects with a change of perspective to 'how can we justify *not* observing practice?' Reflective practice discussions and action learning have also enabled practice to be considered in a more meaningful way by managers and practitioners alike, although consistent feedback about the level of skill and practice required has reinforced the importance of ongoing momentum.

In addition to the pilots, we have the pilot on SPA, the aim of which is to test existing tools that seek to engage offenders more fully in sentence planning. This pilot covers Stepping Stones, the 'Web' and the Birmingham Treatment Effectiveness Initiative (BTEI). Space precludes longer discussion here, but further information is available from the Offender Engagement team (offender.engagement@noms.gsi.gov.uk).

DEVELOPING THE EVALUATION

Evaluation of this programme is somewhat unique and takes a mixed methods approach including internal as well as external evaluation. We developed specifications for evaluating the pilots alongside our detailed plans for taking the pilots forward, in collaboration with our research partners ICPR-Leicester and Sheffield University. The level of interest in piloting the three approaches meant that it was not possible to include all pilot projects in the external evaluation. We worked with trusts and the external evaluators so that a total of nine trusts were included in the external evaluation.

In the case of the pilots relating directly to how offender managers engage offenders, SPA and SEED, the external evaluation includes collecting structured feedback from practitioners and offenders and data on supervision outcomes. In SPA, offenders who started supervision with a project practitioner between March 2011 and September 2011 are included in the external evaluation. In order to report findings by autumn 2012, the evaluators – ICPR-Leicester – will analyse supervision outcomes after six months on these offenders. They are also using a developed OMFQ to investigate offenders' and their supervisors' views of supervision and how these relate to outcomes. These data will be compared with equivalent data on a group of offenders who are not supervised by practitioners in the project (the comparison group).

A similar approach is being taken to evaluating SEED, although the timescale is longer to accommodate the continuous professional development envisaged in the project. Offenders starting supervision with SEED practitioners between March and April 2011 and March and April 2012 are included in the evaluation (pilot projects started immediately after trusts completed the initial training), and supervision outcomes after one year will be analysed by the evaluators (Sheffield University) and compared with a comparison group. Given that the focus is equipping practitioners with *skills* to engage offenders, the evaluators are collecting feedback from practitioners after the initial and follow-up training and observing training and supervision sessions to assess what practitioners were able to gain from the project. An interim report in the autumn of 2012 will cover a great deal of learning from the pilot, and the final report on supervision outcomes is due in the autumn of 2013.

The external evaluation of RSM involves focussing on the experiences of the practitioners and managers in using the resources and activities involved in the model. A web-based before-and-after survey for managers and practitioners will be followed up by interviews with a sample of managers and practitioners to investigate the issues in implementing reflective supervision and a discussion group with senior managers involved in the pilot. The final report – by ICPR-Leicester – will be available in the summer of 2012.

A researcher from within NOMS was able to work with the team to develop an internal evaluation that sits alongside the external evaluation. Working with the external evaluators, we will extract management information to compare outcomes and process data between the project and comparison groups across all 22 projects. In addition, we have offered all projects falling outside of the external evaluation the opportunity to work with the internal evaluator to explore specific aspects of their projects in more depth.

The internal evaluation has adopted a realist approach, the purpose of which according to Kazi 'is the development and improvement of the models of practice' (2003, p. 30). This fits with the whole ethos of the programme that has worked collaboratively with academics, trust senior managers and practitioners. Areas of interest identified include exploring the impact of adopting the model more widely across the trust and looking in-depth at the pattern, rate and seriousness of reoffending and compliance. Practitioners and senior managers have had an opportunity to influence the style and content of the internal evaluation, and the skills and local knowledge of trust research and information managers have been incorporated into the data capture and design principles adopted. According to Sturgeion-Adams (2008, p. 110), involving practitioners in the process can be empowering and move the evaluation purpose from simply a tool to demonstrate success to one that is viewed as contributing to learning.

Flexibility has been a key feature of the internal evaluation, which has enabled us to respond to changes in the environment in which the programme is being piloted. Data capture for each trusts comprises:

- Keeping a record of all offenders included in the project and comparison groups, with sufficient unique identifiers to enable central extraction of data from case management, offender assessment and interventions databases. The measures include outcome (e.g. successful completion of orders) and explanatory (e.g. number of offender manager changes) variables for both project and comparison groups. For one trusts where the project has been implemented across 75% of teams, this list also captures those offenders who were eligible but who were not included. This provides valuable data on unconscious bias when selecting offenders for inclusion.
- Keeping two diaries, one for senior managers and one for practitioners. These diaries are used to record data about changes in the environment, such as management decisions that may impact on morale (e.g. announcement of redundancies), capacity (e.g. sickness of key individuals) or strategic direction (e.g. implementation of the new national standards). Practitioners are also encouraged to record information about key benefits or costs associated with the project.
- Feedback from training events and group discussions (e.g. reference groups) will also be used when preparing the final report.

FUTURE DIRECTIONS

While working with trusts to take the programme forward, we are conscious that the ongoing challenge is to maintain the commitment to quality practice and leadership and management support for effective engagement. Enabling a culture change is a continuing task and piloting a model is the start of a process, not the end. The OEP is seeking to play our part by building on the momentum created by the pilots and the level of engagement from trusts in beginning to make an integrated framework on offender engagement available before the end of the pilots in March 2012, based on what we have learnt from the pilots. The aim is to use the learning from the pilots and evaluation to produce a robust evidence-based framework that can inform NOMS' priorities for 2012/2013 and beyond.

NOTES

1. In Australia, pro-social modelling (acting as a positive role model and encouraging and rewarding pro-social statements and actions) was associated with lower rates of breach and reconviction over four years (49% compared with 73% where there was no evidence of pro-social modelling) (Trotter, 1996). In Maryland, United States, offenders supervised by officers trained in Proactive Community Supervision supported by a pro-social organisational environment achieved lower re-arrest rates than comparable offenders (30% vs. 42% for the comparison group) (Taxman, 2008). In Canada, officers trained in STICS (Strategic Training Initiative in Community Supervision) used relationship building, cognitive techniques and a structured approach to achieve lower reconviction rates (25% compared with just over 40% for other officers) (Bonta et al., 2010).

2. NOMS defines commissioning as 'the cycle of assessing the needs of courts, offenders, defendants, victims and communities then designing, securing and monitoring services to meet those needs, while making best use of total available resources', see http://www.justice.gov.uk/downloads/publications/corporate-reports/noms/intro-to-noms-commissioning.pdf

REFERENCES

Bonta, J., Bourgon, G., Rugge, T., Scott, T.-L., Yessine, A. K., Gutierrez, L., & Li, J. (2010). *The strategic training initiative in community supervision: Risk-need-responsivity in the real world.* Corrections Research: User Report, Public Safety Canada. Retrieved from www.publicsafety.gc.ca

Dowden, C., & Andrews, D. A. (2004). The importance of staff practice in delivering effective correctional treatment: A meta-analytic review of core correctional practice. *International Journal of Offender Therapy and Comparative Criminology, 48,* 203–214. doi:10.1177/0306624X03257765

Kazi, M. A. F. (2003). *Realist evaluation in practice: Health and social work.* London: Sage.

Maruna, S. (2001). *Making good: How ex-convicts reform and rebuild their lives.* Washington, DC: American Psychological Association.

McNeill, F., & Weaver, B. (2010). *Changing lives? Desistance research and offender management.* Retrieved from www.sccjr.ac.uk

Sturgeion-Adams, L. (2008). Evaluating practice. In S. Green, E. Lancaster & S. Feasey (Eds.), *Addressing offending behaviour: Context, practice and values.* Cullompton: Willan.

Taxman, F. (2008). No illusions: Offender and organisational change in Maryland's proactive community supervision efforts. *Criminology and Public Policy, 7*(2), 275–302.

Trotter, C. (1996). The impact of different supervision practices in community corrections: Causes for optimism. *Australian and New Zealand Journal of Criminology, 29,* 29–46. doi:10.1177/000486589602900103

White, L. (2000). Changing the "whole system" in the public sector. *Journal for Organizational Change Management, 13*(2), 162–177.

OFFENDERS AT THE HEART OF EVALUATION

Barry Kushner and Saville Kushner

ABSTRACT

This chapter looks at the role qualitative evaluation can play in the external review of the Probation Service, the development of an evaluation framework for ongoing assessment and how it can be used to develop new elements of the service. How is this different from the use of existing data by the service?

This takes us to the kind of information that is used by the probation service, to make judgements about the effectiveness of its programmes and the impact on offenders. The main contention is that this is in the main quantitative data, and reports on levels of re-offending. The data is standardised so that it can be used to make comparisons between different types of sentence and criminal justice intervention.

Our contention is that this information is limited in what it says for two main reasons. Firstly, quantitative data tends to report on impact, that is whether an offender has committed another crime after engagement with the probation service, or whether there are patterns of behaviour between offences, individual circumstances and the likelihood or re-offending. In short, the data is a snapshot of whether an offender has changed his or her behaviour or not. However, this chapter will illustrate how quantitative

Perspectives on Evaluating Criminal Justice and Corrections
Advances in Program Evaluation, Volume 13, 211–229

ISSN: 1474-7863/doi:10.1108/S1474-7863(2012)0000013014

data misses an understanding of how behaviour changes and why behaviour does not change. As a result, this leaves the service with a limited understanding of how it is working.

Secondly, the chapter will argue that the existing probation framework itself creates quite specific definitions of which data is relevant and which data is not relevant. We will give examples of narratives that offenders offer in group sessions that provide rich material about their lives, pressures and offence. But evidence suggests that this information is not used to inform programmes, re-assess and review an offender's own progression towards re-offending or a life without crime.

INTRODUCTION

This chapter looks at the role qualitative evaluation can play in the external review of the Probation Service, the development of an evaluation framework for ongoing assessment and how it can be used to develop new practices in the sustainable reduction of offending. It is based on a collaborative formative evaluation between the University of the West of England and an English.

At present, the service relies substantially on quantitative – mostly demographic – data for judgements about its effectiveness in reducing offending. This data is standardised so that it can be used to make comparisons between different types of sentence and criminal justice intervention, as well as performance comparisons of different services and regions. Evaluation is mostly confined to measures of service productivity.

However, this information is limited in what it says for two main reasons. Firstly, the existing evaluative data focuses on impact, that is whether an offender has committed another crime after engagement with the probation service, or whether there are patterns of behaviour between offences, individual circumstances and the likelihood of re-offending. The data is a snapshot of whether an offender has changed his or her behaviour or not – and, since it is standardised, it admits only of a limited range of possible explanations and analyses of re-offending behaviours. This leaves the service with a limited understanding of how it is working.

Secondly, the chapter will argue that the existing probation framework itself creates specific definitions of which data is relevant and which data is not relevant, that is pre-specifying and limiting the range of possible explanations for recidivism or reduction in offending patterns. We will give examples of narratives that offenders offer in group sessions that provide informative data about their lives, pressures they face and their offence which often lie beyond conventional datasets. Evidence from the evaluation we will report suggests that this information is not used to inform programmes, re-assess and review an offender's own progression towards re-offending or a life without crime. There is a major confusion between evaluation for accountability and evaluation for understanding and development. What risks being lost in the focus on service *productivity* is the identification of service *quality*. Quality is the key variable for sustainability.

The data for this chapter is drawn from a 12-month evaluation of a UK Probation Trust group-work programme. The programmes are 5–10-week issue-focused group-work programmes for lower-tier offenders. They are constructed on the basis of Cognitive-Behavioural Therapy (CBT) and draw some of the concepts, structure and activities from the longer and more tightly framed Accredited Programmes. The aims of the programmes vary from providing information in the Alcohol Awareness programme to techniques to support personal change such as in the Conflict Resolution programme. As is implied by the title of the programmes, the aim is both to enhance supervision and to reduce the resource (i.e. by supplementing individual supervision with group sessions).

The Probation Trust commissioned a formative evaluation, because there was recognition that there was an information gap in assessing the impact of the service. The senior management felt that qualitative evaluation could add insight into their practice that could support the development of the service. The openness of staff at every level of the Trust allowed us to draw its data from a number of observations of group sessions, including observing early and late sessions in the programme with the same group, from interviews with probation staff at most levels of the service, including senior management, the data team and group-work facilitators. The Probation Trust team was also keen that we interviewed individual offenders and also facilitated a number of focus groups. This led the evaluation team and the Probation staff to ask a simple question: if Offenders are the target of the service, should they not be at the heart of the evaluation of the service?

THE DATA GAP

Our starting point is a review of the data that is currently available to the service, and is most readily used – largely based on re-offending rates. This is the bottom line that most concerns Government. Re-offending is arguably the touchstone of policy and so it is the main driver of a probation service. The current Justice Secretary is not happy: '*statistics show that reoffending in this country is unacceptably high and underline the urgent need for steps to counter it. It is a national scandal that nearly half of all offenders reoffend within a year of release.*'[1]

The introduction by the Government of '*payment by results*' schemes, such as the pioneering scheme at Peterborough Prison, suggests measurement of re-offending outcomes will remain a key driver of the service. And the stakes are high – particularly for community sentences – to show that they reduce offending. Carson, Milne, and Pakes (2007) make the position clear, '*if these reductions are not achieved or are less than expected, rehabilitative interventions of all types may be replaced by more punitive sanctions.*'

But given that both statistics *and* explanations on re-offending are so crucial to the development of rehabilitation programmes, what are they telling us?

The Probation Trust was concerned that the data it holds on offending and the impact of their service was not telling the whole story of their interventions. Our analysis of statistical data used by the probation service suggests that the re-offending rate for those who completed a group-work programme was lower than if they didn't attend one, or left one early. For example the re-offending rate (2009/2010) for people completing a group-work course was 3%, which was 10% lower than the National Offender Management Service (NOMS) re-offending rate of 13%. Yet, offenders who did not complete group-work appeared to have a re-offending rate of over 60%. This suggests that completing the group programme reduces re-offending.

The analysis of the data could have stopped there, but for begging the question, '*what does this tell us?*' On closer inspection, the data raised more questions than it provided answers, mainly because of the complex nature of probation practice, the use of sometimes ambiguous, official NOMS language and the difficulty in measuring the wide range of factors present within the information.

For example, demographic data does not distinguish between probationers who left programmes because they did not receive notification or who felt uncomfortable being part of a group, from probationers who were withdrawn from the programme by the Offender Manager for procedural reasons. Many left programmes due to the term '*revoked on application*', but the term *'revoked'* covers a wide range of outcomes, positive and negative, that include:

(a) A probationer has completed all the requirements of the order and done extremely well and no longer needs to be supervised;
(b) A current order is replaced by another order that is considered more suitable;
(c) The offender has re-offended, making a new order necessary.

On closer inspection even the term 're-*offending*' itself is subject to competing interpretations. For example NOMS data suggests that 63% of probationers, who left the group-work programme early, re-offended. However, one third of these 're-*offences*' were not actually a crime, but the result of court or procedural offences. Many of the probationers who, for example, were recorded as having re-offended had breached their probation order, rather than having committed a new criminal offence. In fact, Police National Computer data shows that almost one quarter of all offending was due to a procedural breach (of the 1,265 recorded offences in 2009, 320 were considered procedural offences).

What is more, the NOMS data does not record the up-to-date data that is on the Police National Computer. New offences going through the criminal justice system do not appear on the NOMS system – in fact, data on the group-work programme attendance was available only to the Probation Trust; immediate data on (re)offending was only available to the police. As a result, estimates for re-offending differ and do not distinguish between re-offending of a lesser offence and the first offence for which the offender was sentenced.

Most official data a probation service is required to generate is focused on impact, whether or not the service has reduced re-offending rates or not. Our research confirmed what the Probation Trust already suspected, that there appeared to be little evidence-based understanding as to why offenders on the group-work programme stopped offending. In fact, it was not difficult for probationers to make sense of, where for example a 30-year-old offender, who was resistant to the programme at first, changed and engaged with it, and took a lot from it. But why? How? The data in itself could not answer the following questions:

- Why did probationers leave the group-work programme or stay on one?
- Did probationers leave one group-work programme, but complete another?

- What was it about the group-work programme that contributed to an offender not re-offending?
- Or was attendance on the group-work programme just an indication of compliance and that the probationer would not re-offend anyway, whether they did the group-work programme or not?
- Is any of this significant or not?

These are tough questions for data to answer, because they are coming face to face with the complexity of the system and the complexity of an individual's behaviour, but were the questions the Probation Trust wanted answers to. Governments and the electorate want to know what works, not so much how it works, and that is where the data becomes an unreliable source of definitive understanding of the probation system and how people change. The answer to the question, *'by what degree has a probation service reduced reoffending'* may be, say, 7% – but 7% of what? Those who passed through a particular rehabilitation pathway? Seven per cent of those who were already receptive to rehabilitation? And was 7% a lot or a little under the circumstances? Do we know enough to be able to replicate the 7% – or improve on it? *Is* it replicable and, if so, under what conditions?

Porporino (2010), who was at the forefront of the '*What Works*' thinking that lies behind the existing probation service interventions, himself wrote, '*the search for evidence-based practices is blind empiricism unless the mechanisms of action of those practices are understood: why and how change might come about.*'

There is information that the Ministry of Justice *wants*, and there is information that the Ministry *needs*. The difference between the two is the data gap.

WHAT DO WE KNOW ABOUT THE SERVICE?

Before answering this question, it is useful to explore the political framework within which data is generated and is utilised. The Probation Service as a whole operates within a prescriptive framework that operates on the basis of '*risk*' and '*need*'. It starts with a standardized assessment and leads to community sentences with standardized programmes of intervention. '*Need*' in this sense is defined by NOMS as '*criminogenic*', which has been crystallised into a set of seven social factors that are likely to cause criminal behaviour (Hollin, 1999). They are areas of social and personal factors that research suggests have a correlation with criminal behaviour, based on the assumption that there is a causal relationship between social factors and offending that can be interrupted by appropriate sentencing.

The strength of criminogenic factors of individual offending is assessed through the standard OASys procedure. Offenders are taken through this assessment by Offender Managers, and based on the answers given, will generate a summary score. This is the second key element of the service – risk, which is defined as a predictor of offending, assessing the '*likelihood of reconviction and risk of serious harm and to prepare a Sentence Plan*' (Howard, 2009).

On the basis of the OASys score, offenders are categorized into levels of need and risk, and this in turn forms that basis of recommendations by Offender Managers of the type of sentence that matches the offender's needs. Magistrates are encouraged to use this assessment to make their sentencing judgment, creating an offender pathway of interventions. For most violent and general offending, it is assumed that '*thinking and behaviour underlies most other risk factors, so scores should help targeting to offending behaviour programmes*'.[2] So for example if OASys identifies a high risk of re-offending, as part of a community sentence it is likely that it will be a condition that offenders attend an accredited programme. These are scripted blocks of 20+ sessions on criminogenic themes, and offenders are recruited onto them based on the nature of their offence.

This is a system that seeks to make personal change through identifying social factors and the applying behaviour modification. As the NOMS framework outlines, '*for most offenders, a cognitive-behavioural/social learning change process is associated with reform and rehabilitation. The key stages of this process are mapped onto the end-to-end offender experience in the model. For most offenders it is this process which has to be nurtured if reform and rehabilitation is to be achieved.*'[3]

This is the application of a theory of criminal behaviour, underpinned by CBT, that has created a sealed system for evaluating individuals that restricts analysis of their lives to a limited range of social factors and restricts interventions to predetermined pathways and scripted programmes.

This has left the Probation Trust with a standardised set of programmes that are administered in terms of '*dosage*' and '*treatment*' that is regardless of the offender's individual circumstances and regardless of their independent agency. A Senior Manager for the programmes, indicating a commitment to quality, felt that standardising the delivery for each offender is important, because '*if an offender is going on a [group programme] in [one town], we should know that they are getting the same level of input as an offender going on a group programme in [another town].*'

Most of our evaluation was looking at the group-work programmes. These were '*Accredited Programme-lite*', with more flexibility for Facilitators, but which borrowed CBT techniques for use in short courses. They are an innovative response by the Probation Trust to the time-limited one-to-one supervision sessions, and potentially a more flexible alternative to accredited programmes. They also offered probationers, a group-work option. These sessions are also carefully scripted. Session Plans provide a detailed description of how each session should progress, with key objectives, and timed exercises and tasks that take the offenders step by step through learning points relevant to the session, so that they realise the session objectives.

This is consistent with the pressure on the service from NOMS to provide a theory-led programme, rather than a Probationer-led framework, and represents a deficit model of intervention, where probationers have a problem that is solved by the correct '*dosage*' of interventions. In this context, psychological theory is used to explain rather than understand behaviour. As assessment of individuals is restricted by NOMS to social, criminogenic factors, the existing evaluation of the system is restricted to how well the programme is implemented and how well offenders respond to their treatment. The theory assumes that if probationers re-offend or do not engage with the programme, it is their failure, rather than a weakness in the programme.

The Probation Trust recognises this as an issue, and is seeking to develop a more flexible range of tools. Staff recognise that within this context statistical data is only required to inform us whether the programme works, not how individuals respond to the opportunity. For example Probation Officers have few tools to tackle non-attendance on one-to-one or group programmes, and our research suggests that this tends to be interpreted as non-compliance. In Probation Trust area, these kinds of offenders are referred onto a motivational programme – which happens to be the worst attended group session – or ultimately they are deemed to be '*in breach*' ('*breached*').

The Probation Trust was seeking a solution to this conundrum and our evaluation and research helped the service ask what the offender is telling us when he or she decides not attend supervision or a group programme. There are multiple possible explanations and it is important to know which is appropriate. Can they not be bothered? Is non-attendance a signal of a resignation that they we always live in the criminal justice system? Do they lack confidence to open up to others? Can they not get beyond the blocks and denials to engagement? Are they poor at communicating? The existing

NOMS framework makes it difficult to establish why an offender is not engaging or to use their lack of engagement as material for further assessment, insight and engagement – another manifestation of the 'data gap'.

Such individual factors and variables in that '*gap*' do not feature in the statistical data collected on group-work programmes or on re-offending. In fact, our observations and interviews with probation staff pointed out that people with mental health problems, older people, young people, victims as well as perpetrators of crime, first-time offenders and re-offenders can all be in the same group. There are people, who are readily engaged in the programme, in the same group as probationers who may be on the programme for the second time, because they did not complete it the first time around. It is interesting to note that for a service that is aimed at reducing offending that in the NOMS framework there is not an intervention that specifically targets or responds to re-offending.

In this system the role of Probation Officer has changed into a more administrative function, as Offender *Managers*, implementing OASys and overseeing and monitoring the application of the offender framework. The probation service is in danger of relying so heavily on prescription that it limits professional judgment. Porporino (*ibid.*), seeking a partial apology for his part in this system, now reflects, '*in this exuberant momentum towards a directed and prescriptive*, change-the-offender agenda *in corrections, however ... we may have blinded ourselves to other ways of approaching the challenge, ways where offenders themselves could be treated with greater respect, as the true experts regarding how they might change.*'

DATA ON QUALITY FILLS THE GAP

In this section we will look at data from our evaluation that offers greater analytical purchase over offending and re-offending behaviour. The examples which follow – along with others – were provided in co-operation with the Probation Trust staff and were presented to the service as part of a proposal to adopt a more educational, rather than psychological, approach to rehabilitation, and to place rehabilitation programmes on a more evidence-based and responsive footing.

Each group-work programme has a set of objectives and a script that details the activities that should take place in the session. We observed offenders bringing intimate examples of the complexity of their lives to these sessions. In most of the observations of group-work programmes that we conducted, we found that the skills of the group Facilitators and their relationship with the Offenders enabled them to talk openly about their relationships with their partners or their children, about their drug-taking, their parents, violent incidents, employment, living conditions, past – all rich material that offers contextual information about their lives. However, the sessions do not appear easily to allow Facilitators the scope, the time or the resource to pursue these in depth – even when the offender is engaged with the process.

For example, in a Conflict Resolution session the Facilitator was explaining the concept and application of anger reduction, and asked Offenders to give an example where they had controlled their anger. A young Offender replied that he was allowed out of jail on a tag, on condition that he lived at home. In the event he had an argument with his father, who threw him out of the house, and so he ended up back in jail. The Facilitator thanked him for the example and commended him on controlling his temper by not attacking his father, and moved on to another offender's example of anger reduction.

But look at the complexity of that story. What does it say about his relationship with his father or his family? Did he feel a sense of betrayal, disappointment or was he letting himself down in front of his father? Didn't he care whether his father was upset or not? Does he not value his life enough to fight more to stay out of prison? What does that say about his self-esteem, confidence or identity? What was his mother's reaction? And are any of these questions relevant in him understanding why he offended, does the existing pathway allow the opportunity for this to be addressed?

Our evaluation team observed occasions when offenders presented alternative theories and understandings to those who fell within the session outline. For example in a Conflict Resolution group session Facilitators are deconstructing anger, into concepts like anger cues and cycles, and moving onto techniques to reduce an angry response. They suggest counting, taking deep breaths. Offenders draw on their own experiences, and challenge not only how difficult these techniques are to use in spontaneous situations, but also how appropriate they are.

Here is a further example of an offender theorising, taken from a gorup session, where participants were being introduced into the vocabulary of the behaviour modification approach:

The Facilitator asked the group to think about what should be done, to which the response included a wide range of alternatives:

better drug treatment – it's much quicker now and you can access it earlier

The only thing that's stopped me offending is my mum, my family. It upsets her if I get into trouble and it makes me think about it.

One member of the group disagreed vehemently with this and stated that he hates his mum and he wouldn't stop doing something because of her. The Facilitator reminded him of the effect his father has on his behaviour, however. 'Yes, I'd stop doing it because of him.' Another participant interjected by addressing the Facilitator (and the group as a whole) 'it would stop you, too, if you knew his dad – he's huge!'

In this example, Offenders introduce the importance of significant relationships for their behaviour. On occasions, these contributions create a dissonance between what Facilitators are trying to achieve within the session plan and what offenders are saying. In the next exchange, the Facilitator is explaining the concept of '*cues*' that trigger or preface anger and how to spot them. If the Offender can spot an anger 'cue', he can avoid anger, and an adrenalin rush is one of them. M is explaining why he hit his father-in-law.

Facilitator – how do you think you handled it? How did you rate yourself at the bottom?

Probationer – It was ok

Facilitator – but it brought you here, yeh. So do you think there are there are things you could have done differently that would have made a difference

Probationer – I could've talked to him, you know. Any bloke sees another bloke hit a woman, you're gonna go nuts, ain't it?

Facilitator – I understand. It's a very, very difficult situation to deal with, but of course the negative consequences are now yours and not his, aren't they. So that's what we want to avoid for the future. So what were your cues then [Probationer]? What were your signs of anger at the time?

Probationer – Um. Just [pause] lash out that's all

Facilitator – But you would have seen that happen and heard what he was saying. There would have been this massive adrenalin flow through your body, as we all get

Probationer 1 – I thought he ain't gonna get away with that and that was it

Facilitator – so any of this stuff

Probationer 1 – shaking I was

Facilitator 1 – right

Probationer 1 – very shaky

Facilitator – did you stick that down that you were shaking, because that's the adrenalin. The adrenalin on the muscles will cause that to happen. OK and what anger reducer of these 3 might possibly have helped?

Probationer 1 – [pause] none of them really

Facilitator – some of these will help, some of them won't, you know. It's very individual, but you do have to practice with it. Do you think possibly a few deep breaths might have helped?

Probationer 1 – might have done

Probationer 2 – in Mike's situation though you can't let that bloke get away with what he done. So all that's a load of nark in that situation

Facilitator – In Mike's situation

Probationer 2 – Yeh, yeh

Probationer 2 – I'm sorry. If saw a bloke raise a hand to a woman, I'd beat the crap out of him. Standard. It's not right

Facilitator – I admire that and that's a nice thing to say. But we don't want is you guys getting into trouble for it, yeah. So it's about.

Probationer 2 – Obviously we don't want to get into trouble for it, but you've got to do something about it, haven't you

Facilitator 2 – what else could you do though? You've only got one option. What else could you do in that situation, if you didn't want to end up back here in more trouble?

Facilitator – Yeah. We will go through that as we go through the programme. I hope there are other alternatives and we'll identify them, as we go through the process

Probationer 2 – To be honest I think I'd quite happily face the consequences

Facilitator – And that's a choice you'd make Probationer 2

Probationer 2 – Yeah

Facilitator – But it's not what we want for you, yeah

Probationer 2 – But that's …

Facilitator – But we all make our choices don't we?

In this example the Probationer is explaining the situation and how difficult he found it, and the Facilitator is punctuating the narrative, teasing examples of the adrenalin rush. This analysis is interrupting the flow of the story and the questions feel awkward and at odds with a serious domestic situation. The session plan did not easily allow exploration of the feelings, emotions and relationships present, and any conflict in the Probationer's mind. In this example, the Probationer describes the offending as a solution to a problem. Hitting his Father-in-law was the only way he knew to stop his father-in-law hitting his mother.

In this example a Facilitator is providing her own example of how she controlled her anger with her sister, who was babysitting her daughter.

> *Facilitator – My daughter still has a dummy at the age of 3, which I am trying to stop her from having. And I got home and um, had a really, really busy day. Got home and my sister said 'oh. Look at this, Alicia, show mummy what you've learnt instead of a dummy.' And she went (L is sucking her thumb) Ah well (laughs). I was like, 'what!' (laughs). ... Like I said me and Sarah are not angels, so there's gonna be, you know, times when we don't handle ourselves very well, and actually told my sister that I thought she was stupid. OK. I said –*
>
> *Facilitator – I know. I said, 'what are you stupid?' So anyway, we had a bit of an argument, she left. Both you know, heated argument. Afterwards, I sat down, thought about it and realised that it was just only a joke, and I rang her and I apologised. OK*

The theoretical underpinning in the group sessions suggests that the processes of decision-making are the same regardless of the type of action. But the group is not convinced that this story has relevance in their own lives and falls silent. The examples of anger that they gave were more intense, laced with aggression and conflict. The dissonance in these examples lies between trying to use theory to *explain* behaviour conflicting with the experiences of Offenders attempting to *understand* behaviour. At times, it makes Offenders feel that Offender Managers do not understand them, '*it's just like they ain't got no problems in their life whatsoever innit?*'

These examples suggest that whatever theory or approach underpins an educational practice dissolves in classroom experience. Other realities take over, such as personal theories and dispositions, relationships, local circumstances and personal histories. There is an assumption that the cognitive, behavioural techniques operate regardless of the social context that people find themselves in poverty, stress, danger.

Three members of a Relationship for Men group offered three different perspectives of their offending and the solution. They were attending because they had all hit their partners. One felt that the course has made a change and given an insight into his own behaviour, which a couple of other members agreed with, '*You can only change yourself can't you? No-one can change anyone.*' A second Probationer thought that change in him should take place in a social context, '*I can't say I can change myself, I wish I could but, look on, basically look on life in a different way. I am trying to work on a relationship. I look on it in a different way. A different angle. With a bit of luck it will work out.*' Another put domestic violence within the context of the pressure and stress in relationships, '*it is all about money.*' This suggests a programme that opens up discourse, to embrace the complexity of human behaviour and circumstances.

Dig deeper, and the offenders went on to say that those convicted of an offence of domestic violence would benefit from their partner going through the programme with them. They understood that some of the techniques for anger management could be useful, but suggested that it lost value because it did not sit within the context of their own relationship. For example, one offender, who seems particularly resistant to the programme, felt it is difficult to apply the programme, that is the triangle, when their partner doesn't know anything about it.

> *These sessions would be a lot more helpful if a) our partners were here and b) if it actually related to the actual offence.* Another goes on to explain that, '*As it is, we have all held our hands up to what we've done, and like, if our partner was sat here and we said "look, we're in the wrong by, by what we did, but you need to open your eyes to this", you know what I mean, I reckon that would be a lot more helpful, and then I'd probably be telling people "you're on what programme, yeh do it, it's good. That will help you."*'

Not all offenders on these programmes are bent on re-offending. A young offender, 19, got drunk on a night out and got into a fight. His offence was committed almost 18 months before he came on to the group-work programme, but by the time his case came to court, he was assessed, started on probation and waited to start a group-work programme contract, he had got his dream job working in a kitchen and had settled down. '*I don't want it to go any further. I've got my job now. I don't want to lose my job. I don't want to have to. I can't take any other day off during the week. I have to go down today, um, plus I want it out the way.*' He appears to have moved on from his offence and doesn't seem to be getting anything more out of the sessions.

We can see from these examples that the complexity of individual circumstances stretches the scope and impact of the existing framework – in a way encouraged by the group-work programme initiative. The Probation staff at every level of the service are aware of the dissonance, the material that offenders offer in group and 1-1 sessions, and were seeking a way to include this in a probation intervention. So what are we missing?

PLACING INTERVENTIONS ON A COMPREHENSIVE EVIDENCE BASE

Need is the starting point. OASys does not account for the previous social history AND domestic circumstances of offenders. It does not include the complexities of the individual narratives of each offender, previous physical, mental or sexual abuse, poverty, poor parenting or having committed a one-off crime. By definition these needs and characteristics of individuals are restricted from sentencing and removing a level of individuality from the understanding offending behaviour, sentencing and probation programmes.

With funding tight and getting tighter, Offender Managers are under time pressure to produce pre-sentence reports. This inevitably has its limitations, as Offenders are unlikely to open up the complexity of their lives in a 2 hour pre-sentence meeting with a Probation Officer, and Offender Managers know this only too well, as one explains, '*you're not going to spill your guts to somebody at the first time you've met them.*'

Without assessing personal need, how can a programme address personal change? An Offender Manager told us, '*if you can't get to what underpins the behaviour, then you're not going to change their behaviour, so and that's why I think the information you've got at the pre-sentence report will give you one set of criminogenic needs, and once you get to know them, you realise well actually there's other stuff that you need to be looking at. You can't pigeon hole any of the offenders. You just can't do it. It doesn't matter, on paper at the presentence report stage it might look like he went out, he got pissed, he punched somebody. It's all alcohol. He could be sexually abused at home. He could be, having no money; he could be in a domestic violence relationship.*'

Offender Managers were telling us that to get into position where probationers divulge intimate and personal information, the relationship with Probationers is important. The same offender manager having told us about personal needs of individual probationers went on to say, '*you don't know any of that, until you get to know them.*'

This is repeated by other Offender Managers we spoke to, '*you've got to build up a relationship with [offender]*', another Offender Manager offers us, '*because you're not going to trust them. You know quite often, the women specifically, they are quite damaged, you know, they've got no confidence. They've got very low self-esteem. They're not going to sit there and say 'I get beaten up every night'. It just doesn't happen.*'

One Senior Manager was clear that change in an individual '*hinges on the relationship they have got with their probation officer, because I think if there is no relationship there, you're going to get bugger all out of them, because they not going to want to change.*'

The issue for the Probation Trust is that there is not the time for this to happen in the modern probation office and building relationships is not part of the NOMS offender pathway. Some Offenders with a long history of involvement with the Probation Service make a similar observation. One recalled a time 20 years ago when Probation Officers, ' *had a bit more time. They wanted to get to know me and wanted, they seriously wanted to help me. And thank god they did.*' He contrasts that with today's service, '*but this time it's not been like that. It's not been like that at all. And I am someone in the middle of a break up in the relationship, er, and I'm a single Dad. Never thought I'd be a single Dad at the age of 48 to a three-year-old boy and having to go through a family court ... I don't feel there's the help. I feel it's far more punitive this time.*' '*I didn't find it when I walked in and first spoke to my Probation Officer, I didn't get that, "right what can we do to help you". It was far more, right, it was treating me as a criminal. Don't get me wrong, I am, I was, done something wrong, put my hands up to it, pleaded guilty, but it wasn't there to try and [pause] help me, it didn't feel like that. It felt that, right we've got you here, 9 months. You're gonna do this, this, this and this. You're gonna do this course.*'

These are insights from offenders and practitioners available only from qualitative methods that raise the following gaps in elements of the existing system in terms of introducing personal individual need as a basis for interventions, allowing probationers' own narratives and competing theories to come out, to provide them with an understanding of their own offending behaviour, rather than professional explanation of it. The research also highlights the role of building relationships in effective interventions.

The current system, as it exists and prescribed by NOMS, is parcelled into different segments – supervision, community payback, accredited programmes, group-work. Where is the thread that links all these elements together? Porporino has changed his view, and takes us to a certain point in considering the nature and quality of appropriate interventions to support offenders, and reflects that '*we might be better off if we allowed offenders to* ***guide us*** *instead, listened to what they think might best fit their individual struggles out of crime, rather than continue to insist that our solutions are their salvation.*'[4] So where will this take us?

A SERVICE GUIDED BY OFFENDERS

We brought our findings in the form of an interim report to the Probation Trust, which organised a collaborative workshop that included staff at all levels of the service – Senior Managers, Offender Managers, Programme Managers, Facilitators and Administrators. We presented the views of Offenders and Offender Managers, and our interpretation of what we saw and listened to, as well as the questions these raised.

The primary question is, if you were to design a probation system from scratch, based on the need to change personal behaviour, what would it look like? We entered an open and insightful discussion of the role of CBT, the importance of establishing positive relationships with offenders, the need to link up supervision with group-work and other elements of probation. We used examples from the observations, interactions and interviews we conducted, together with the examples and thoughts of the probation staff. The discussion moved to the need to devise a programme or a framework that encompassed the insights that offenders contribute. There was a reluctance to abandon CBT as a methodology, but an acceptance that it is not enough – acknowledgement of the data gap.

The workshop reached a consensus that *engagement* with offenders is the key to having an impact – but how can this be represented in the programme? From this workshop and others, these conversations continued in team meetings, training and planning meetings. Senior Managers were developing an evaluation framework that attempted to capture the key elements of the probation programme that affected change in probationers, as part of the ongoing development of the service. There was an acknowledgement, too, that high-quality data on individuals not only offers evaluative insight into service change, but also can be effective in individual rehabilitation.

The evaluation of the service led to the development of a new probation framework that has coherence, because it places engagement and individual need at the heart of the programme. It also aligns with an evaluation framework that continues to capture good quality individual data, including the personal development of offenders and how their own personal change can build from there. Each element of the service is brought together through the Probationer. At the heart of the proposed new approach is data on the quality of relationships and interventions – data that starts with the complexities and capabilities of the offender, rather than starting with an imagined solution.

CONCLUSION

The Probation Trust commissioned a qualitative evaluation of their group-work programme, because they were seeking to evolve the service away from the prescriptive constraints of accredited programmes, but were unsure whether it was an effective intervention that NOMS could accept.

Senior staff, Offender Managers and Facilitators felt that there was a data gap that could aid their understanding of how their work was having an impact on offenders. There was recognition that their experience and skills were not being utilised effectively to develop programmes, challenge and engage with offenders.

Senior management embraced qualitative evaluation to provide an insight into their work, the feelings and evaluation of offenders, and to develop a framework that could be adopted to assess the impact of their work. In fact, both the Probation staff and the evaluation team discovered that the insights from the research opened up a new probation framework. It provided a reflection of current practice and the constraints the service currently operates within, to develop a framework based on offender engagement and their personal development.

This is what putting offenders at the heart of evaluation can offer, and what a service looks like, when, as Porporino suggests, you allow offenders to guide us.

NOTES

1. Kenneth Clarke's response to 2011 Reoffending Compendium 10 May 2011.
2. The Noms Offender Management Model 2005.
3. The Noms Offender Management Model 2005.

REFERENCES

Carson, D., Milne, R., & Pakes, F. (2007). *Applying psychology to criminal justice*. London: Wiley.

Hollin, C. R. (1999). Treatment programs for offenders: Meta-analysis 'what works' and beyond. *International Journal of Law and Psychiatry*, *22*, 361–372.

Howard, P. (2009). *Improving the prediction of reoffending using the Offender Assessment System*. Ministry of Justice Research Summary 2/09. London: Ministry of Justice. Retrieved from http://webarchive.nationalarchives.gov.uk/20110201125714/http://www.justice.gov.uk/publications/docs/oasys-research-summary-02-09.pdf

Offender Engagement Research Bulletin Promoting Offender Engagement in Sentence Planning, Issue 7, Ministry of Justice (Undated Publication).

Porporino, F. (2010). Bringing sense & sensitivity to corrections: From programmes to 'Fix' Offenders to Services to Support Desistance. In J. Brayford, F. Cowe & J. Deering (Eds.), *What else works? Creative work with Offenders* (pp. 61–85). London: Willan Publishing.
The Noms Offender Management Model 2005.

FROM TEXT BOOKS TO FOOTPATHS: MAKING REAL-WORLD RESEARCH STICK AT THE COAL FACE

Ian Lambie and Julia Ioane

ABSTRACT

When research is complete and findings concluded, is research really just about publishing findings? Have you ever wondered whether your research will have any real *impact in the world? In our opinion, we believe a bigger obstacle awaits us at the end of a research project. This being the implementation of research findings. We share with you our combined experience spanning over three decades of research – the challenges and learnings we have gathered along the way as we aim to translate research findings into real world, everyday practical reality. Our research experience is generally about human behaviour and psychology within the forensic population. As a result, the implementation of findings is crucial to inform policy makers, practitioners, local community agencies and government departments about the way to work with this population. In this chapter we provide a practical step-by-step approach to how we aim to implement our findings in research. We look at the problem of*

Perspectives on Evaluating Criminal Justice and Corrections
Advances in Program Evaluation, Volume 13, 231–243

ISSN: 1474-7863/doi:10.1108/S1474-7863(2012)0000013015

linking between theory and practice alongside what is currently in practice today. We discuss the challenges we have faced and what we have done to 'Making real-world research stick at the coal face'. *We wish you all the best with your research and hope that you find it as challenging and rewarding as we have!*

INTRODUCTION

Before we begin this chapter we thought it best that we provide some background of who we both are. We would probably best classify ourselves as clinicians-researchers who carry out both research and do clinical work. While trained in clinical psychology, our practice draws on a variety of theoretical and clinical approaches including experiential, psychodynamic and humanistic. We believe that culture plays an important part in any clinical treatment and as such this is also an important part in evaluation research. We have worked for many years in the community and continue to do so. While Ian works at a university he is well linked to the community and has a small private practice where he carries out assessments and therapy with adolescents and children. Julia works full time in a community treatment programme for adolescents with sexually harmful behaviours. Both of us have previously undertaken research in the community on a variety of topics including arson, sexual offending and violence offending. While most of the research has focused on adolescents, some of it has also included adult offenders.

So what specifically is this chapter all about? This chapter focuses on making research findings stick at the coal face in everyday clinical work. Drawing on our experience – successes and failures – we provide a series of steps that will guide you as a researcher through the evaluation process and increase the likelihood that what you recommend matters and has some impact in the 'real world'. We believe that people find learning easiest with chunks of material as opposed to pages and pages of narratives. As such we have scattered boxes throughout with key take-home messages that we hope you will find useful. You will see that we purposefully haven't cited a lot of other people's work but rather relied on what we have learnt from our own projects. Those that we have cited we feel are excellent resources that you will find useful. But this should not been seen as exhaustive as there are many others that are no doubt excellent and we encourage you to read widely.

THE PROBLEM – LINKING BETWEEN THEORY AND PRACTICE

In any evaluation or applied study, what one often reads in a book and/or learns in a university lecture is often very different to what takes place in everyday reality. So what is it that we would refer to as unanticipated obstacles that one has to navigate around that is often not talked about.

For us the biggest factor that makes research 'happen or fail' is people! Personalities play what we believe are the biggest 'black box' in any research project. Here are some key things that we feel are important in successfully undertaking an evaluation project.

Getting the Right Evaluation Team Together

Researching forensic populations is never an easy task as we all know, so one key place to start is getting the right evaluation team together. This means skill sets but also personalities. We have often asked ourselves: does the person doing the job suit the role being asked of them? On one evaluation project where the community treatment programmes for sexually abusive youth were being evaluated, the project was split into two key areas. One focused on the outcome evaluation, while another focused on completing the process evaluation. Being a national project, it was massive, taking lots of time, energy and not the least money! While I (Ian) would like to think that I had the project well organised and a clear, logical plan set out, I am sorry to say that this was not the case but was lucky in the staff that I had to do the project. The research assistants chosen for the role played to their strengths and fitted with their personalities. For the outcome evaluation I had someone who had good statistical skills and who was not scared of working with numbers. They had very little, if any, clinical experience but liked detail and were very thorough. On the other hand, the person undertaking the process evaluation part of the study (which entailed interviewing young people, caregivers and programme staff) had 20 years experience working as a probation officer, was older and a mother, had the experience of working with young people and finally knew the cultural consultant (this was a great advantage as they had a strong relationship with each other) who was at many of the interviews. The point is that if I had reversed the roles and asked each to perform the others' role, I know they could have done it but not as comfortably as the roles they had, which they were more naturally suited to carry out.

Forming a Small Group of Key Stakeholders Before the Project Commences

There is a saying which goes like this: 'What you put in is what you get out'. No truer word comes into our heads than when we think about evaluation research. One of the biggest obstacles when undertaking applied research in the justice area is getting the buy-in of staff and their support for the project. While they might think the idea of doing research is great, often when the practical reality comes into play it is a very different story. We believe that the ease with which your project runs will, in many ways, rely on the stakeholders that you get involved in the planning stages of the project and how you get their buy-in. While it is often easy to form a group, you have to ask yourself, 'Have I really got the right people I need?' This might not necessarily be the people who you like but when you honestly think about it, can these questions be answered:

...

1. *Do they support the research being carried out?*
2. *Will they support the project continuing until it is completed?*
3. *Will they assist me in transforming the findings into action?*
4. *Will they assist me in making my life less of a headache?*

We believe that if the above questions have been answered and you have a good feeling inside then you can start with some confidence of what lies ahead. When conducting evaluation research, as the time progresses and the project develops in the ideal world the stakeholders take an ever-increasing role and responsibility for translating the project's outputs into tangible outcomes.

Leading by Example and Managing the Team Well

In many ways, how well a team operates often comes down to how the team is led and managed throughout the research. For us, this comes down to both the personal qualities and project management skills in the team leader. Some of these characteristics include the following:

...

1. How much experience they have in working in the criminal justice sector.
2. How well they can manage and support people in their particular role.
3. Their knowledge of research and evaluation skills.
4. Their passion and commitment for working in the criminal justice sector and completing the work to a standard as high as possible.
5. Their interpersonal skills – that is, their ability to tap into the individual strengths of their evaluation team members and harness them, as well as their ability to make the research assistants feel valued.
6. Putting resources into upskilling the team members as required.
7. Managing budgets well.
8. Providing supervision and support on an ongoing basis.
9. Providing unexpected rewards (e.g. shout them lunches, buy them coffees) throughout the entire project.
10. Maintaining high professional and ethical standards for the whole team.

For us, having the above skills in a research team leader are key to the success of any evaluation project.

Current Practice

We know how hard it can be for practitioners to stay abreast of the current literature and thinking in the criminal justice field. Unfortunately this comes from our own personal experience despite being trained in evidence-based practice and the importance that reading journal articles play in one's ongoing professional development. What is clear to us is that using the literature and tapping into 'experts' who might be able to act in an advisory role on the project is important.

In the evaluation programme described above we utilised a number of experts who had experience in different areas. These included a cultural consultant, as one of the primary objectives of the study was to determine how appropriate the services that were being provided were for Maori[1] youth and their Whanau.[2] The cultural consultant was included in each interview for every Maori young person and their Whanau. This ensured that the process was culturally safe for each participant, that the client was placed at ease by having someone from their own culture present and finally it allowed for any questions relating to cultural issues to be addressed.

The other expert as part of this project that we engaged the services of was an economist. This person undertook the cost effectiveness part of the evaluation and was solely responsible for ensuring that this part of the contract was completed satisfactorily. We acknowledged that this part of the project required specialist skills and was outside the scope of our expertise. We believe that as part of evaluators' ethical standards it is important for them to acknowledge what they don't know and undertake whatever steps are required to fill this gap.

CHALLENGES

However, despite our best intentions for research to inform good practice in our work, challenges remain. Apart from general limitations that we often find in research relating to things like small sample size, lack of reliability, lack of validity or the inability to generalise across other sample populations, the challenges we attempt to list are from our own experiences with linking theory or research into practice.

The Price to Pay

Findings or recommendations are often seen as the 'be all and end all' of research, but, they will only be worth the paper we write on if they cannot be implemented. In the real world, resources are needed to implement findings and, often, accessing the appropriate resources to do this can be unrealistic or too costly to support.

Linking With the Real World

Sometimes our findings may not be relevant to the real world and often not in alignment with organisational policies, visions and/or mission statements. For example, my doctoral research (Julia) looked at Pacific Island youth who offend violently. Now, I admit that this was a personal interest of mine; however, while this may have been a motivating factor for me, I needed to see what aspect of my research may be relevant to agencies and organisations working with Pacific Island youths who offend. Is the problem identified in literature and research a reality in the community that needed to be investigated? Fortunately it was.

Timing Restraints

This should be of no surprise to anyone. Deadlines are important when planning research; however, it is always important to expect the unexpected. Often the dilemma we have faced in the past is do we continue with the project in order to meet the deadlines, or do we delay the project in order to include other areas which we believe to be beneficial to our research but will take longer to collate? This is the balancing act in research and brings us back to the question of 'What is the purpose of the research?'. We do not want to do a 'half-pie' job or simply 'tick the box'. We want research that is realistic with a pathway to implementation.

Those in the Know

Experts as we like to call them are people who have knowledge and/or experience about the area we are researching. In most cases these are the people who are more likely to support your research and advocate for its implementation if appropriate. However, politics can often be a hindrance to research particularly if findings are not positive and do not align with the objectives of policy makers. Therefore, while it is important to understand the purpose of the research, it is equally important to ask yourself for *whom* is this research important to, *who* are the decision makers for this population and tailor your research findings to address this.

Quick Fix Solutions

This is what we all like to see – a solution that is going to be quick and easy to implement with fast results! If there is a fantasy in research then this is it, and while researchers may be aware of this, our influencers in the real world need to come to grips with this. The reality is, most of our research is about humans and humanity. There is nothing simple or easy about us. We are the most complex living organism on this planet so to think that there are quick fix solutions out there for us, is a lovely thought to have but not a reality. Findings, solutions and the impacts of our implementations take time.

So, how can we respond to these challenges?

MAKING REAL RESEARCH STICK

The aim of this chapter has been about 'making real research stick at the coal face'. In other words, making sure that our research is able to be implemented in the real world, rather than merely being printed into journals and books ready to be placed on bookshelves. Once again, the following recommendations are from our own experiences with research.

Be Real

While it is always great to research an area that one is passionate about, one must also be realistic and challenge oneself into thinking whether this is going to be something of value to the general population. Secondly, it is always worthwhile to sit down and plan as to where you want your research to go. Who will benefit from my findings? How can I get the message to this group? How can I implement my findings? Research and findings are an integral part of research; however, the practical aspect of your research must remain at the forefront of your work at all times. We have found that identifying possibly pathways and practical methods for implementing your findings should be part of research. By doing this allows for your research to be more genuine and applicable to the real world.

Research Your Research

As you all know, reviewing the literature is very important to see what is needed to research. Be specific in your literature review. First, write down the questions you are seeking to answer in your research review. One thing that we have found useful on top of the general literature reviews of local and international research is to look at government and local government reports. Access such websites and look at their internal publications. Sometimes they are not publicly accessible but if you contact them and explain the reason for your request, they can be quite helpful. This can also be a future contact for you as you progress in your research.

These publications can provide you with what is working well and what is not working well in reality, therefore highlighting what may be areas for potential research.

Get Out into the Real World

Real research needs to involve real people. Now by this we mean getting involved with the work and put a face to your research. Get out there in the real world and see how it operates. If I (Julia) think back to my research on Pacific Island youth offenders I made it a point to see things at 'grass-roots level'. It is not enough to study your target population from behind a computer screen or from reading a book. I worked as a youth worker for a residential facility that accommodated the most serious and violent youth offenders in New Zealand. I observed youth in youth-court settings for a period of time to get a 'feel' of their world. It was this personal connection that made my research come to life as well as giving me the honour and privilege of stepping into their world. In my Pacific Island culture, your behaviour is often the loudest message that portrays your character. I did not want to be another academic or another researcher looking at our people, making recommendations yet never having worked directly with them. It also became a motivating factor in my work because the faces of the individuals I had met and worked for gave me a sense of real purpose to my work. In addition, this real-world experience can often lead to pathways to connect with the experts. People like to share with those who 'walk the talk' of their work.

Talk to Those in the Know

As we have previously mentioned, connections with the experts is going to be important for your research to really 'stick'. We have found that consultation with practitioners, agencies, policy makers, community groups and government departments allows for your research to be seen and heard. It also provides an opportunity for your research to be reviewed right from the start as to whether it may have some implications in the future. There is no point doing research in an area and wanting your findings to be implemented, if it is not seen as a priority in the real world. While this may be a laborious task or one that can be quite time consuming, we can assure you that once the relationship is made, these experts can be an ally for you as your research progresses. They can connect you to further experts, they can offer you sound and objective advice that is often not in the literature and they can open their world to you as a stepping stone in the right direction. They are likely to be more open to hearing your views post research as they have personally invested themselves into your work. Let us face it, we live in a society where people and reputations can be the decisive factor as to whether one is to be heard. Ongoing consultation with those in the know is likely to make it easier for your findings to be presented with a possible view to implement.

Make it Real

Great! You've finished your data collection, you've written your findings and your recommendations, and you've presented them to the world. So now what? The next step we believe is the *implementation* of your findings or making your findings 'stick'. Now before we go on, we make it clear that it is not your role as a researcher to ensure your findings are implemented, but we believe it is your role to connect the dots between research and practice. You have identified *what* it is that needs to be implemented; the next step is to perhaps suggest *how* it may be implemented. This again is where your connections with the experts and those working at 'grass-roots level' are very useful. Talk to them and discuss confidentially the findings of your research and your thoughts as to how it may be implemented. They can share with you as to whether the *how* can be a reality. For example, one of the findings in my Pacific Island research suggested that Pacific Island families needed to raise expectations of their own Pacific children. How on earth do we do this without being insensitive or causing offence to our own community? Therefore, talking to those who work with our families can provide insight as to *how* we can make this a reality. Your relationships with these experts provide an opportunity for your findings to be translated into the real world.

Another example was the recommendation for a centralised database of information about our youth who offend. This has been an ongoing recommendation from previous researchers, yet unfortunately, nothing has been done. This is an example of research findings not being translated into clinical practice despite the recommendations to do so. However, the problem is that this goes in the 'too hard' basket in the real world given limited resourcing, and this is another area that researchers need to be aware of and accept.

Once you have discussed your findings and your suggestions for implementation with the experts the next step is to write these into your research report. It is always beneficial to 'go the extra mile' in your research in order to make it easier for the reader. Provide practical steps of how you would implement your findings as this is likely to be make it more 'alive' and 'real' for the reader. Let us face it, people are more likely to engage in a process if it is transparent and clear to follow.

Acknowledge Others

We have always found that once the research is complete and the findings shared appropriately, the relationships don't necessarily end or need to end. We always make it a point to personally visit those who have helped us along the way and thank them for their assistance. Often, these visits end up being a pathway for further discussions of findings and future research. We will usually take a small gift or morning tea with us and acknowledge their contribution to our research. It also provides a nice ending to the research relationship but also allows for the relationship to remain open. This is the personal touch that has a long-lasting effect on colleagues and comrades. As an example, there is a particular senior sergeant in the police force who was instrumental in my doctoral research. Even though my research ended, our relationship continues to remain with current research projects being worked on collaboratively.

So here it is, our suggestions of what could help make real research 'stick' in our world. We provide a summary that may assist as you begin your own research:

Making Real Research Stick

1. *Be real*
   Ask yourself honestly; is there a real purpose to my research? Is there a need for this area to be investigated in the real world?
2. *Research your research in the real world*
   Access both local government and government reports about your area of interest. Gain an understanding of what those in the real world say about the area you are planning to research.

3. *Get out into the real world*
   Get your own personal experience of your research. Get out there and either work with them or observe them as they go about their usual world. It is these experiences that you cannot read from text books or journal articles.
4. *Talk to those in the know*
   Get out from your desk and arrange to meet with the practical experts. Get them included in your research because they are the ones working in the real world. Keep them engaged throughout your research process as they are likely to identify any barriers that you may overlook given their experiences of the world you are researching.
5. *Make it real*
   Following your endless efforts to add "reality" throughout each step of your research, this is the crucial part. Identify practical and realistic steps as to how your research findings could be implemented and write about them. Make the connection between research and practice.
6. *Acknowledge others*
   Remember to personally thank those who have assisted you in your journey with research.

CONCLUSION

In this chapter we have provided you with some key steps that we hope will make your job of undertaking evaluation easier and more 'doable'. A key message from us would be to not give up despite whatever challenges you might face in the real world. Keep it up and don't give up. One of the things that made it easier for us was to acknowledge when things were challenging and to discuss with the research group. This allows for everyone the opportunity to voice and share their concerns and the impacts it might be having on their work. Remember, we are all human. It also helped that personal experiences with the group we researched became a 'light in the tunnel' during those challenging moments. It was their faces that gave the motivation that there was someone we were doing this for.

Undertaking research in the community with community partners is really important if we are to translate research findings into clinical practice. Often carrying out the actual research is the easier thing but ensuring that research findings translate to change in clinical practice is hard ... but not impossible.

> If it was easy it wouldn't be worth doing
> *John F. Kennedy*

NOTES

1. Indigenous population of New Zealand.
2. Maori name for family.

ABOUT THE AUTHORS

Brad Astbury is research fellow in the Centre for Program Evaluation, Melbourne Graduate School of Education at the University of Melbourne where he lectures within the Masters of Evaluation course. His interests lie in evaluation theory and social research methodology. Brad has conducted evaluations in a number of areas, including corrections, education, health promotion and various family and community service interventions.

Matt Barnard is social researcher who specialises in conducting mixed-method research and evaluations focused on vulnerable populations including children who have suffered abuse or neglect, drug-dependent adults and problem gamblers. As head of evaluation at the NSPCC, he is currently overseeing an extensive programme of 20 evaluations of innovative services being rolled out by the charity. The evaluation approaches range from randomised controlled trials and quasi-experimental designs to in-depth process and formative evaluations. Before joining the NSPCC, Matt was a research director in the crime and justice team at NatCen Social Research where he led a wide range of research and evaluations. Many of the studies were commissioned by the UK's Home Office and Ministry of Justice, including the Drug Treatment Outcomes Research Study, a major national evaluation of drug treatment in the United Kingdom for which he was the lead researcher on the qualitative component. He has particular expertise in qualitative research methods, having helped developing NatCen's analysis of qualitative data course and taught it for many years. He has also led the development of Critical Qualitative Theory, a new articulation of NatCen Social Research's approach to qualitative research.

Robert F. Boruch is University Trustee Chair Professor at the University of Pennsylvania with appointments in the Graduate School of Education and in the Statistics Department of the Wharton School. At Penn, he is a member of the Graduate Group in Criminology in the School of Arts and Sciences and the Graduate Group in the School of Social Policy and Practice. He joined Penn's faculty in 1989, following service as a professor of psychology, statistics and education at Northwestern University in 1969–1988.

Boruch is a founder of the international Campbell Collaboration and a co-founder of the Evaluation Research Society, now named the American Evaluation Association. He has served on the Board of Trustees for the W. T. Grant Foundation and on advisory boards for the Rockefeller Foundation, the Robert Wood Johnson Foundation Smith Richardson Foundation among others. He has served on advisory committees for the US Department of Education, US Government Accountability Office, National Center for Educational Statistics, National Science Foundation, National Institutes of Health and on committees for the US National Academy of Sciences. He has also served on advisory boards or panels for the World Health Organization, UNESCO, OECD and others.

Erica Bowen is senior lecturer in psychology. She has worked in the field of evaluation since 2000, focusing her attention on evaluating domestic violence perpetrator programmes, and primary interventions for violence in intimate relationships. Erica has worked with a number of UK probation areas. Her work has typically adopted a 'comprehensive' evaluation approach through which impact and process are considered with a view to validating programme theory. She is a council member of the UK Evaluation Society.

Sarah Brown is reader in Forensic Psychology Development, and Editor of the *Journal of Sexual Aggression*. She started her academic career evaluating community-based sex offender treatment programmes. Since that time she has been involved in a number of projects involving statutory and government agencies regarding the assessment and management of high-risk offenders. Sarah's research interests include: sex offender treatment programmes, empathy, attitudes towards offenders and criminal justice responses to them.

Joe S. Cecil is project director in the Division of Research at the Federal Judicial Center, the research and education agency of the federal judiciary. Currently he is directing the Center's Program on Scientific and Technical Evidence. As part of this programme he has served as principal editor of the Center's *Reference Manual on Scientific Evidence*, a third edition of which was recently published in collaboration with the National Academies. He has served as a member of several panels of the National Academy of Sciences, including the Committee on Identifying the Needs of the Forensic Science Community, and presently is serving as a member of the Committee on Science, Technology & Law. He is currently directing a research project that examines the difficulties that arise with expert testimony in federal courts, with an emphasis on clinical medical testimony and forensic science evidence. Other areas of research interest include access to federal courts, federal civil and appellate procedure, jury competence in complex civil litigation and assessment of rule of law in emerging democracies. Dr. Cecil received his J.D. and a Ph.D. in psychology from Northwestern University.

Elaine Ellis has been working as performance unit manager with NOMs in the East of England for 5 years. Prior to this she held a number of research and information posts within the Home Office and the Office of Criminal Justice Reform. Her role in the Offender Engagement Programme has been to undertake an internal evaluation. Elaine is also an associate lecturer at the Open University.

Nigel Hosking is senior probation officer with the London Probation Trust and is currently seconded to NOMS. He qualified as a probation officer in 1983 and has worked in most probation settings including field teams, prisons and community service. He has a background in offending behaviour programmes, having worked as a practitioner delivering programmes, treatment manager, national trainer (for the Reasoning and Rehabilitation Programme) and programme manager. He developed a one-to-one programme for offenders in Romania, which was subsequently adopted by London Probation, before joining the Offender. He has previously published an article on group dynamics in the *Journal of Psychiatry* and is the co-author of a chapter in *Probation supervision. New directions in theory, research and practice*.

Jordan M. Hyatt, J.D. M.S., holds degrees in criminology and law from the University of Pennsylvania and Villanova University School of Law, respectively. He is currently the senior research coordinator at the Jerry Lee Center of Criminology at the University of Pennsylvania. His research focuses on the impact of cognitive-behavioural therapy and social networks on high-risk probationers, randomized experiments in criminology and on the integration of risk-assessment into sentencing decisions.

Wendy Hyett joined South Wales Probation as a trainee probation officer in 2003. She qualified as a probation officer in 2005 and worked primarily with Prolific and Other Priority Offenders (PPOs) until she moved into a role as project manager. She has worked as a project manager for the past 4 years, first within Wales Probation Trust where she managed local implementation of national projects including Intensive Alternatives to Custody (IAC), and more recently within the NOMS Offender Engagement Programme where she has led on the Reflective Supervision Model of work with Probation Managers.

Julia Ioane is of Samoan descent and is a registered clinical psychologist in Auckland, New Zealand. Currently, Julia works for SAFE Network Ltd. which is a community treatment programme for people who have sexually offended. Julia assesses and provides therapy for children and adolescents within this forensic population. Prior to this she worked with youth offenders in residential facilities and youth in community mental health settings. Julia's research interests are youth forensic with a focus on sexual, violent and arson-type offending. Her doctoral research looked at Pacific Island youths who offended violently in comparison with New Zealand European and Maori violent youth offenders. Her current research projects involve children who deliberately light fires, adolescents who sexually offend and Pacific Island youths with violent offending behaviour.

Barry Kushner is an independent regeneration consultant supporting the development and sustainability of third-sector organisations, with experience of developing and delivering services in social care, with specific experience in Youth Justice. He has conducted several research and evaluation projects including on homelessness, safeguarding and the probation service.

Saville Kushner is professor of public evaluation at the University of Auckland. He is a leading proponent of democratic and rights-based approaches to programme evaluation. He has worked extensively in the criminal justice sector and served as adviser to the Home Office on national police training.

Ian Lambie Ph.D., P.G.DipClinPsych, DipBus is an associate professor in clinical psychology at the University of Auckland, New Zealand. There he teaches clinical, forensic, child psychology. He has been providing treatment for adolescent offenders for 20 years and has published nationally and internationally in this area. His specialist clinical and research interests are youth forensic psychology and in particular severe conduct disorder, adolescent sexual offending and arson. Ian has a private practice where he specialises in working with youth offenders. He is a consultant to the New Zealand Government on youth offending and a member of the Ministry of Justice Independent Advisory Group on Youth Offending chaired by Chief Youth Court Judge, Judge Becroft and a member of the Ministry of Social Development Expert Group on the treatment of Conduct Disorder.

In 2001 Ian was the youngest recipient ever to receive the New Zealand Psychological Society Public Interest Award for his longstanding community work with adolescent sexual offenders in New Zealand. In 2006 he was awarded the Ann Ballin Award from the New Zealand Psychological Society for services to clinical psychology in New Zealand. In 2011 Ian was awarded the William Friedrich Memorial Child Sexual Abuse research and treatment award from the American Institute on Violence, Abuse and Trauma.

L. E. Marshall, Ph.D. has been treating and conducting research on offenders for more than 15 years. He has helped design preparatory, regular, denier, low-functioning, maintenance and juvenile sexual offender programs, as well as anger management, domestic violence, gambling, self-esteem and cognitive skills programmes. Liam has many publications including three books and more than 50 peer-reviewed journal articles. He has made numerous international conference presentations on sexual offending, sexual addiction, violence, ageing and problem gambling issues. Liam has delivered more than 70 trainings for therapists who work with sexual and violent offenders in 15 countries worldwide.

Liam is a reviewer and board member for a number of international journals on sexually problematic behaviour, and gambling problems. He is currently a therapist, and training and research director for Rockwood Psychological Services; he is a consultant to the Royal Ottawa Health Care Group Secure Treatment Unit and to the St Lawrence Youth Association.

W. L. Marshall, O.C., F.R.S.C., Ph.D., C. Psych, is director of Rockwood Psychological Services which provides treatment for sexual offenders in various settings. He has over 380 publications including 20 books, and he has served on the Editorial Boards of 17 international journals. Bill has received several awards and in 2006 he was appointed an officer of The Order of Canada which is Canada's highest honour for a civilian which was awarded for Bill's national and international contributions to making societies safer.

Sue Rex has been in NOMS since 2005, apart from a short period of secondment. Having started her career in policy work at the Home Office, she took leave to undertake a Ph.D. at the Institute of Criminology, University of Cambridge. This was followed by research and teaching, and a wide range of publications relating to community penalties including two edited books and an authored book on *Reforming Community Penalties*. She joined the Offender Engagement Programme at its inception early in 2010, initially managing the research programme and later taking on responsibility for managing the entire programme.

David Smith, a former probation officer, has been at Lancaster University since 1976. He became professor of social work in 1993 and professor of criminology in 2002. As well as writing on methodological issues, he has researched and written on youth justice practice and policy, inter-agency co-operation in criminal justice, racism and racist violence and minority ethnic groups' experiences of probation and criminal justice. He recently conducted an evaluation of a pioneering programme in Liverpool for perpetrators of racially aggravated offences, and was principal investigator, with Paul Iganski, on an international research project on programmes for the rehabilitation of hate crime offenders.

Herb Turner III has three decades of experience conducting scientifically valid research in education and related areas. He is founder, president and principal scientist of ANALYTICA Inc., a woman-owned and minority-led small business that specialises in using scientifically valid research designs and methods to address policy-relevant education problems. He has extensive experience providing technical leadership and assistance (TA) to research teams on all phases of federally sponsored research including the Regional Educational Laboratory (REL) Programme, the Investing in Innovation (i3) Fund and the Social Innovation Fund (SIF). In these and similar initiatives, he has provided TA to over a dozen teams working on large-scale multistate RCTs, authored methodological and statistical guidance documents and served as lead strategist for developing registries to support efforts that produce well-designed and well-implemented studies. Previously, Dr. Turner served as scientific project director for the Campbell Collaboration. Dr. Turner is also an adjunct assistant professor at the University of Pennsylvania's Graduate School of Education where he teaches data processing and analysis and other quantitative research method courses. He has published in several peer-reviewed journals on randomized trials and systematic reviews.

Timothy Victor has more than 20 years of experience in industry and academic research. He has served as principal methodologist on studies in the areas as diverse as of education, nutrition, psychometrics and medicine. He completed his doctoral training at the University of Connecticut and the University of Pennsylvania. He has expertise in the areas of statistics and psychometrics. He has conducted extensive research in the field of psychiatry and neuroscience. He has held positions of scientific leadership at GlaxoSmithKline, AstraZeneca and Aetna. Dr. Victor maintains academic appointments at the Philadelphia College of Osteopathic Medicine and the University of Pennsylvania where he teaches experimental design, statistics and psychological assessment. He currently holds the position of vice president of Science and Strategy at Kantar Health where he oversees multinational research programmes in healthcare and medicine. Dr. Victor's research interests include computational statistics, measurement theory, the design of randomized controlled trials, large-scale survey design and observational research. His current projects include the design and implementation of an international health survey and scale development across a broad range of diseases.

INDEX